Praise for *Informatio*

* From *Management Gurus Internati*
Voted one of the **World's Top 30 M**

From *Kirkus Discoveries*:
Bontis offers a broad overview of the information explosion and intelligent advice on how to avoid being suffocated by it.

As a technophile, Bontis feels the pain of those suffering from the excessive, indiscriminate need to consume today's flood of information because he knows that information contains knowledge and in our knowledge-worker economy, knowledge is what we have to sell as employees. Still, too much information can be debilitating physically, emotionally and in our social and familial lives. The trick is to filter the important stuff from the noise.

Bontis, who writes in what is essentially a comfortable speaking voice, takes a leisurely and anecdotal approach to the issue of information bombardment. He paints the historical and technological background of the problem; draws attention to its manifestations on individual, group, organizational and institutional levels; provides numerous examples of his points; and then tenders quality prescriptions to control and facilitate the gathering of applicable knowledge.

Readers could simply jump to the last few chapters for Bontis' toolkit, but his tour of the information highway is entertaining and instructive, gently meandering into neuroanatomy, Anglophonic pitfalls and more—at one point offering a dramatization of how a car crash might play out in the techno-soaked future—as he explores the reasons behind such knowledge-management snafus as the response to Hurricane Katrina and the BP oil spill. "In essence, we need to refine the amount and type of information pulled to us and pushed toward us at every instance.... Choosing which information arrives at your mental desktop is a conscious choice."

He achieves his goal through a combination of software and social networking. The software includes e-mail-rule wizards, push alerts that garner targeted information and Wikinomics tools. He combines these with the human interactions of knowledge cafes (something like show-and-tell), knowledge auctions (rewards for sharing information) and alumni networks to keep all that accumulated knowledge capital in the flow after retirement. As a final piece of advice, he suggests learning to speed read. Thorough, practical and optimistic—stress relief for the info deluged.

—Kirkus Discoveries

Dr. Nick Bontis bombards us with a timely, informative, common sense tutorial on today's information dilemma. Technological changes, too much information, too many unknown sources, and the decline of face-to-face communication have changed the way we receive and disseminate information. I travel over 200 days a year and am seldom in the same time zone as my office. I depend on technology to receive and send accurate, current, concise, confidential and relevant information. Nick's book is a must-read for all my senior staff! On a personal note, I have experienced many times Nick's passion for the art of communication and his ability to convey his approach to information management both to large audiences and in boardroom settings. Most importantly, whether it's in person or in this book, he delivers his essential message in a way that we can all understand.

—Ron Foxcroft, founder and CEO, Fox 40 International

Today's knowledge seeker is deluged with information 24/7. The conflict between knowledge assimilation, effective human interactions and private, tranquil "me" time afflicts all information consumers in the twenty-first century. Thankfully, Nick Bontis brings some insightful wisdom to these issues. Lock yourself away for a day and read *Information Bombardment*. You won't regret it! Better still, your family and friends will thank you. Mine did!

—Dr. Edward A. Minich, former president and CEO, Otis Canada

Nick Bontis spins a compelling tale of the knowledge world. He covers everything from the alphabet to the Internet in an easy-to-read style. Implications and applications range from the individual to the organization. It is truly a comprehensive story of one of the most fundamental issues in life: knowledge.

—Dr. Jac Fitz-enz, founder, Human Capital Source

Nick Bontis addresses a problem that has left society unable to cope effectively: information bombardment. His enlightened insight is brought to life by his humor and personal stories about a phenomenon that impacts our daily lives at multiple levels, affecting our health and relationships. Besides clearly outlining the issues, Nick provides actionable prescriptions to help us succeed in today's technologically complex world.

—Don Pether, retired chairman, president and CEO, Dofasco

This is the elegant telling of the "what, so what and now what?" of the Information Age. Dr. Nick Bontis serves up powerful facts and revealing insights that remind us that technology makes a great servant but a poor master.

—Jim Letwin, president and CEO, JAN Kelley Marketing

Nick Bontis is an inspirational individual who demonstrates in-depth understanding of our rapidly changing, knowledge-based world. *Information Bombardment* combines Bontis' academic acumen with witty, personal-life experiences, leaving the reader informed and entertained. Above all, the reader is inspired to reflect personally and organizationally with an eye to strategic changes that will help to maximize productivity and success.

—Murray T. Martin, president and CEO,
Hamilton Health Sciences

Dr. Nick Bontis has an uncanny ability to take complex technological concepts and distill them into sound bites that are as easily understood and equally valuable to the technocrat as they are to the novice. This book is a must-read if you want to stay on top of the digital revolution tsunami that has already formed off the coast and is heading quickly to every shore the world over.

—Martin H. Charlwood, president and CEO,
Uniglobe Travel; vice chairman, Century 21 Canada

If there's one thing human beings crave above all else, it's information. I know, you thought I was going to say "sex." The truth is that we're hunting down information much more than we're prowling for sex. In this world of Twitter, Facebook, blogs and Google, information is anywhere and everywhere. How do you handle it, deal with it and manage it all? Thankfully, Nick has written *Information Bombardment* to help you get it all sorted out and in order. If your e-mail inbox is a never-ending game of Tetris, this book is for you!

—Mitch Joel, president, Twist Image;
author of *Six Pixels of Separation*

Information Bombardment is more than just a book that you will keep prominently on your bookshelf. It is a lifeline resource that will assist you in getting back your most important asset: your time. Using on his considerable academic research and consulting practice, Dr. Nick Bontis weaves a fantastic journey through time while examining how information, and our constant hunger for it, is consuming our lives. He provides various personal stories, case studies and business examples of how we can accelerate knowledge-worker productivity across four levels of analysis: individual, group, organizational and institutional. Above all, the book is written in a straightforward style and endowed with page-turning momentum. Furthermore, Dr. Bontis provides the reader with invaluable Web resources after every single chapter so that your learning continues long after you have finished reading the book for the first time.

—Frank Andreoli, MDRT member, Andreoli Financial Services

There is no end to information, and there is certainly no way to slow down the speed at which it is growing today. Nick Bontis helps us quickly understand that this is a race that cannot be won. From the outset this book will have you wondering how we allow ourselves to be caught in this trap. The author provides a clear understanding to help us deal with our insatiable desire to always be connected in the Information Era at all levels.

—Alex Rechichi, president and CEO, Extreme Brandz

Information Bombardment is a unique look at how an overload of information impacts individuals, organizations and institutions. Bontis warns that too much information not shared and synthesized properly can be dangerous but also provides examples of how information turned into intelligence can be powerful and even life-saving. This book is a must-read for anyone with a Blackberry device, and the "Rule Wizards" section is great for e-mail addicts looking to better manage their inboxes. The book touches the reader at a personal level and reminds us all that there must be a balance between our information intake and what matters most in our lives. Nick offers sage advice on living a better life by managing knowledge rather than being bombarding with information.

—Jeffrey A. Berk, chief operating officer, KnowledgeAdvisors

Information Bombardment by Nick Bontis is an absolute must-read for today's knowledge workers and their leaders. Unlike most books in the domain that contribute to the problem, *Information Bombardment* is an enjoyable read that offers actionable ideas to combat the malady. Nick's brilliant balance of firsthand stories, real-world examples and technological detail provides amazing clarity to a rather complex and expanding phenomenon. Well done!

—Dr. John P. Girard, professor, Minot State University

This book is a rare combination. Both heartfelt and helpful, it is a timely and thoughtful guide to living and working productively in a world of digital immersion.

—Dr. Carla O'Dell, president, APQC

Information Bombardment is more than a discussion of today's information overload. In his book, Nick Bontis provides marvellous insight into tomorrow's information avalanche and how individuals and organizations might prepare for this unstoppable eventuality. His masterful book is well worth the read.

—Dr. Jerry Blanton, cofounder, Carrier Team One, AMSEC

Sit down, strap on your seat belt and prepare yourself for a journey through communication and intellectual history. Be prepared to take off in a time of cave drawings and land in the whirlwind of modern-day hyper-communication. What does it mean, where is it taking us and is it too much? Will we adapt or will our human circuit breakers eventually shut off and turn the thinking over to artificial intelligence? Nick Bontis takes us through past discoveries and future predictions that most of us don't consider in our day-to-day lives. *Information Bombardment* helps shine a personal and entertaining light on the undeniable wall of hyper-communications and information that comes our way daily. Ready or not, you should read this book.

—Michael Kovacs, president and CEO, Harvest Portfolios Group

In this entertaining and insightful read, Nick Bontis offers a troubling diagnosis of society's information addiction—a disease that's negatively affecting people and organizations in the form of costly information irrelevance, personal stress and inefficiency. Nick's expansive review of this problem forces a therapeutic reflection of the costs of our preoccupation with information. His simple yet powerful methods to manage, disseminate and process information are effective remedies. A must-read for busy managers!

—Meaghan Stovel McKnight, director of IT, Bell Canada

Nick has written a thoughtful and practical guide to dealing with information overload, not only for individuals and groups but for organizations too. The book moves along at the same pace as Nick's presentations and is equally engaging and entertaining. I know right where I'm going to start to solve my information overload problems!

—Stephanie Barnes, chief chaos organizer,
Missing Puzzle Piece Consulting

Everything is different now! Knowledge mobilization is in the final stages of transition from a privileged few to everyone; all the time. Think about researching two books in the library—now think about researching a million books. If you wish to educate or employ workers in the digital economy; if you are involved in policy development, or if you simply want to understand, let alone compete, you need to read this book by Nick Bontis from cover to cover.

—Paul K. Bates, dean, DeGroote School of Business

This book is a lifeline for the modern knowledge worker. Nick Bontis combines practical advice with high-minded theory to tackle the negative effects of information overload and provide a guide for working smarter in the Digital Age. In the process he delivers an engaging, wide-ranging and piercing exploration of how living in the Information Era impacts individuals,
groups, organizations and societies.

—Mike Prokopeak, editorial director,
Chief Learning Officer and *Talent Management* magazines

Information Bombardment is unique in its approach to today's challenges with information both personal and professional. From diagnostics on how we got here and predictions of where we are headed, Nick offers sound advice and tools to help us all manage our time more effectively, so we can spend more of it on the things that are truly valuable—family, friends, ourselves—and maintain successful, profitable and satisfying careers.

—Rebecca Mountain, principal, Impetus Consulting

Professor Bontis' insightful observations, compelling examples and lively writing style are just what we need to survive and thrive in the knowledge era. His helpful advice on how to transform challenges into opportunities fills a gap in this vital field of study and practice. Clearly, it's time to reboot our perceptions and expectations of information sharing and knowledge translation.

—Heather Pullen, manager,
PR & Communications, Hamilton Health Sciences

Information Bombardment is worthwhile reading in the age of information overload. Nick Bontis' insightful, entertaining presentation reminds us that knowledge is power—and it has the power to overwhelm knowledge workers and the institutions who rely on them when it is not managed closely. The book's clear action plan is a diet for the information obsessed and a highly recommended way to make information useful again.

—Ted Hastings, president, Cyberplex

As you draw from the hundreds of stories and personal accounts that are a hallmark of this brilliant book, you realize that there is a piece of Nick Bontis in all of us. That is why one is compelled to turn each page and learn just how to deal with information bombardment. In this intensely personal and vivid book, Nick offers a rich, historical perspective, powerful metaphors and insights that reveal our technologically complex lifestyles. But Nick also creates a space for us to contemplate just what we might do to make big changes that can make qualitative differences in our lives and in the lives of those for whom we care.

—Dr. Arshad Ahmad,
3M national teaching fellow, Concordia University

With this powerful statement from his book, *Information Bombardment*, Nick Bontis sets the stage: "We have entered an accelerated period of change. The knowledge era in which we now find ourselves has created changes within our world that far exceed the speed of change in generations past." Nick Bontis clearly explains our knowledge environment, how we got here, the consequences of information bombardment, and some comprehensive, practical solutions that will help us become more effective users of knowledge. The book is an easy read of a complex subject; for me, Nick's primary contribution to the discourse is his connecting the dots with suggested navigational aids within the potential chaos of unmanaged information bombardment. This book is a must-read for us all!

—Dr. Christopher R. Hardy, director,
Defense Acquisition University

Thirty years ago, the data wasn't available; today, we sometimes wish someone would just make the data overload stop! The end result is the same: individuals, organizations and institutions still struggle to turn data into valuable, actionable knowledge. Nick's book is very timely in its calls for us to evolve beyond gorging ourselves at the data buffet and to move towards a more mature, discerning use of information to enrich our individual and collective lives.

—Dr. Philip E. Hunter, Saratoga Canada lead, PricewaterhouseCoopers

When we use our gadgets—mobile phones, tablets, iPods, notebooks and others—we don't even think of their effects on our behaviors and our environments. Nor do we think about how these things affect our social interactions with others. Clarifying these issues is the essence of Nick Bontis' book, *Information Bombardment*. It covers the whole range of influence, from the individual to the institutional level. Nick Bontis presents an entertaining proposition worthy of the attention of every reader, regardless of education or business position.

—Dr. Ante Pulic, founder, Croatian IC Center, University of Zagreb

Harnessing and grasping the information we receive on a daily basis, both at work and at home, has become a chronic challenge as we are forced to adapt, digest and learn on the fly. Nick Bontis has deftly condensed many areas of our digital world into a guidebook that describes the e-universe around us and how to manage it intelligently. I found myself connecting with many of the real-life scenarios Nick shares in *Information Bombardment*. He offers a refreshing look and viable options that we may integrate into our busy professional and personal lives. A great read!

—Mitch Bauer, owner and president, Bauer Systems

Thoughtful, insightful and visionary... Nick Bontis outlines the good and the bad of knowledge bombardment and our endless thirst for information. This book explores these fundamental concepts, providing insights into our modern world and ultimately into our own inner workings. Like a true specialist in his field, he not only defines the issues but offers valuable solutions to help keep us afloat in the sea of knowledge, improve our quality of life and bring about much-needed balance. A must-read for anyone in the academic field.

—Dr. Atul Humar, director,
Transplant Infectious Diseases, University of Alberta

Nick's book provides some great insights into the information challenges we all face in everyday business. He helps us understand how we got here and then provides some practical and useful tools to help us manage our way through the tidal wave of information. This is a must-read for anyone in business!

—Richard Koroscil, president and CEO,
Hamilton International Airport

Information Bombardment is a useful and practical guide for knowledge workers. Nick Bontis compiles common, everyday experiences and offers micro and macro views of the implications of information overload in your personal and professional lives. It is an entertaining read!

—Vasilis Tsaitas, investment manager, Enolia Premium Capital

Dr. Nick Bontis offers cover to people and organizations pinned down by an incessant barrage of information. He exposes the human forces driving a worldwide addiction to unfiltered information and its assault on our quality of life. And, with a hopeful smile, he invites us to be more discerning in our choices as the first step to liberating time for family, friends and reflection. Use this important book to design an information management strategy that puts you in charge.

—Richard W. Allen, managing director,
Hamilton Economic Summit

Nick is at his best when he writes like he presents: dynamically and energetically. I found that the stories throughout *Information Bombardment* leapt off the page while clearly illustrating the principles that are critical to all of us wishing to thrive in the Information Age. These are stories that will make you ponder if we will ever take control of the constant barrage of information we face daily. Nick's personal tales of how life can get out of balance certainly resonated with me, and I am encouraged by the prescriptions he offers as a cure. Now I need to implement these words of wisdom!

—Don Williamson, president, The Williamson Group

Information Bombardment is a rare book—a pleasure to read and rich with insight and anecdote.

—Dr. Chun Wei Choo, professor, iSchool, University of Toronto

Every business, not-for-profit organization and individual is trying to understand where we've been and, more importantly, where we're going in the digital world and the knowledge economy. Dr. Nick Bontis' latest book connects the dots for all of us in a user-friendly way while including very helpful additional resources at the end of each chapter.

—David Adames, executive director, Tourism Hamilton

In his uniquely candid and inimitable way, Dr. Bontis gauges the costs of information bombardment and our obsession with information in regard to our time and quality of life. He offers relevant and practical—though not necessarily easy—solutions to help all of us better manage the onslaught, get the value we need, and move on. Read it from cover to cover, or "take a page from the book" and read only the relevant bits. Either way, it's well worth the investment of your time and attention.

—Howard Deane, cofounder, Acme Metric Company;
former CKO, KPMG Canada

During the 1960s and 1970s, knowledge workers often spent hours trying to locate key information for decision making. A generation later, the problem is too much information! Knowledge workers today spend hours sifting through mountains of data and information in order to reach critical decisions. Analytical software is limited in its ability to identify the right piece of information at the right time. Coworkers and networks of "experts" may be able to contribute insights, but often they, too, do not have access to all of the information needed to solve a problem or reach a critical conclusion. Nick Bontis expertly addresses these concerns and more in *Information Bombardment* and provides knowledge workers with a set of practical solutions to enable each person to improve productivity while also creating a more holistic work and personal-life experience.

—Rory Chase, managing director, Teleos

Nick Bontis has written a book that is highly accessible, thoroughly engaging and wonderfully illuminating. He takes us on a provocative tour of the information universe. He effectively charts the pervasive and universal impact that the relentless flow of information is having on our harried lives. The practical prescriptions he advances are a welcome restorative towards achieving better balance, success and mastery of our lives.

—Bryan Elliot Davis, president,
Kaieteur Institute for Knowledge Management

Information Bombardment may well be the number-one challenge facing society today. Dr. Bontis eloquently and entertainingly points out the insanity of our "need to know" world and the negative impact that it can have on our productivity and our personal lives. After leading us though a twenty-first-century self-diagnosis of our collective problem, Bontis prescribes some practical tips for survival. Turn off your smartphone and read what he has to say... It just might save your day.

—Paul Salvini, CTO, Side Effects Software

Dr. Nick Bontis, a veritable force of nature, provides an all-encompassing review of information bombardment. In a wonderful paradox, he both bombards us with information and provides us with the tools to manage the very bombardment he creates. A wonderfully engaging read for those of us who are addicted to information, Dr. Bontis' survey of the magnitude, nature and management of information bombardment ranges from a discussion of reality TV and *American*

Idol to academic studies of intellectual capital. *Information Bombardment* provides a worthy diagnosis of one of the key challenges that an increasing proportion of the world's population faces individually, organizationally and institutionally, with thoughtful suggestions as to how we might avoid some of the most dire consequences.

—Dr. Anthony K.P. Wensley, Faculty of Information, University of Toronto

When I first met Nick Bontis eleven years ago, he changed the way I saw the world of business. Those who know Nick, and those who have heard him speak, know what I am talking about. His grasp of the digital information revolution is legendary. Now he has brought his trademark insight, passion, candor and humour to a larger audience through this compelling and highly recommended book. *Information Bombardment* should be on your must-read list.

—David H. Brett, CEO and founder, Knexa

Dr. Nick Bontis presents compelling evidence of the creeping negative impact of information bombardment on individual life, organizational efficiency and institutional productivity. His exposition is from a practitioner's perspective, hence every knowledge worker can relate to it. He presents numerous life-saving, pragmatic and actionable solutions for all knowledge workers who wish finally to achieve the dream of working smarter, not harder.

—Dr. Rafik Loutfy, former vice president, Xerox Corporation

This book is a must-read for all knowledge workers to help them explore how to work smarter. Dr. Nick Bontis helps us make sense of the reality of information bombardment and how to cope with it effectively. With humor and multiple perspectives through a historical timeline, he offers practical advice for individuals and the organizations for which they work. This book is both fun to read and easy to use.

—Dr. Edna Pasher, author,
The Complete Guide to Knowledge Management

INFORMATION BOMBARDMENT

Rising Above the Digital Onslaught

Nick Bontis Ph.D.

Information Bombardment: Rising Above the Digital Onslaught

Published by Institute for Intellectual Capital Research

For more information:
Nick Bontis
nick@bontis.com
www.InformationBombardment.com
www.NickBontis.com

Photograph on cover taken by Roy Timm
roy@roytimmphotography.com
www.RoyTimmPhotography.com

Book design by Arbor Books, Inc.
www.arborbooks.com

Printed in the United States of America

Library and Archives Canada Cataloguing in Publication

Bontis, Nick
Information bombardment : rising above the digital onslaught / Nick Bontis.

Includes index.

ISBN 978-0-9867945-0-6

1. Human information processing--Popular works. I. Title.
BF444.B65 2011 153.4 C2011-900163-2

This book is dedicated to my "big fat Greek family":

Τια Μαρια, Ντινο, Τσαρλι, Σταυρουλα
Δεσποινα, Χαριλαος
Εφη, Κωστα
Παναγιωτα, Δημητρι, Στεφανο, Δεσποινα

May we continue to enjoy each other under the warmth of the sun, and may God bless our health and happiness.

TABLE OF CONTENTS

Foreword

Designing Our Lives for the Networked Age

For three decades I've written about the challenges of thriving in the information shower of the Digital Age. But today something extraordinary is happening: the continuous quantitative changes are becoming a qualitative change.

Information and computing technologies are moving on to "the second half of the chessboard"—a clever phrase coined by American inventor and author Ray Kurzweil. He told a story about the emperor of China, who was so delighted with the game of chess that he offered the game's inventor any reward he desired. The inventor asked for rice.

"I would like one grain of rice on the first square of the chessboard, two grains of rice on the second square, four grains of rice on the third square, and so on, all the way to the last square," he said. Thinking this would add up to a couple of bags of rice, the emperor happily agreed.

He was misguided. While small at the outset, the amount of rice escalated to more than two billion grains halfway through the chessboard. The final square would require nine billion billion grains of rice—enough to cover all of earth.

After decades of doubling and redoubling, we're now achieving gargantuan leaps in all facets of information technologies, such as processing power, storage capacity and bandwidth. Examples are everywhere, from Intel's computer chips to low-cost consumer electronics. When the MP3 player debuted in 1998 it stored less than a dozen songs. Now 160-gigabyte iPods store 40,000 songs.

Google CEO Eric Schmidt noted that between the dawn of civilization and 2003 there were five exabytes of data collected (an exabyte equals one quintillion bytes). Today five exabytes of data gets collected every two days. Soon there will be five exabytes every few minutes. It's an understatement to say that we're in danger of drowning.

But there is more to this than information overload. Because of the mobile Internet and the rise of pervasive computing, the shower continues all day long. Soon everything will be constantly connected to the Internet, including us. The growing number of little gadgets we carry will soon morph into one uber-gadget that is constantly online. These little Blackberrys/personal digital assistants/digital cameras/MP3 players/video cameras/GPS devices will continue to shrink in size and increase in functionality and ease of use.

Today this is obvious when your lunch companions check their Blackberrys for messages. But soon you won't be able to tell that they're even doing this. Their eyeglasses will have little video screens that can bring up any image they want. While you talk, they can check their e-mail or watch the news. Of course you can do the same, calling up the text of *Macbeth* when you think dropping some Shakespearian bon mot will impress your audience.

Most of us wonder what this environment is doing to the way we process information, learn and even think. Young people—digital natives—seem to be more adept at dealing with this new environment. I'm hopeful that the changes to their brains, caused by their growing up digital, will be positive ones. But many people worry and justifiably so, as there is much that we don't know about the human brain and human behavior. Will we all end up in "the shallows," as Nicholas Carr describes them, where we lose our capacity for deep thought? Will we abandon reading deeper and longer works and end up flittering around from one data source to another like a bee in a garden of flowers? Will this affect our relationships with others as we are consumed by thousand of weak social-media ties and have less time for those we love? Will this new world change not only how we think and relate but how we are—and the values we have and stand for?

I've written that we need to adopt a much more take-charge attitude about how we manage these tools and all this information, and, for that matter, how we live. More than ever before we need to step back and consciously design our lives. We need to decide explicitly what we stand for and whether we are the slaves or the masters of the new technologies.

When I was a kid, life for my parents was blissfully simpler. There was one daily newspaper in our house and three television channels. Dad went to work. Mum didn't. Workers put in their hours in factories or planned their days at the office, and the only source of interruption was the telephone. We had clear values—taught by our mothers in our homes and reinforced weekly at church. There was no pornography in the house or, for that matter, even on the newsstands in our town.

This was the late ’50s, and the cause célèbre was whether Ed Sullivan would show Elvis grinding his pelvis on his hugely popular Sunday night variety television show. The decision: no. All images of Elvis were from the waist up.

Smart companies are taking initiatives to help their employees cope with the new technology-rich world. They train their employees in time management and in becoming members of a values-based enterprise. They ensure that integrity is part of their corporate DNA. They design business models, structures and processes to ensure that work systems best serve the organization and maximize the effectiveness of its people.

Smart people and families should do the same. On the personal front, most of us, in our daily lives, in our work and in our families, muddle through this new data-rich, networked world, hopping from device to device, app to app, decision to decision or crisis to crisis without an overarching strategy. All of us should be applying principles of design to our lives and making conscious choices about how to upgrade our capacity to filter data, when we should use new technologies and what we believe in.

Adopt a values statement for yourself and your family—and constantly revise it as the world and conditions change. Don’t complain about technological overload. Know how to adjust and even turn off the shower. Harness the power of new technologies and transparency for the good; design them rather than letting them control you.

I hope you find ***Information Bombardment: Rising Above the Digital Onslaught*** to be a helpful contribution to this rather epic challenge.

—Don Tapscott

Don Tapscott is the author of fourteen books including ***MacroWikinomics: Rebooting Business and the World*** *(with Anthony D. Williams). He is an adjunct professor at the Rotman School of Management, University of Toronto.*

Preface

I have been wanting to write this book for a while. But I could never find the time. It seems that we all have the same challenge. Our lives are so busy. Since the first of my three children arrived several years back, I have been in pursuit of what I believe is the ultimate quest: how do I work smarter, not harder? This way, I can spend my time doing the really important things in life.

This book is about getting closer to that pursuit. The target reader for *Information Bombardment* is the modern knowledge worker with several e-mail accounts, the latest smartphone and an insatiable appetite to know—that is, to consume all available information. Unfortunately, while we pursue all the bounty of the digital world, we fail to realize the accompanying negative consequences. Why can't we sleep at night? Why do my fellow employees fail to collaborate with each other? Why can't my organization tap into to all of its cumulative expertise? Why did it take so long to respond to Hurricane Katrina?

While there are numerous books that discuss the knowledge economy, mobile technology, knowledge management and even intellectual capital, this is the first practitioner-focused book to address why we yearn for information to the point of unhealthy and unproductive bombardment. More importantly, this book provides some guidance about what we can do about this problem moving forward.

A knowledge worker (i.e., the typical reader of this book) is defined as someone who is valued for her ability to interpret information like a lawyer, a nurse, a researcher or any office worker. She consumes at least three times as much information as a generation ago and, while working in front of a computer, she can multitask across thirty-six applications in an hour. She is not afraid of digital technology and is often the first to own the latest gadget, which she uses to collaborate with her online community. She is the subject of my analysis.

At the individual level, I am very interested in the impact of all of this information bombardment on her health, her brain and her relationships. At the group level, do her friends share everything with her or do they choose to hoard certain tidbits of information? At the organization level, how does her firm leverage her full intellectual capital potential? Finally, how can her knowledge-sharing behaviors influence institutions and society at large?

This book is divided into three parts. Part one addresses the context and issues related to information bombardment (chapters one through eleven). Part two provides implications of the impact of information bombardment at multiple levels of analysis: individual, group, organization and institutional (chapters twelve through sixteen). Finally, part three provides actionable prescriptions that you can follow for all levels of analysis (chapters seventeen through twenty).

QR Codes

A QR Code is a two-dimensional barcode that is readable by smartphones. Scanning the QR codes at the end of chapters and sections in this book will conveniently point the browser on your mobile device to the specific website that will provide you with further information.

To download a QR code reader for your smartphone:

Step 1 Pick one of the following URLs listed below based on the model of your smartphone and insert it in the browser of your mobile device.

http://reader.kaywa.com
Motorola, Nokia, Sony Ericsson

http://get.beetagg.com
iPhone, BlackBerry, Samsung, Siemens

http://get.neoreader.com
Asus, Dopod, Hewlett Packard, LG, O2, Palm, Panasonic

http:// www.2dscan.com
For most other manufacturers

Try searching "QR code reader" on www.google.com for others and check out the App Store for Apple products and App World for RIM products

Step 2 After downloading and installing the appropriate QR code reader for your smartphone, launch the application and steadily place it above the QR code for a few seconds.

Step 3 Test your application with the following QR code which should take you directly to the book's main website www.InformationBombardment.com

Acknowledgements

I have received a great deal of emotional and intellectual support while writing *Information Bombardment.* For every person acknowledged, scores of others go unmentioned. I am grateful to all of them.

First, I would like to thank my speaking agents: Martin Perelmuter at Speakers' Spotlight (www.speakers.ca/bontis_nick.html) in Toronto and Wesley Neff at the Leigh Bureau (www.leighbureau.com/speaker.asp?id=341) in New York. They both advised (yelled at) me on numerous occasions over the last several years to shut up and just write the damn book. Well, finally I did.

Second, thanks to my academic colleagues who provide conceptual stimulation and a constant reminder why research and teaching must go hand in hand. Hearty handshakes go out to Mary Crossan, Chris Bart, Peter Vilks, Alexander Serenko and Paul Bates. Plus, a shout out to all of my past, current and future students. Thanks for allowing me to shape your minds three hours at a time.

Third, I would like to acknowledge my business partners, through whom I learn to apply my crazy ideas. High fives go out to Don Tapscott, David Brett, Jac Fitz-enz, Michael Kovacs and anyone else who has entrusted me for consulting services. I truly appreciate your business.

Finally, my sincerest gratitude goes to the editing, production and marketing team that helped transform this book from idea to reality. Cheers go to Doug Childress, James Uttel, Jessica Gorham, Olga Vladi, Larry Leichman, Andrew Carreiro, Ryan Burgio and Sourov De. Weren't those weekly Skype calls just awesome?

About the Author

Dr. Nick Bontis is the world's leading expert on intellectual capital and its impact on performance. He helps organizations leverage their most important intangible asset for sustainable competitive advantage.

Nick has been immersed in the field since 1991, when a cover story in *Fortune* magazine, titled "Brainpower," changed the course of his life. Risking a secure future, Nick left a promising banking career to pursue a PhD in the field. His groundbreaking doctoral dissertation went on to become the number one-selling thesis in Canada. At a relatively young age, his accomplishments thus far could fill a volume.

As a professional speaker, Nick has delivered keynote presentations on every continent for leading organizations in both the private and the public sectors. His dynamic, high-energy presentations provide personal and team recommendations for improving individual and organizational effectiveness, leaving audiences with the tools, inspiration and impetus to accelerate performance. His customized programs are a mix of practical managerial tools, rigorous academic research, strategic consulting, entertaining humor and a blast of youthful exuberance.

As an academic, "Nicky B" (as he is known by his students) is an award-winning, tenured professor who delivers enlightening content with energy that virtually zings off the walls when he steps into a room. He currently teaches strategy to undergraduates, knowledge management to MBAs and advanced statistics to PhD students at the DeGroote School of Business, McMaster University. He has won over twelve major teaching awards and was named faculty researcher of the year twice. Maclean's magazine has rated him as one of McMaster's most popular professors for six years in a row! TVO recognized him as one of the top ten lecturers in Ontario. OUSA awarded him Ontario's top professor award. He is also a 3M National Teaching Fellow, an exclusive honor only bestowed upon the top university professors in the country!

Nick earned his PhD from the prestigious Ivey Business School, University of Western Ontario, where he received the university's top scholastic achievement award. He also won a Canadian silver medal in the running long jump with a remarkable leap of seven and half meters—that's nearly twenty-five feet! Nick also competed on the UWO varsity men's soccer team, receiving both MVP and leading goal-scorer honors. As an athlete, Nick received national all-star status and several high-profile awards all while performing in the UWO symphony band as a euphonium player.

As a consultant, Dr. Bontis is the director of the Institute for Intellectual Capital Research—a leading strategic management consulting firm. His services have been sought after by leading organizations such as the United Nations, Microsoft, Health Canada, Royal Bank, Telus, Accenture, the US Navy and IBM. Tom Stewart, former editor of the Harvard Business

Review and *Fortune* magazine, recognizes him as a "pioneer and one of the world's real intellectual capital experts." Nick is also on the advisory boards of several organizations, including a variety of educational-based institutions designing and implementing executive development programs across the country. He is also on the board of Hillfield Strathallan College—one of Canada's leading independent schools, and Harvest Portfolios Group—an investment firm located in Oakville, Ontario.

As a writer and associate editor of the *Journal of Intellectual Capital*, Nick has won international acclaim for his groundbreaking research papers and management cases. He is ranked as one of the most-cited authors on intellectual capital and knowledge management in the world. As an entrepreneur, Nick is chief knowledge officer of Knexa Solutions—the world's first knowledge exchange and auction, based in Vancouver. Canadian and US patent applications have been filed for Knexa's dynamic pricing system.

Dr. Bontis also draws on his wealth of practical, hands-on business experience. He started his career at Human Resources Development Canada and later at KPMG. He then moved on to work for several years at CIBC Securities, Inc. in a varicty of areas including marketing, securities analysis, recruitment, strategy and software development. He received the CIBC Chairman's Award for outstanding contribution to the bank.

With his unique combination of substance and sizzle, Dr. Bontis is guaranteed to ignite, entertain and enlighten audiences, empowering them with both the tools and the inspiration to perform at a higher level of accelerated performance. He currently resides in Ancaster, Ontario, with his wife Stacy and their three young children, Charlie, Dino and Tia Maria.

Please visit the following links:

www.InformationBombardment.com
www.NickBontis.com
www.twitter.com/NickBontis
www.facebook.com/NickBontis
www.youtube.com/NickBontisMedia

CHAPTER 1

Seeking Balance in a Digital Storm

The day was absolutely perfect. My family and I arrived on the island of Santorini in the middle of the Aegean Sea. If you have never been to this little piece of paradise, I encourage you to do so if you get the chance. Sculpted out of one of the earth's largest-known volcanoes more than 3,500 years ago, Santorini is a small archipelago off the coast of Greece. Layers upon layers of different-color lava rock form ledges of terrain filled with cascading villas leading downward to the ocean. The glistening views from the whitewashed-stone terraces are spectacular, and the sunsets over the volcanic caldera are breathtaking. It has always been one of my most favorite places in the world.

My wife and I, as well as our three children, were making our annual summer escape to the island. But the day wasn't to be as perfect as I thought. Despite having physically escaped Ontario, there was still a chunk of me that couldn't leave. I hadn't checked my e-mail in over forty-eight hours, and I was about to go crazy. All those important messages and pieces of information that I fictionalized in my head were simply sitting in my inbox unattended. But there was another problem: on this exquisite Greek island, amidst the lavish beaches and gentle breeze, I couldn't get any reception on my BlackBerry.

How was I going to find out what I was missing without connectivity? I needed information, and I had been cut off. I was severed from the digital world!

"Daddy, come play soccer with me," Charlie, my older son, begged, tapping on my leg.

"Hold on," I replied. "Give me just a second. I'm trying to get some stock market quotes off my phone."

"Let's search for seashells, Daddy," came another request from Dino, my younger son.

"Can my dolly swim with us?" piped in my daughter, Tia Maria.

"Nick," my wife Stacy called from a few yards away, "what are you doing? Let's take a walk down the beach and catch the sunset."

"Just a second, everybody," I said, trying to buy some time. "I think I am getting a signal. I will be done soon."

I missed the sunset, regarded as one of the most romantic in the world. I missed an opportunity to play soccer, collect seashells and swim in the water. I lost these precious moments with my family on one of the most beautiful islands in the world. For what? For the endless search of knowledge. Or, better yet, for the need to quench my incessant addiction to information. I was held hostage by digital chains. I was craving my data fix as if it were air, food and water, yet in the process I failed to balance the most important things in my life.

Think back to the apex of the industrial era circa the mid-1960s. Steel workers at Dofasco, one of my hometown's largest employers, would go to the factory when the whistle blew. At day's end, the whistle would blow again, signaling them to go home. At night the workers would spend time with their families and then enjoy some leisurely pursuits. But when does the whistle blow today? Honestly, the whistle blows only if we shut off our smartphones. Most of us have more attentive relationships with our BlackBerrys than we do with our spouses and friends.

"Good morning, my love. Do you have any e-mails or alerts for me this morning? How's your battery, sweetheart? Are you feeling well connected?"

The first thing we do when we wake up and the last thing we do before going to bed is check our inboxes. Is it absolutely necessary that we yearn for a quick glimpse just to make sure some juicy piece of information didn't come across that might suddenly change our lives? Digital devices have crossed all boundaries of our lives, and some of us can't live without them. While we suffer from the dangers of a *crackberry* addiction, how do we achieve a healthy work-life balance?

Santorini is actually thought by some historians to be the long-lost island of Atlantis that was written about by Plato in the fourth century BC. A tremendous volcanic eruption left only an island remnant of what was once a thriving Minoan civilization. But eventually Hellenization spread back into the area, and great thinkers and philosophers like Plato, Aristotle and Socrates dreamed of a flourishing utopian society that would be the genesis of civilization. They sought knowledge and wisdom, or what the Greeks referred to as *sophos,* believing this was the key to progress. Yet there I was, ignoring the things that should have been important to me in exchange for the promises of a handheld device. On one end of the spectrum, I was surrounded by the genesis of civilized culture amidst the azure waters of the Aegean Sea, and on the other end I stood with my BlackBerry raised to the sky, trying to get a signal. Is this what my ancient Greek forefathers envisioned?

Bathing in Bits

The Kaiser Family Foundation recently released a study that found the average young American spends more than seven hours a day using some type of electronic device. Facebook, Twitter, instant messengers and smartphone apps are just the most recent newcomers to the attention-grabbing environment of today. Technological advances have allowed us to be connected constantly to streams of information from around the globe so that we don't have to miss a binary beat. We are literally bathing ourselves in bits, and some of us are drowning.

What drives us to do such a thing? Do we really gain that much more from interfacing with a cold, hard piece of metal than with other people? Some people would say definitely yes. Without question we have entered the knowledge era and left the industrial era and agricultural era behind. No longer do we use our brawn and physical skills to harvest the land. Instead, we use our brains. Without knowledge we are left defenseless. Ignorance carries a huge price tag in the knowledge era. If you're left out of the loop, it is likely you're going to be left behind.

The big problem is that most of us have no idea how to filter, organize and prioritize all the information we receive. While much information is useful, we are constantly being bombarded with a huge amount of *noise*. Junk mail, spam, sales pitches, gossip and propaganda saturate our attention spans. If you were to open up a new Hotmail account today, it would take on average about eight minutes before you received your first spam mail. More than likely it would be about how cheaply you can buy Viagra or about some guy in Nigeria who is in dire need of your financial support. How many of these e-mails do we need?

The bottom line is that we cannot help ourselves. We are so fearful of being left out that we sacrifice things that are important to us simply in order to stay informed. That means we have left the door open for *information bombardment* to occur. With more than a billion Internet users in the world, there are plenty of eager people to provide you with vast amounts of information—both useful and useless. Unless we learn to get a handle on how to discern the quality of this information and our *real* need for the information, the negative effects of information bombardment are bound to happen. In fact, they already have.

I didn't really need to check my inbox on vacation. All of my colleagues knew I was away on holiday. Nothing was pressing whatsoever. Yet this need to know had somehow become more important to me than spending time with my family or even allowing myself to relax. The longer I went without an Internet connection, the more anxious I became. The more anxious I felt, the harder it was to relax and enjoy myself. I had become addicted to knowing the latest and greatest piece of information that might have come across my path. I had allowed my inbox to be more important than anything else. I was bathing in bits and drowning. Meanwhile, my family was starving for another scarce resource.

Today's Scarcest Resource

If you take a survey and ask a thousand people what the most limited resource is today, the majority will respond by saying "time." But time doesn't change. Time has always been the same. You don't have more time one day and less the next. There are always twenty-four hours in a day, sixty minutes in an hour and sixty seconds in a minute. Therefore, time cannot be more or less scarce with each passing generation or even millennium. Time is limited, but it is constantly limited to the same degree. Time isn't the primary problem, however; how we use our time is.

In the knowledge era, our attention spans are the scarcest resource. Do I give 100 percent of my attention to my boss as he speaks at a corporate luncheon? Or do I share my attention between him and my e-mails as they come across my BlackBerry? If I share my attention between both, then I get rewarded by being more efficient and more productive. This, in turn, may lead to a promotion or greater opportunities for me. Today, incentives are in place that encourage me to share my attention among different and sometimes competing demands. The amount of time I have doesn't change, so how can I get more out of time? Easy: split my attention by optimally allocating my priorities. This is more commonly referred to as *multitasking.*

I have a theory. I believe that one's age is inversely proportionate to the number of windows that are simultaneously open on one's desktop computer. For example, my father Harry is a successful accountant who taught himself how to use a computer in his sixties. On an average day at work I have watched him open his Outlook and read e-mails from his clients. Then he closes Outlook to open up a Google search browser to find the phone number of his favorite restaurant on The Danforth (Toronto's Greek area). Then he closes the browser and opens a media player to listen to Paschalis Terzis (his favorite singer). The peculiar part of this whole process is that only one window is open at a time.

In contrast, my first-year university students typically

have ten or more windows open simultaneously as they write up their assignments in Word, crunch some numbers in Excel, surf the Web, post photos on Facebook, burn a CD, download an MP3 file, tweet their emotions and more. Over the past couple of generations, the environment has rewarded those who compartmentalize their attention spans into small chunks and multitask. Today, a whole generation of children naturally multitask because it is a sign of the times. They have grown up us digital multitaskers.

But multitasking has had its costs. My children are starving for my attention. My wife spends romantic sunsets on immaculate beaches without me holding her. And, deep down, though I refuse to hear it, a small voice within me is screaming for some exhalation and relaxation. Instead, I choose to give the bulk of my attention to a silicon chip within a plastic case connected to streams of data that I do not even truly need. Like many of you, I have been socialized into feeling that these bits of information are critical to my survival. So I give them my attention while relationships and quality of life suffer. Have you tried cuddling in bed with your BlackBerry lately?

False Promises of Technology

Back in the days of the agricultural era, multigenerational families worked together on farms to grow crops that fed the population. In the early twentieth century, thirty million people provided food for 100 million Americans. But over the ensuing decades, guess what happened? The children of these farming families learned to read, to write and to think. Seemingly overnight, there was an exodus of farm workers as young, bright men and women chose to pursue other professional careers.

Did the world then starve? No. Technology came to the rescue with new farming equipment (e.g., bulldozers, genetically modified seeding systems, and irrigation architecture designed by these newly educated men and women that could more efficiently and effectively assist with food production). By the end of the twentieth century, ten million people could now feed over 300 million Americans. Who could argue that technological advancement wasn't a good thing?

To a point, innovation is certainly a wonderful thing. However, at some point we begin to give away too much of ourselves in the process. Today, we have satellite and cable television systems that provide us with dozens if not hundreds of channels to sample. We have satellite and Web-based radio that let us choose a specific genre of song anytime we want. Of course, with the help of Google, our ability to search for any answer with the tapping of a few keys places us in the midst of a sea of information. This all sounds good, right?

Let me pose a question to you: Do you think it is simply a coincidence that the rise in ADHD (attention deficit hyperactivity disorder) over the last thirty years occurred during the same time that society experienced an explosion of information? I don't. I remember how when I was a kid, there were less than ten channels on our RCA television set. If I wanted to change the channel, I had to get my lazy self off the couch and rotate the dial. As a result, I would endure long segments of time viewing one program without shifting my focus of attention. Today, with a universal remote control in my hand, I find I spend only a few minutes at best on a channel before moving to another. Or, better yet, my kids use the picture-in-picture functionality of a 1080p 3D LED display to watch five channels simultaneously (of the several hundred available) in rich 9.1 Dolby digital surround sound.

The infusion of information into our environments has forced us to share our attention, and it has taught us to become better multitaskers. But in addition it has taught us how to rapidly shift our attention from one item to the next. Did you know that most people can scan an e-mail's sender and its subject line and decide whether or not to delete it within 1.2 seconds? Pretty cool skill, eh? No one taught us that in school. But while that is extremely efficient, the act enforces brief bursts of attention. It is becoming harder and harder to attain skills in focused and long-lasting periods of concentration. This is the kind of attention my wife and kids are craving.

Why do I keep clicking forward through the television channels even though I find a show that is somewhat intriguing? The answer is the same reason why I am dying to get a signal from my BlackBerry on vacation: I don't want to miss any little juicy piece of information or entertainment. There is *always* something better on television than what I am currently watching! Technology has enabled us to have access to vast amounts of variety within multiple forms of communication. Yet without the ability to filter and prioritize this information, the same technology is causing our quality of life to decline.

Technology has always caused paradigms to shift, but some of technology's promises have not always been true. Do you remember the big promise technology made when the computer replaced the typewriter?

"Think of all the paper we will save. Everything will be stored and transferred electronically, so all that waste will disappear. We will all work in paperless offices!"

This has hardly been the case. We currently use more than 100 million tons of paper each year in the US alone. When you check in at the airport, in most cases you still must go to a kiosk to print out your boarding pass to get through security. Despite your medical records at your doctor's office being electronically stored, health-care payers often still require paper documents to justify proposed charges. Instead of saving paper and allowing society to become paperless, electronic technology has done the opposite. Even though we may print out a smaller percentage of the total stored information available, the entire quantity of information has risen exponentially. The end result is that we have more paper floating around than ever before.

While information bombardment and the demands of attention sharing are evident in recent technological advances, technology is also rapidly replacing—or displacing—many areas once thought to be ruled only by the human brain. Stories about machines replacing factory workers are nothing new. Likewise, machines eliminating positions that primarily organize, categorize or distribute products are quite common. But what about machines that can actually *think?*

In 1997 IBM designed a machine called Deep Blue that successfully competed against the world's best human chess player. Compared to other computers, its processing power allowed it to calculate up to 200 million chess moves in a second, and it could anticipate all potential permutations up to twenty moves ahead. Garry Kasparov, the reigning world grandmaster, took on Deep Blue in a six-game match. In the end, Deep Blue successfully beat Kasparov after the champion made an early mistake in the last game. It was the first time a machine had ever accomplished this feat.

Do you think it is impossible for computers and their artificial intelligence to surpass the capacity of the brain? Let's think about this in practical terms for a moment. The brain has approximately 100 billion nerve cells called *neurons.* At a base level, it is safe to assume that each neuron has a storage capacity of at least one byte of information. That means the average brain can store at least ten gigabytes even before we consider connections between neurons. If you then add the ability to store information between neurons in neural networks, experts estimate the total brain capacity may be as high as 1,000 terabytes (a terabyte is 1,000 gigabytes!). That is a huge amount of storage ability and processing power.

Certainly there is no way a computer processor and storage device could house that much information. Wrong. The Library of Congress and many other large databases are rapidly approaching this figure. Ancestry.com reports a total storage capacity of 600 terabytes after it added US census data from 1790 through 1930 to its online database. Its total figure is rapidly approaching the theorized total brain capacity to hold and process information. It's no wonder we are beginning to feel the effects of information bombardment. I'm getting a headache just thinking about it.

As nanochips get smaller and the devices we use become more powerful and faster, it is likely that these devices will begin interacting and communicating amongst themselves. Not only will we have information from other people to digest but we will also have an entire new body of artificial intelligence to keep up with. Think about it: is your life better as a result of all the technology around you? Or has it simply provided a way with which to bombard you with more information in a shorter amount of time? If quality of life is truly better, then we should all be enjoying the pleasures and sunsets of Santorini.

Information and Your Health

Ever since the development of the Internet, a great deal of buzz has been publicized about being informed about your own health. You should know about any disorders you have, the side effects of your medications, your family history and more. An informed patient knows the right questions to ask his or her doctor before they even meet. Yet the ironic thing is that information itself is one of the biggest health risks today. Our constant thirst for information places demands on us mentally that affect us over the long term.

Did you know that thirty percent of the population in all industrialized societies suffers from some type of insomnia? Almost one in every three people! More than ninety percent of these people cannot sleep because of stresses occurring in their lives. They may have had a recent emotional loss or experienced some type of trauma. But many simply are struggling to keep up with all the information they contend with each day.

As a management professor at the DeGroote School of Business at McMaster University, I have my own share of deadlines to meet and pressures with which to contend. But through it all, I am constantly available to give my attention to my BlackBerry or computer should instant messaging, e-mail or video conferencing requests arrive. What I didn't realize was the amount of mental energy it took to be so constantly vigilant. When it came time to go to bed at night, coming off this digital high was nearly impossible.

The chemical released in our bodies when we are so hyper-vigilant is called *adrenaline*. Adrenaline is great for situations when you must fight and defend yourself or escape a hostile situation, but to be in a constant state of *adrenalization* is not a good thing. In addition to causing you not to sleep, being constantly adrenalized can lead to anxiety disorders, high blood pressure and even heart disease. Information bombardment doesn't only affect your social relationships; it can affect your physical and mental health as well.

Are you working to live or living to work? A balance between working and personal time is important in order to be healthy, but the number of people actually paying attention to this balance is shrinking every day. That doesn't mean that constant information-seeking isn't important in today's knowledge era, but there needs to be a happy medium to be maximally productive.

In the US, most employees get two weeks of vacation a year, but most of us don't even take that. In contrast, many Mediterranean countries take six weeks of vacation a year. In Greece, the entire month of August is a time for relaxing and leisure. No wonder why, when my family travels to Santorini, all the people there have smiles on their faces. The goal is to work smarter, not harder.

Vacation and leisure time have to be part of our priorities. Yes, sometimes we just have to turn the BlackBerry and the computer off. We clearly forget that all of these machines can be unplugged! That sounds pretty scary, eh? But in order to succeed in the knowledge era, we will need to find this balance in order to maximize overall productivity and quality of life. It's time to unleash the digital chains that bits and bytes have over us and take back control of our lives.

My mother, Despina, spends almost every waking moment of her summer months tending to her lovely garden. She has a fantastic green thumb that is the envy of all of her neighbors. In fact, some budding horticulturists in the community have visited her simply to get advice on what flowers they should plant in their own gardens. My mother is always willing to part with her wisdom, which she has cultivated over several decades. In her case, the beauty of her knowledge is like the beauty of her garden: it is always more valuable when shared with others.

Knowledge or Null Edge?

Here is a fact: knowledge is power. We use it to wield authority over people, groups, communities and even nations. We need it to succeed in our personal lives and in the workplace. The boundaries of geography and physical limitations no longer apply. Knowledge goes beyond these constraints and encompasses an ever-expanding body of information that is increasing at exponential rates. But as knowledge expands, time does not. This leaves us having to decide how best to manage the information with which we are bombarded and to which fragments to lend our precious attention spans.

I see us at a crossroads of sorts, or perhaps the edge of a cliff would be a better analogy. Each of us is confronted with endless bits of data second to second—the current temperature outside, the forecast for tomorrow, the exchange rate, the stock market level and whatever else we want to know. We thrive on it and have become dependent on it. But the costs have reached a point where we are suffering in the quagmire. Is it all necessary? Must we have it all at our fingertips right now? We obviously survived without it before, yet now we eagerly yearn for it and digest it bit by byte. All the while, our families, our friends and our health pay the consequences. This is the place I call *null edge.*

We can choose to embrace the knowledge era and gain control over the information bombardment that attacks us from every angle, or we can fall off the edge of the cliff and drown in an ocean of data. The digital chains of information bombardment will drag us over the edge unless we begin to prioritize and discern what is most important.

There is an old adage that states that when you are young, you have plenty of time but no money; when you are middle-aged you have money but little time; and only when you are elderly do you have both money and time. I don't think this has to be true. I am often shocked when I hear colleagues complain that they have little time to do task A or B. It is the number-one complaint I hear in the workplace. Under my breath, I basically scoff at how poorly they are allocating their attention spans. One of the main objectives in my life is to maximize wealth and quality of life while minimizing energy expended. This is what we all want, isn't it?

I have been to Santorini many times now, but my vacations are much different from before. I still check my e-mail periodically, but I don't let information control my life. I take in the treasures that the island has to offer and think about what my Greek ancestors might have thought as they walked on the same beaches, swam in the same seas and watched the same sunsets. Could they ever have fathomed that our world would exist as it does today? Would they believe the magnitude of information each of us deals with on a daily basis? Despite all of this progress in technology, and despite bathing in bits and bytes, are we really better off?

No matter how you answer these questions, the fact remains that we all have to deal with information bombardment, and how this is done affects all of us at different levels. We now have no choice. We must do something about this yesterday. If not, we are in for dire consequences. On a personal level, our family lives and our health will be harmed. In groups and organizations, efficiency, productivity and profitability are at stake. Our nations and the global community continue to pay a high price. Information bombardment has already lead to catastrophic disasters like the failure to prevent 9/11 or to assist families quickly enough during Hurricane Katrina or the earthquake in Haiti. These are very real practical implications.

So what can we do? Plenty. But in order to understand how to tackle information bombardment, we first have to understand how we got to this point in our history. Our knowledge base hasn't been steadily progressing through the generations. In fact, we have entered an exponential period of information explosion never before experienced. Unless we start to develop the tools with which to manage ourselves in the knowledge era, we indeed may be looking to an era of null edge. The choice is ours.

FURTHER READING

Kaiser study: http://www.kff.org/entmedia/mh012010pkg.cfm

Insomnia: http://www.ncbi.nlm.nih.gov/pmc/articles/PMC1978319/

Attention deficit hyperactivity disorder: http://www.nice.org.uk/nicemedia/pdf/CG72FullGuideline.pdf

Paper used in US: http://www.afandpa.org/

Brain capacity: http://www.moah.org/exhibits/archives/brains/technology.html

Computer storage: http://www.cbsnews.com/stories/2006/06/22/tech/main1740956.shtml

Scan QR code for direct link to website, hypertext links and other resources:

CHAPTER 2

Phoenicians, Gutenberg and the Mark I

It's five o'clock in the morning and my alarm is going off. Sluggishly I sit up and reach over to my night table. Before I even glance over to see if the alarm has awoken my wife, I am already checking my BlackBerry to see what e-mails I received during my slumber. My wife's good-morning kiss will have to wait. I cradle my BlackBerry gently and check the screen with wild anticipation. Wow, only forty messages in the last five hours! I skim through my inbox and isolate the critical action items. Awesome—all of my messages are good news. There is nothing critical, upsetting or time-sensitive that requires my attention for the next fifteen minutes. What a relief! I now feel calm and at ease, ready to start the new day.

Then I check out the last five hours' worth of tweets, typically from my European and Asian followers. Then a quick read through my global news reader, weather updates and my personalized stock ticker, and I am off to the washroom. Within the hour I have completed a rigorous sprint on my incline treadmill and I have showered and dressed, all the while catching up-to-date local news.

Within the following thirty minutes, I have negotiated the streets and highway with my GPS and its dynamically updated traffic re-router. An optical character reader scans my license plate for the obligatory highway usage fee. In the background I listen to my satellite radio and make mental notes of the morning's top economic and business news. The RFID parking tag on my windshield automatically raises the gate in front of my building and a local schematic points out the only remaining parking spot. The security card opens my office door and I finally sit in my ergonomic chair.

At my desk I will immerse myself in dozens of papers to grade as well as a handful of new research papers that I must edit before classes begin at eight-thirty sharp. Hardly four hours will have passed, yet I will already have digested a tremendous volume of information. This is simply a typical, average day for most knowledge workers. Who are we? Individuals who leverage their intellectual capital for economic benefit.

How did we get here? Was it always like this? No, it wasn't. Information bombardment is a relatively new phenomenon. When Plato wrote about the island of Santorini and the legend of Atlantis, he wasn't being constantly interrupted by a beeping pager or a ringing cell phone. The biggest thing he had to worry about was a student asking him a question or two about his philosophical musings. Our current world barely resembles the tranquility of the world that existed back in ancient times. The reason for this lies in the fundamental concept of *knowledge codification.*

In simple terms, knowledge codification is the process of externalizing our tacit expertise to give it permanent form. In other words, we take what we know and write it down to distribute it to another place or person more easily. Telling a story about an event as someone takes notes is a means of codification. Writing a news account of a recent happening for others to read is codification. Even sending an e-mail to a fellow employee about why you don't like a company policy is codification. Knowledge codification is what allows us to learn about the world around us, whether it pertains to cultures, beliefs, values or facts. It is also the reason why we find ourselves bombarded with information today.

Prehistoric Codification

Let's go back 200,000 years in time to the Paleolithic Era, when people lived in caves and communicated with each other through a series of grunts, groans and gestures. Cave people were primarily hunters and gatherers and lived a nomadic lifestyle, roaming from place to place. No alphabets, symbols or even common languages were present among various gatherings of people, and therefore codification of information was very limited. Instead of schools and books, information was communicated through songs, folklore, oral stories, behavioral patterns and traditions. The pressures of the day had more to do with finding enough food to survive and avoiding predators than it did with information processing.

"Hey Joe, got some meat?"

"No, ate it all."

"Let's go hunt for some more."

"OK."

Perhaps this is oversimplified, but the bottom line is that our ancient ancestors weren't checking their e-mails, checking the morning news or even grabbing magazines. Their needs were simple and the amount of information they had to deal with was limited. They could easily distribute their knowledge to other members of their society through oral traditions and experience. I doubt anyone suffered from attention deficit disorder then.

Around 10,000 BC, societies began to shift from a nomadic lifestyle to a more regionalized way of living. With the introduction of the agricultural era, food supplies became more plentiful and the use of metal tools made travel more cumbersome. More importantly, this new means of existence provided an entirely new set of skills and knowledge. In addition to the skills of hunting and gathering, methods of crop cultivation and harvesting had to be passed on from generation to generation in order for progress and survival to occur. Apprenticeships and rites of passage began to emerge as means to distribute knowledge to younger members of the group. The need to become more efficient at codifying information was slowly becoming evident.

Codification Shift #1: The Alphabet

Around 3,500 BC—incidentally, the same time period during which the volcanic eruption formed the island of Santorini—a group of people in Mesopotamia began to develop the first writing system using letters and symbols. I imagine two guys were sitting around having to memorize some epic poem when suddenly one of them had a better idea.

"You know, Pete, I'm tired of trying to remember all these rhymes and stories. It would sure be nice if we could see them instead of having to memorize them."

"Yeah, the pictures on the vases and walls just don't help me remember what I am supposed to say."

"Hey, how about we make a picture for each sound and then we won't have to remember them?"

"Good idea! You make a sound and I'll give it a symbol."

This shaped the foundation of writing, which eventually led to the first set of hieroglyphics in Egypt circa 3,400 BC. The Phoenicians then developed the first widely used alphabet circa 2,000 BC. Letters and symbols were carved in stone and written in ink on different types of plant leaves. Instead of having to rely on memorization and inherent human error in recollection, written documentation was now available to be passed on from person to person. This change was a significant shift towards allowing knowledge codification to occur at a more accelerated rate. The time it took to write a passage of information compared to memorizing it was significantly less.

The Egyptian hieroglyphics led to the Phoenician writing system, which was the basis for the full writing scripts subsequently developed by the Greeks. Literacy began to flourish slowly throughout the region. Eventually, literacy spread through Europe and Asia, setting the stage for the formal codification of culture and history. The alphabet clearly was a major milestone in accelerating the dissemination of information more efficiently.

From the first development of a writing system in 3,500 BC, it took 1500 years for an established alphabet to be accepted and used. It then took another 900 years before the use of an alphabet was widespread among the many regions of the civilized world. Despite this, literacy rates within the ancient Greco-Roman empires were around fifteen percent at their height of power. Can you imagine progress being this slow today? I get frustrated now because the BlackBerry I bought a year ago no longer has the most up-to-date features available. This puts things in perspective, doesn't it?

Gradually, the ability to read and write became incorporated into the European traditions of education. During the Early Middle Ages, Catholic monasteries were the main sources of literary education, which was primarily religious-based. These institutions evolved into religious universities, with secular universities beginning to appear around 1,500 AD. The concept of a teacher educating students one on one was radically changed as books and manuscripts became increasingly available. Now entire lecture halls could be filled with students, allowing one teacher to pass on his or her expertise in a more efficient and scalable manner.

Believe it or not, books were copied by hand in those days. In both monasteries and scriptoria, scribes would diligently copy one book at a time. On average it would take a scribe a year to copy Martin Luther's version of the Bible. Can you imagine ordering a book on Amazon.com and receiving it a year later in written form? Regardless, alphabets and the ability to rewrite books changed the way codification occurred and allowed the spread of knowledge well beyond regional confines. The distribution of information was markedly expanded from the prior methods of memorization and verbalization.

Codification Shift #2: The Printing Press

Johannes Gutenberg, a goldsmith in Germany, is the man credited with creating the first printing press. It was invented in 1440. Using his skills of metallurgy, advances in newer paper styles and oil-based ink, Gutenberg successfully designed a movable-type printing press that revolutionized society forever. Despite the fact that pages and characters had to be set individually, the printing press was much faster than handwritten scripts. Books could be created in a fraction of the time and had a greater degree of readability compared to cursive script.

You might find it hard to imagine just how far-reaching the effects of the printing press were on society at large. For example, the ability to mass produce the Bible and distribute it throughout Europe facilitated the Protestant Reformation. The ability of scientists throughout the world to compare and share their experimental findings through printing-press documents led to the scientific revolution. The Renaissance, which was just beginning when the printing press was introduced, flourished as information regarding art, literature and history was disseminated throughout Europe and Asia. In other words, more efficient codification systems led to worldwide changes in global culture.

I need to point out one important aspect of the printing press in addition to its enhanced knowledge codification abilities. Prior to the printing press, Cambridge University's library housed a total of 122 books. Most of us today have at least that many books in our own homes. But what is noteworthy is that the value of each of these books was equal to the price of a small farm or vineyard at the time. Hand-copied books weren't cheap! The human-labor hours involved in copying a book were significant, and the cost alone prohibited the universal spread of information. This all changed with the invention of the printing press.

With the prices of books falling, the supply of books rising and the demand for greater literary materials skyrocketing, an explosion of literacy occurred during the Renaissance period and spread rapidly throughout the industrialized world. Newspapers began to appear, as did periodicals. Information was available to people from sources that had never been accessible previously. In essence, the printing press allowed a democratization of information that had not been present previously. Instead of codified knowledge being only available to clergy and those of the upper class, information was now available to everyone.

What is the single most important skill needed to reap the benefits of codified information? One must be able to read! Before the printing press, estimated literacy rates were less than twenty percent. But in the centuries that followed the introduction of the printing press, these rates rose dramatically. For example, literacy rates in France rose from thirty-five percent to ninety-five percent between 1720 AD and 1880 AD. The literacy rates in New England at the time of the American Revolution were more than ninety percent. Eventually, the ability to read translated into better skills in writing. The ability to codify knowledge was growing dramatically.

Despite taking more than 3,000 years to evolve from an alphabet to the printing press, the changes that took place after the printing press were rapid. Within a few centuries, the codified information available to everyone was exponentially increased compared to centuries earlier. It seems that a snowball of information was gaining momentum, but no one could have predicted what would happen next. Up until that point, we had barely scratched the surface in our abilities to codify knowledge.

Codification Shift #3: The Computer

We take computers for granted today, but this was hardly the case a few decades ago. The very first programmable computers were actually developed in the 1940s through a series of discoveries and technological advances. Electronic computation and storage of data defined what is now considered the modern-day computer. But you would hardly recognize those machines compared to the slick, compact devices of today.

IBM created the Mark I computer in 1944 for Harvard University. It was the first digital and fully automated computer designed with electromechanical systems. Its presence marked the dawning of the modern Computer Age. Just to give you an idea about its features, consider the following factoids about the Mark I:

- Weight: 10,000 pounds
- Length: 51 feet
- Height: 8 feet
- Wires: 500 miles in total length
- Wire connections: 3 million
- Time for addition and subtraction operations: 3 per second
- Time for multiplication operations: 1 every 6 seconds
- Time for logarithmic operations: over 1 minute

This computer occupied a small office building and had a tiny fraction of the computing ability of today's cell phones. Even so, this represented a tipping point for codification. With the invention of the Mark I, the world would never be the same.

Over the next decade, vacuum tubes replaced wires, and computers became more compact. By the 1960s transistors enabled even smaller computers. Transistors had the benefit of not only being smaller but also faster, more reliable, less expensive and less energy-consuming. By the 1970s, microprocessors and integrated circuitry revolutionized computer size and power again. These advances allowed computers to be small enough for individual use and consumption. Thus was born the personal computer.

With each step of technological advancement, the ability to codify information grew significantly. Today's modern computer is able to handle billions of instructions per second without any problem. Though program codes may take teams of people to write, software and hardware programs provide incredibly fast abilities to manipulate, compute, store and relay information. Don't think this processing power is limited to your laptop or home computer. Even the smartphone you hold in your hand is a fully computerized microprocessor in its own right. What used to take up blocks on the street now fits snugly in your palm.

Sometimes I envision some dark room back in the early 1400s, lit by oil lamps, where some poor scribe diligently labors to copy precisely the written text of some worn manuscript. Page by page he works occasionally wiping his forehead and trying to refocus his weary eyes. Can you imagine walking into that room with your BlackBerry, scanning the pages with its digital camera and then sending the images over to a wireless printer? The poor scribe would probably die of shock! Imagine what may lie ahead for us given the same passage of time.

Today, we not only have isolated information present on our computers; we also have instantaneous access to information all over the world. Using telecommunications technologies, every computerized device (including peripheral devices like printers and scanners) is capable of having its own IP address, enabling it to network with other devices. This is the basis of the Internet, allowing you to send and receive e-mails from multiple locations. The World Wide Web is exactly that: a huge interconnection of electronic signals sending and receiving vast amounts of data. The capacity for codification today can hardly be compared to the same abilities in millennia past. It's no wonder we are faced with the dilemma of how to survive information bombardment.

The Concept of Singularity

Technological singularity is a term that has been in use since the mid-1960s, and it pertains directly to our conversation about information bombardment and codification. As you can see, the progress since prehistoric times until today has been quite dramatic in terms of the ability to pass knowledge from one generation to the next. However, even more evident is the speed at which changes in codification are now occurring. What once took centuries to evolve now takes only a few years.

The time from one evolutionary period to the next has accelerated significantly. For example, during the Paleolithic time period, the economy of societies took 250,000 years to double in size. Fast forward to today and most software is outdated within a year. Technology has pushed the envelope when it comes to speed of change. But what if technology changed so fast that machines grew smarter than humans? In fact, the capacity of the human brain (despite its enormous processing power) has been relatively fixed for the last several millennia. In contrast, the processing power and memory-storage capacity of machines keeps growing exponentially. At this point, artificial intelligence has only been limited by the ability of the human brain to create it. But at some point this may change. What if machines gained greater intelligence than human designers and became more proficient at building more intelligent machines? This is the premise behind super-intelligence and the concept of singularity.

I. J. Good, a British statistician, described an intelligence explosion at some point in the future. This critical point would occur when a computer gained the ability to be more intelligent than the human brain. The increased computational capability of the world's fastest computers through the last 60 years supports the rapid trend towards this tipping point. Once it is reached, Good suggests, an effective change in reality could be quite sudden and quite dramatic. The machine that possesses this superintelligence, along with its subsequent superintelligent machines that it creates, will continue to advance the ability to process and store information at escalating abilities surpassing all human capacity.

Imagine getting out of bed for the day only to be controlled by the information systems around you. Your wardrobe is chosen based on the weather, the agenda and the fashion of the day. Your breakfast is selected based on your health factors, the food's nutritional content, worldwide scarcities and other environmental factors. Your route to work is determined, as well as your mode of transportation, based on a network of communications occurring between several super-smart computer systems. At what point do we choose to manage the information in front of us versus assigning that responsibility to artificial intelligence and super-smart machines?

Perhaps this is a bit too futuristic for you, but without question computers are gaining ground in the area of information codification. Part of the reason we are confronted with so much data every waking moment is the technological advances in computer science. We have become so good at codifying knowledge that the volume of information surrounding us is becoming overwhelming. It can cause us to become paralyzed and unproductive. The natural tendency would be to let a machine handle it for us instead, and in many cases this is a good thing. But in some situations we simply need to learn how to manage information better ourselves.

Where Do We Go From Here?

By now you may be getting the feeling that the accelerated rate of information codification is a bad thing. Certainly this is not the case. Without the ability of supercomputers processing mountains and mountains of data, we never would have been able to determine DNA genome sequencing, which has elucidated many important facts about human diseases. Without rapid information codification, space travel and revelations about global warming would have been out of our reach. We also trust that interconnected computers and their enormous information-processing power are essential in establishing safeguards against spoiled terrorist attacks and the threats of natural disasters. We can also look to the collective processing power of cloud computing to inform us about possible life in space and the origins of the first big bang. The villain is not information codification itself but our failure to manage it effectively.

Just as information can be helpful in solving problems and preempting disasters, the failure to manage information well can result in catastrophic effects. I am sure you remember the events in New Orleans a few years back, during Hurricane Katrina. The US Army Corps of Engineers, the Federal Emergency Management Agency (FEMA), the New Orleans mayor, the New Orleans Police Department superintendent and even President George Bush all had information that could have prevented the unfortunate happenings occurring in the wake of the storm. But what happened? Information wasn't shared and was grossly mismanaged. Not only did people suffer and lose property as a result, but many people lost their lives.

Progress brings both the good and the bad. We now live in an age where information is abundant, and that alone brings responsibilities that we all share. History shows us that our ability to codify knowledge is growing by leaps and bounds. Part of this progress has occurred due to technological advancements, but this isn't the only reason. You and I are in part to blame for this information explosion. After all, we asked for it. Our insatiable desire to know has fueled the fire that led to our current capacity to distribute information so effectively. Our ability to codify information is only one piece of the puzzle.

FURTHER READING

IBM Mark I: http://www-03.ibm.com/ibm/history/exhibits/markI/markI_intro.html

France's illiteracy rates: http://en.wikipedia.org/wiki/File:Illiteracy_france.png

Prehistoric education: http://starfsfolk.khi.is/allyson/africa/traditional-education.pdf

Middle Ages education: http://www.frinstitute.org/allschools1.html

Mesopotamia writing origins: http://www.mesopotamia.co.uk/writing/story/sto_set.html

Hieroglyphics: http://en.wikipedia.org/wiki/History_of_writing

Technological singularity: http://en.wikipedia.org/wiki/Technological_singularity

Gutenberg press: http://inventors.about.com/od/gstartinventors/a/Gutenberg.htm

Scan QR code for direct link to website,
hypertext links and other resources:

CHAPTER 3

I'm Thirsty—More Knowledge, Please

When I was a young boy, there was no such thing as a universal remote control. In fact, my parents' Zenith television didn't have any kind of remote channel changer whatsoever. If I wanted to change the channel, I had to get up from the couch and change it manually. Of course, you know what happened: I would simply watch whatever happened to be on that channel. In other words, the television programs had more control over what I watched than I did. Eventually, a device called a *converter* came along. This was not the digital-to-analog converter you may be familiar with today. The converter of which I am speaking had to do with the remote ability to change the television channel. A converter was a box with several push buttons that was connected to the television by a long wire. By pressing a button I could change the channel from the comfort of my couch. Wow! What a change in the way television could be watched. I now had more control. I now had power over how my time watching television was managed. Enter modern-day information on demand.

It may seem like a small change, but the ability to dictate what I wanted to watch by pressing a button was a tipping point. This small technological advancement allowed us to express our thirst for knowledge and make choices to satisfy our thirst. Technology provided us with the tools, but our thirst for knowledge drove the explosion of information that exists today. The more information we received, the stronger our thirst became. We now crave knowledge to the point of information bombardment. We simply cannot get enough.

Why is this? Is it simply human nature? Is it because we need information to survive? Why is our thirst for knowledge so intense? Understanding the answers to these questions can allow us to appreciate how we got to where we are today. Too much knowledge is not necessarily a bad thing, but appreciating what information is (and is not) useful can be critical to surviving in the knowledge era.

Knowledge As a Means of Survival

The codification of knowledge, as discussed in the preceding chapter, demonstrates that information passed from one generation to the next is essential if progress is to be made. It would be highly inefficient if each successive generation had to establish the same processes, technologies and literature all over again. Each generation provides a building block of knowledge that allows the next to reach a little higher. So, in a significant way, our thirst for knowledge is founded on the needs to progress and survive. Essentially, this is the concept of *perpetual incrementalization.*

The basis of law and civilization was founded on this concept. The establishment of legal codes and a set of laws allowed societies to function. By legally defining relationships between people and between groups, acceptable standards for social behavior were established. This was essential for any civilized society and enabled communities to progress. Information has always provided a means for social advancement.

More than 5,000 years ago, the ancient Egyptians established legal codes by which their societies lived. Likewise, ancient Greeks devised laws to define citizenship and to help prevent territorial wars between nations from one generation to the next. Without the development of these laws and their corresponding codification, progress would have been stymied. Empires and nations would continually be redefining geographic boundaries and how people interact.

But what about today? How has our increased codification of information affected our survival? Remember, knowledge is power, and we all desire to become more powerful whether it is socially or professionally. The employee who has greater knowledge about a vital process in an organization is most likely to be advanced or rewarded. The academic researcher who generates more knowledge about a certain phenomenon becomes synonymous with that topic. The business manager who has greater knowledge of the marketplace is likely to excel above her competitors.

In the knowledge era, survival is dependent on information and the efficient use of it. As a result, we all crave information in order to enhance our chances of success. For example, card counting is widely considered a profitable method for tilting the probability of blackjack success away from the house and in your favor. By counting the number of face cards still available in a deck, optimal decisions about making appropriate bets can be maximized. Of course, in this case, knowledge is power, but it is also frowned upon in Las Vegas!

While using information to get ahead is a worthy pursuit,

much of what we absorb does not really help us at all. Let's face it: none of us really need to know what Britney Spears is doing on Twitter in order to get ahead in life or to be more satisfied. But at the same time we have insatiable appetites that won't be quenched until we know what the pop superstar did on Saturday night. Human survival may be at the very core of information cravings, but at the same time basic human interest drives our thirst for knowledge as well. No one likes to miss out on some juicy piece of information.

Nobody Wants to Be Left Out

When I was in kindergarten, one of my classmates was caught saying a four-letter word he shouldn't have been saying. Though nobody actually heard him say it or saw him get into trouble, the rumors about his misfortune spread like wildfire around the school. Some kids said that the teacher had made him eat a full bar of soap. Other children said he was kicked out of school forever. Neither was true, but even at the age of five years old none of us could get enough information about this boy's circumstances. We all wanted to know the scoop.

The bottom line is that no one wants to be left out in the cold. No one wants to be ignorant. It is human nature to want the latest gossip about the people we know. At times this practice can become malicious, but at a very basic level this behavior highlights a natural instinct we all have to be knowledgeable. The more interesting a piece of information is, the more we crave to know it. The key is what defines which pieces of information as interesting and which pieces as not. What piques our interest in some forms of gossip and generates no interest at all in others? On a day-to-day basis, most of us seek to survive through the social maze of people we encounter. Our friends, our colleagues, our employers and others influence us the most. A piece of information about one of them—or a piece of information that may interest one of them—is more valuable than studying the inner workings of a microprocessor.

Additionally, we all constantly seek to validate ourselves in one way or another. If we learn that Tiger Woods has had a social indiscretion (or twelve), then it makes us feel a little better about ourselves by comparison. Suddenly I am not such a bad person if someone as famous as Tiger Woods can make a mistake. Perhaps this use of information isn't the healthiest, but the thirst to know these juicy tidbits of knowledge reflects a very human characteristic. Without a doubt, many of us use information every day to help us manage our own egos and self-esteem. Realizing this simple fact can help you identify ways in which you can manage daily information better.

Human interest is the key factor in driving our thirst for knowledge. Suppose you're in auto mechanic school and you know that fifty percent of the final examination is going to be about carburetors. Now you have a greater incentive to know how a carburetor works because it affects you significantly. Your interest level is increased because without this information you will be considered ignorant and will fail the exam. You don't want to be left out of your graduating class and ultimately without a job, do you?

It is clearly human nature to crave knowledge, but the degree to which we thirst for a given piece of information depends on how it impacts us. Whether we choose to share information or hoard it depend on a series of instantaneous calculations we each perform subconsciously. This concept will be elaborated upon later in the book, but this speaks to the fact that knowledge provides strength while ignorance reveals weakness. Each of us learns these very simple lessons very early in life. Therefore, we all seek more and more information as we try to avoid being left in the dust. This alone has driven our increased desire for information to the point of bombardment.

Be Careful What You Ask For

When did we get to the point that AM and FM radio were no longer good enough for our listening entertainment? Without a doubt, the difference in quality between traditional radio and satellite radio is significant, but I don't believe this was the distinguishing feature that led to a change in our preference. Sirius XM radio not only gave us exquisite sound quality; more importantly, it gave us choice. I can now select from hundreds of musical and talk genres to satisfy several of my informational cravings.

Do you know which type of radio stations now serve the greatest number of people? In most cities throughout the US and Canada, news talk radio occupies the most popular stations, with sports radio not far behind. It's bad enough that basketball fans religiously watch their favorite teams play several times a week, but now they talk about them all day long on blogs and radio talk shows as well. The key is that the most popular stations are the ones that provide us with the greatest amount of information. We no longer simply use radio for musical entertainment. We use it to fill our heads with tidbits of data. Why do you think morning radio talk shows are so common—when the majority of us are captive listeners trapped in our cars?

Technology provided the tools by which we were allowed greater choices, but our thirst for knowledge catalyzed the explosion of choices available to us today. Satellite and cable television now offer hundreds of channels which we eagerly devour as if it were some delicious dessert buffet. The more channels, the better. No longer do I have to sit prisoner in front of my television watching the scheduled program because I am too lazy to get off the couch and change the dial. With a click of a button, I can peruse any information source I want. I am in control now.

Exactly when did this ability to choose different pieces of information change? Remember the Persian Gulf War in 1991? For the first time ever we were able to see a war unfold live on television, as missiles and artillery lit up the skies over Baghdad. Despite a presence since 1980, CNN established itself with that broadcast as the premier source of twenty-four-hour news and surpassed the other three major networks as the best news information source. Its ratings were on fire! We had spoken in a loud, collective voice. We wanted information, and we wanted it live.

We still can't get enough. Each of us has tuned in to CNN at some point since then to absorb information about the latest happenings in the world. The terrorist attacks of 9/11, the 2008 presidential election, the Mumbai hotel bombings, Hurricane Katrina in New Orleans, the earthquake in Haiti, the BP oil leak in the Gulf of Mexico and many other global events have been made available to us through CNN. The other networks have had to follow suit. In order to meet demand, the media has been more than happy to supply the elixir to slake our thirst.

Today we have a news channel for everything imaginable. ESPN blossomed as the sports news network. MSNBC provides up-to-date financial news. Even Comedy Central provides a humorous slant on the current events of the day through *The Daily Show* and *The Colbert Report.* We don't just want news. We want it delivered in an entertaining format as well.

When I was growing up, the popular television programs were situation comedies. *All in the Family, M*A*S*H*, The Cosby Show, Three's Company* and many others were the mainstay programs in most family households. But what types of programs have now replaced them? Situation comedies provided entertainment without information, but reality television provides both. This fad of television programming was a sign of the times. We only had so much attention to allocate to gathering information, so in order to become more efficient we sought to combine entertainment and information together. Reality television made perfect sense.

Take, for example, the show with the highest ratings: *American Idol.* Not only does it offer the rags-to-riches, feel-good story of plucking an obscure singer and plopping her into the middle of the Hollywood hype machine but it collects millions and millions of pieces of information in the form of call-in (and click-in) votes. *American Idol* was the first show to marry the universal appeal of an amateur talent show with the power of audience-driven information.

What we have learned in the last several decades is that we can control our attention spans and direct them to the precise outlets of information we crave. We no longer buy entire music albums or compact discs. Instead we purchase specific songs for our iPods and MP3 players. We don't wait for the six o'clock news. Instead we switch over to the constant news channel for current headlines or go online to read about a story on demand. This is simply the beginning. The ability to focus our attention even more accurately through the Internet is rapidly replacing other mediums of information.

No longer is content in control of our attention. We are now in control of the content, and we have the power to satisfy our own specific thirsts for knowledge. But in getting what we asked for, we are now faced with a new problem: information bombardment. How do we decide which information is important? With increased control over information came increased responsibility. The challenge we now face is being responsible in managing the information we are faced with every day.

Allocating Your Attention Span

If there is any type of need in a capitalist society, you can be sure some entrepreneur will find a way to meet that need. That's simply supply and demand. As our thirst for knowledge grew, and as technology provided greater means to access information, the world around us accommodated our ever-increasing cravings. Let's face it: if there weren't a market out there for 300 television channels and satellite radio, these options wouldn't be there. The supply has simply been in response to the demand for information.

But as a result of this new marketplace of information, we now find ourselves in a compromised position. In essence, we now suffer from two conditions related to information bombardment. I like to think of one of them as acute and the other as chronic, but both are related to one another. Notwithstanding, we have to address both in order to survive the Information Age successfully.

From an acute standpoint, we all suffer from an excessive and indiscriminate need to know. We need to know the latest Hollywood scandal. We crave the latest consumer information on new products and services. We thirst for the latest styles and fashions. On and on it goes, but the bottom line is that we don't know where to draw the line. In an effort to appease our biggest fear (the fear of being ignorant and left out), we walk around like huge sponges, hoping to absorb every little piece of information we can. But as sponges, we can only hold so much. We become engorged, we leak, and we can no longer effectively absorb.

Of course, the supply side figured this out long ago. Why do you think twenty-four-hour news is available? It exists because collectively we absorb information as fast as we can. The more current, the better. Not only is constant news available to us but the information is positioned in such a way that we cannot help but want to learn more. These enticements are everywhere, and the information suppliers have become very skilled at drawing your attention. For example, the average person is exposed to over 3,000 advertisements in an average day.

I found myself standing in line at the grocery store the other day, and one of the tabloids read, "Elin's painful choice"—referring to the wife of Tiger Woods and her decision about whether or not to divorce the golf superstar. Did I need this information? Was this journalistic piece going to educate me in order to be more successful? Doubtful. Yet I still had the urge to pick it up and glance at the article. I have been socially conditioned to want to know. I subconsciously thought I could somehow apply this information about this famous couple's struggles to my own life. I could hear the editor of the tabloid saying, "Gotcha!"

All forms of telecommunications and media have become very savvy at soliciting our attention. We all know how the game works. Advertising dollars make the world go 'round. Have you looked at Google's cash balance lately? The market is driven by marketing. A television company, a newspaper, a Web site or a radio station must pay for operations by acquiring high-paying advertisers. Of course, advertisers only want those information providers that gain the largest audiences. So what happens? We are constantly given little tidbits of information (or perhaps a better term is *information bait*) so that we tune in for the full story at a particular time. It's akin to providing one drop of water to a person stranded in the desert. He will always desire more. Eventually we satisfy our thirst, the media gets viewership or readership, and advertisers reach a target market. Everyone walks away happy. Right?

So much information abounds today that it has become impossible to absorb it all. That doesn't mean that we don't try our best. Unfortunately we make the effort at the expense of other things in our lives. We reduce the time spent with our spouses or partners so we can surf the Web just a little longer. We skip quality time with our children to catch that breaking news report. Or, most commonly, we cut off another hour of sleep by catching the late-night sports highlights of the day. The problem is that this is a quantitative answer to a qualitative problem. We don't need to make more time to accommodate larger piles of information. We simply need to prioritize to which pieces of information we lend our attention.

This leads to what I see as the more chronic problem regarding information. Progressively, from the days of the hardwired television converter to today's remote control and towards on-demand viewing, we have been socialized into giving brief bits of attention to various forms of media. A few seconds here to catch a movie trailer preview, a minute or two there to hear the recap of the Manchester United soccer match. Our attention tends to bounce all over the place.

Other than a full-length movie or some project required at work, when was the last time you allocated all of your attention to one task for more than thirty minutes? Be honest. That means not looking up once to check your e-mail or your cell phone or to hop over to another channel or Web site for a quick peek. I imagine most of you cannot recall such a time in recent years. Attention deficit disorder is not a genetic problem—it's a social phenomenon. Our information culture is teaching us to have shorter attention spans.

While our immediate problem is the inability to discern which information is most needed, the longstanding challenge is overcoming a natural tendency to move quickly from one topic to another. Multitasking has contributed greatly to this tendency as we distribute our attention among several different actions at once. Today's teenagers (also known as Generation Y, Net Geners or Millennials) are becoming very proficient at multitasking. They have to excel in this area in order to keep up with all the latest technologies, social networking demands and the academic challenges placed upon them. But, as each of us relinquishes a little piece of our attention to something else, we run the risk of sacrificing quality for quantity.

Don't get me wrong—I am all in favor of multitasking. In fact, I was among the first professors in my faculty to have three flat-screen viewing panels on my desktop and enough RAM on my computer to run a small country. Being able to accomplish several things at once promotes efficiency and is a good use of your time. However, when multitasking is performed without regard to quality, the savings in efficiency no longer matter. In the knowledge era, not only do we have to learn to discriminate between pieces of information better but we also must learn how best to allocate our attention spans. The length of time we lend our focused attention to a task and the extent with which we spread our attention among several things are critical factors in determining how effectively we manage information bombardment.

Information Obsession

I love soccer. It is my true passion. My office is adorned with team scarves from all over the world. I am still an avid soccer player and continue to compete at a relatively high level (sometimes against my own eighteen-year-old students). I coach my sons' soccer teams, follow live matches on the Web during the day, constantly check scores and standings on my BlackBerry, and watch at least one hour of highlights each and every night. I consider myself a true student of the beautiful game.

When Greece went on its improbable journey to win the European Championships in 2004, I celebrated for days.

When Toronto FC (Canada's first professional MLS franchise) launched in 2007, I went to the open try outs and competed for a spot on the team with 1,000 others. During the World Cup every four years, I am in heaven. You might say I thirst to know about the sport of soccer.

Now, suppose I let my enthusiasm for soccer get out of hand. I begin skipping my own university lectures to watch soccer games; I join an online fantasy soccer league and start betting on match outcomes; and I even leave my family for weekends on end to travel with my favorite club. You can rightly assume that at some point my boss, my students, my wife, my family and my friends will begin to get irritated with me. No longer is my interest in soccer healthy. Instead, it has become an obsession to the point that it is affecting my quality of life.

Fortunately, soccer does not rule my life. However, for many people, the thirst for information is becoming an obsession and an addiction. The Merriam-Webster definition of addiction describes a "compulsive physiological need for and use of a habit-forming substance." However, medical terminology for addiction refers not only to the physiological need but also the psychological need. From the medical perspective, an excessive desire for information that disrupts normal social functioning can clearly be an addictive disorder. In other words, information is the habit-forming substance about which some of us become compulsive.

Several surveys have sampled people using the Internet and found that a significant percentage suffer from this type of information obsession. Overall, about one in every eight people described having relationship problems because of Internet use, tried to conceal the amount of time they were using the Internet or felt preoccupied with the Internet even when they were offline. The common threads here are the desire to get information and the fear of being left out. These emotions have consumed these individuals to the point that their quality of life is suffering.

Being able to balance your life and your responsibilities is important. When one aspect of your life becomes out of balance and begins to impact other areas, you become less proficient, less productive and, oftentimes, less happy. Information is an essential part of our lives, especially today, and it can be a wonderful thing. But even too much of a good thing is detrimental. A healthy thirst for knowledge is one thing, but an uncontrolled addiction to information is another.

The question is how to quench our thirst for knowledge without drowning in knowledge at the same time. As we have been increasingly bombarded with information, we have not developed the skills necessary to regulate, discern and prioritize it. Most of us still have an underlying belief that we can digest all the information available to us and still manage our personal time effectively as well. Even if we committed all of our time and attention to absorbing information, we would not be able to keep up with the constantly changing databases of information.

Unlike in past generations, data is now changing so rapidly that we cannot stay informed of all the latest discoveries and happenings. Though our thirst for information has grown tremendously, the capacity by which knowledge is stored has increased significantly more. It therefore seems logical that the answers to information bombardment lie in managing our thirst rather than increasing our consumption. For those of you who choose the latter, you should know what you're up against. You might just be amazed by exactly how fast the world's knowledge base is changing.

FURTHER READING

Radio rankings: http://www.stationratings.com

Center for Internet addiction: http://www.netaddiction.com

Tabloid headlines: http://www.thefrisky.com/tag/tabloid+cheat+sheet

Attention span test: http://psychologytoday.psychtests.com/cgi-bin/health/transfer_health.cgi?partner=pt&test=attention

Scan QR code for direct link to website, hypertext links and other resources:

CHAPTER 4

Cumulative Codified Information Base

Did you know that over ten billion songs have been sold on iTunes? Considering no one had heard of iTunes ten years ago, this figure is a pretty astounding statistic. Did you realize that every sixty seconds, twenty hours' worth of video material is uploaded to YouTube? Again, this is an impressive fact given that the company didn't exist prior to 2005. Many products and services are taken for granted today, and several that most of us consider cornerstones of today's society have only been around for a few years. It's hard to imagine that companies like Facebook, Twitter and eBay didn't exist a little more than a decade ago, considering how ubiquitous they are now.

At the same time, some companies have rapidly fallen from grace over the same time period. The movie rental superstore Blockbuster, which was founded in 1985, dominated the movie rental market in the 1990s. Super Bowl advertisements and sponsorships of major college sports championships were standard for this once-prestigious corporation. But in the last ten years, the company has suffered major losses and is now worth only a small fraction of its historical high. The same can be said for retail music stores and many major newspaper organizations. What happened? Why did some companies rise almost overnight and others vanish in the same time period?

Before getting into the complete answer, I would like to introduce a term that can put things into better perspective. Since human beings sought to progress from one generation to the next, the codification of existing knowledge has been important (we reviewed this in a previous chapter). Codification allowed the passage of information gained from one era to be passed on to another era because it transformed data into permanent form. As previously mentioned, the alphabet, the printing press and the computer were undoubtedly the most significant inflection points enabling our ability to codify knowledge. They allowed us to springboard from one information base to another.

But how do we measure this codification of knowledge? How do we quantify all the information we have ever written down and stored over time? The term *cumulative codified information base,* or CCIB, is how scientists have attempted to place some perspective on this concept. In simple English, the cumulative codified information base of the world is simply all the stuff we have ever written down since we first started writing down stuff. That's a lot of information! You thought it was hard surviving university calculus…just imagine trying to grasp on the world's entire cumulative knowledge base.

Despite the challenge, plenty of astounding geniuses have made valiant attempts to do so over the centuries. These men and women are sometimes referred to as *polymaths, Renaissance men,* or simply *geniuses.* Without question, names like Plato, Aristotle, da Vinci and Einstein are included in this group of people. Each had a pretty good handle on the world's extant knowledge base during his time. But what would happen if they lived currently? Would they be as successful today at mastering their craft?

Between technological advancements and our thirst for knowledge, the amount of codified information has exploded. The volume of data has expanded greatly even within this century compared to prior centuries. But rather than look at the total volume of information, another statistic seems to be more relevant. The speed at which information is changing and being recorded reflects our current situation more than any other factoid. Plato had his entire lifetime to master the philosophical and scientific advancements of his contemporaries. His writings were evidence of all that he had encountered and envisioned. He was not faced with the challenge of having to unlearn old facts and master new ones because of the rapid acceleration of the world's intellectual capital. This is why the rate of informational change is just as important as the amount of new information being processed.

Eleven Hours

In the 1930s, a group of astute researchers sought to determine how quickly knowledge was growing in the world. Based on the growth of physical libraries during that era, library scientists projected that the cumulative codified information base (CCIB) of the world would double every thirty years. I would suspect that we are all fairly comfortable with this figure. My father didn't understand many of the things I learned in grade school and university because the information base had changed since he had been in school. Twice the amount of information existed for me to learn compared to when my father was in school. This may explain the generational gap between parents and their children. Completely acceptable.

But what happened next? The rate of information growth began to increase significantly. Computers were introduced in the 1950s and began to allow for more-efficient codification processes. The secrets of DNA were revealed and new theories of medical science, as well as new medications, appeared. Space programs accelerated our understanding of the universe as well as our own planet. No longer was the growth of information occurring at a comfortable pace (i.e., from one generation to the next). The pressure to know was on. What you learned in school twenty years ago was no longer good enough. New models continually replace old theories. Just as we once thought the world was flat. We can never assume that all we know is finite.

By the 1970s, information scientists reexamined the doubling rate for the world's cumulative codified information base. Believe it or not, the figure had shrunk from thirty years down to seven years! By the time a child went from first grade to eighth grade, the amount of information in the world had doubled. What were we supposed to do? How many of our children have textbooks that are more than seven years old? Are we supposed to rewrite every textbook every five years to accommodate this new birth of information? Considering that it takes a year or two to rewrite a textbook, even one hot off the presses will already be somewhat outdated.

In October 2003, Chinese astronaut Yang Liwei travelled into space, looking to confirm one piece of information he had been taught since grade school. Reportedly, the Great Wall of China was the only manmade structure that could be seen from outer space beyond the earth's orbit. I imagine that upon his return, he had a conversation with his Russian cosmonaut and American astronaut buddies about his findings.

"So, Vladimir, did you see the Great Wall of China when you orbited the earth?" Yang asked.

"Nyet, I did not see it."

"Neil, did you see the Great Wall of China during your space expeditions?" he continued.

"Nah, man. I don't think there was any manmade structure that could be seen from up there."

What had once been taken as a source of national pride for many Chinese citizens had now been proven to be a myth and a falsehood. So, what was Yang Liwei supposed to do? Go back to China and change every textbook ever published to convey the real facts about the visibility of the Great Wall from space? That would be impossible to accomplish in his own country, much less throughout the entire world. What we as humans know is changing so fast we cannot alter our traditional outlets of codified information quickly enough to provide current accuracy.

Let's jump ahead by seven years. By the end of the year 2010, the cumulative codified information base of the world doubled every eleven hours! What we knew to be true yesterday is only a fraction of what is true today. Either new information has been added or old information has been updated and corrected. In fact, in a special report by *The Economist,* it was estimated that we created ten times more information in the past twelve months than we did five years ago. As data changes so fast, we struggle to keep our head above the sea of information in which we are drowning. But the struggle is futile. Unless we find a stronghold on pieces of information that matter the most, we are certain to succumb to the rising tide.

Imagine what this means for your personal life. You might go out to dinner on a Saturday evening and sleep late the following morning. By the time you wake up, a full world's worth of information has doubled again. While you slept, the world continued to know more, and you haven't stayed up to date. You are unaware of what happened in the world in the last eleven hours. Did a war start or end? Did some new medical breakthrough take place? Did some technology become obsolete or enhanced? The pressure we feel today to keep up with all the new information is a direct reflection of how fast knowledge is changing. How will we survive when the cumulative codified information base doubles every eleven minutes?

Practical Life Issues

Dr. Stevenson is a cardiothoracic surgeon in the middle of an open-heart surgery. The fifty-two-year-old man anesthetized in front of him is known to have four narrowed coronary arteries. None of the blockages are amenable to stents or angioplasty, based on a thorough diagnostic workup, so Dr. Stevenson proceeds with a four-vessel bypass grafting operation. Screening laboratory findings, examinations and patient history all suggest that the operation is the best solution. Information input, analysis, decision and output. All seems pretty straightforward.

But as Dr. Stevenson begins the procedure and starts grafting the second bypass, the new microscopic computer attached to the patient's heart arteries begins to indicate that the plaque composition isn't common. In fact, the plaque suggests that the patient has a primary clotting disturbance found only in 0.5 percent of the population. Dr. Stevenson rapidly orders an anticoagulant but must proceed cautiously so the patient doesn't bleed. As Dr. Stevenson resumes, the computerized databank monitoring all up-to-date events on the operating suites announces that patients with this type of plaque composition have four times the complication rate of other patients. In fact, five percent die during the operation.

Dr. Stevenson is required to make instantaneous decisions in a very complex situation. He no longer has the luxury of analyzing the data in a leisurely manner and putting it into some decision-making algorithm. Now he must make immediate decisions about how to proceed as information about the patient is constantly changing and being updated. The surgeon is being bombarded with information. Even scarier is the fact that Dr. Stevenson will be held accountable for his knowledge of this information and whether or not he made the correct decision. Can you see the cumulative codified information doubling right before your eyes?

Perhaps you don't hold a man's heart in your hand as volumes of information confront you, but, regardless, you have your own information bombardment with which you must deal. We all experience it whether we realize it or not. Fifty years ago, a young man might have gotten a job at a local company, learned the company's procedures and products, and eventually retired from the same company forty years later. The demands of keeping up with industry information and changes were small compared to today. In contrast, most of us today must read and stay abreast of changes within our businesses and in our lives simply to maintain the status quo. If not, we fall behind and become outdated.

These changing patterns of information have caused us

to make some very important decisions about the data we encounter. As the volume of visual, auditory and written information overwhelms us, we must choose which information means the most to us. In addition, we often decide what things we will sacrifice in order to gain this new knowledge. Many times, our choices are not very healthy.

Researchers who have looked at the effects of time pressure on decision making have noticed some very important facts. As information is concentrated into shorter time periods, we are forced to deal with it in less comfortable ways. First, we tend to look at information with higher priorities only as time becomes progressively limited. We selectively focus on some details while discarding others. Secondly, we don't assess the information with the same depth of analysis. A shallow assessment often suffices. Lastly, we tend to fall back on familiar strategies that are known to work for us. The luxury to devise new creative strategies is lost as time is crunched.

These methods of dealing with the time pressures of information processing are not necessarily bad. If we don't prioritize and become selective, then certainly we will drown in the quagmire. But the key is to realize how we prioritize information and what strategies we choose in selecting key pieces on which to focus. A strategy of sleeping fewer hours a day and trading in family time for work time is not healthy. The increased doubling rate of the world's CCIB has forced us to approach daily information more selectively. It is important that we choose the best way of dealing with information bombardment if we want not only to survive but also to succeed in the knowledge era.

Human Capacity for Information

Do you know what a *zettabyte* is? A zettabyte is one billion trillion bytes. That's an unfathomable amount of ones and zeroes. In a recent study that looked at all American households in 2008 (and, incidentally, this study did not include any information received in the workplace), the total amount of data received each year in total was 3.6 zettabytes, or 10,845 trillion words. Averaging this figure out for every American over 365 days, the daily information consumption per person was thirty-four gigabytes of data, or 100,500 words. There are more than 100,000 words in this entire book, which means that if you did nothing else, you would be reading at least one book a day all year long! Most netbook computers have a total memory capacity of about seventy-five gigabytes. So this means you would be confronted with half the computer's information base every single day. Wow! Don't forget—this analysis did not include the capacity of the human mind to retain any of the information with which it was presented. However, it did reveal the real threat of volume that the average individual deals with every single day. Despite the brain's incredible abilities, we do not have the capacity to retain this volume of data. Although the average human mind's capacity is easily measured in trillions of bytes (or gigabytes) by conservative estimates, a finite limit exists in our ability to absorb and recall information accurately. Centuries ago, the average person did not have to deal with the same volume or speed of change.

Most of you have taken reading comprehension tests at some point. You know the drill. You have a passage to read in a limited amount of time and then you are tested to assess how much you comprehended. We all are aware that with greater time pressure we are able to understand and recall less. Why is this? The brain's capacity to receive information is tremendous, so why does our comprehension decline as the length and complexity of the passage in a given amount of time increase?

The answer is our attention span. Despite the hundreds of billions of neuron connections in the brain, much of these connections are involved with sorting out what is important and what is not. This concept is called *signal-to-noise ratio.* Just imagine how much information, positive and negative, the brain is receiving at any given time. It's receiving touch information from every nerve ending in your skin, visual information from your retinas about all your surroundings, auditory information from your ears regarding the tiniest sounds, and so on. It is even receiving internal information from the body and its normal functioning. Quantifying this amount of data (even in zettabytes) is unfathomable!

Clearly, we are not conscious of all this information coming into our brains. In fact, we are only aware of a small fraction. A significant amount of energy is spent determining which information gets passed along to our attention centers. A significant information signal linked to emotional or intellectual importance is amplified in the brain in order to get our attention. In contrast, other pieces of information are suppressed if they are deemed unimportant in comparison. In other words, the noise of insignificant information is quieted while the signal of important information is enhanced.

Consider this example: You walk into your place of employment and your boss is upset about something. Your brain begins receiving information as you listen more intently. You examine your boss' appearance and behavior. You glance around at your coworkers to assess their reactions. All of these signals are important. They can help you determine whether your boss is upset with something you did or with something unrelated to you. The color of socks your cubicle partner is wearing is low on the list of information importance. A drooping plant in need of water in the corner is not a priority. The fragrance of your assistant's new perfume drifts through your brain. Despite receiving all of the above information, only the important information concerning your own immediate needs is amplified within your brain so that you may focus your attention on these observations.

The human capacity to receive information is certainly amazing. However, the brain's ability to pay attention to select pieces of information is limited. The brain uses a filtering process to identify things that are important while ignoring seemingly useless data. How we choose to use our attention spans is the most important facet in dealing with information bombardment. Like our brains, we can choose which information should receive our utmost attention.

The cumulative codified information base is currently doubling too quickly for us to keep pace, but effective tools are present for us to handle this dilemma. By developing better filtering mechanisms for selecting which information is passed on to our attention centers and which is ignored, we can optimize our own daily information management.

Computer Capacity for Information

In 2007, IBM announced the biggest supercomputer in the world to date. Named the Blue Gene/P, this supercomputer could process more than 3,000 trillion calculations per second. Its processing power came from more than 880,000 processing cores that allowed this incredible computational ability. In fact, this was equivalent to the processing power of a stack of laptop PCs measuring 1.5 miles in height. That is a lot of processing power!

Estimates of the human brain, with its ability to process information, have suggested a speed of 100 million megabytes of information per second. Comparatively, the Blue Gene/P has a processing speed roughly thirty times this amount. In other words, IBM's supercomputer can process three trillion megabytes per second. Not only did this new supercomputer contain greater capacity to store memory data but it also has harnessed greater processing speeds and operations. It's no wonder chess champion Garry Kasparov was no match for the evolving new supercomputers of our current age.

You might understand that we have already arrived to a time when the capacity of machines has surpassed the human capacity of information processing. With this in mind, you should not be surprised that the doubling rate of the entire world's knowledge is rapidly increasing. As these supercomputers' abilities are applied to greater pools of data, a continued explosion of information will occur. Integration and comparative analyses between information and data by these supercomputers will accelerate how quickly new knowledge forms. Are we really ready for this degree of information bombardment? More importantly, how much power do we give to these super-artificial intelligent machines in determining our fate?

The concerns about technological singularity previously mentioned pose these same questions. As computer intelligence expands, a time may indeed come where the human capacity for knowledge is tremendously overshadowed. Who will make decisions then—man or machine? In the knowledge era, information is the bargaining chip. We are at a point where we can choose how best to handle the onslaught of information coming at us from all directions. But if we fail to handle information bombardment well, we might find that we lose the opportunity to control our future. Do we want to control information or allow information to control us?

IBM's Blue Gene/P is amazingly compact as well. Its height is about six feet with a width of only four feet. Remember the original IBM Mark I in the 1950s that occupied a city block and took several seconds to perform one mathematical division? Those days are long gone. As technology has advanced and the cost of computer components has declined, the capacity to concentrate superhuman computing powers into smaller and smaller spaces has become a reality. Exactly how long do you think it will be before such a supercomputer will be the same size as the human brain?

So where do we go from here? The cumulative codified information base continues to expand at rates that are beyond our human capacity to absorb knowledge. Supercomputers now exceed our own abilities to store and process information. Whether we like it or not, information is hitting us so fast we can hardly catch our breath. What used to take years to develop and distribute now takes seconds. It is time for a paradigm shift.

While the increase in the cumulative codified information base hindered our ability to absorb all of the world's information, it did teach us new skills. We were forced to focus our attention discriminately, prioritize data in hierarchies and negotiate our attention spans among competing interests. We could no longer afford to give our attention to processes that took long amounts of time or focused on insignificant information. These new skills certainly affected companies like Blockbuster. Part of the reason Blockbuster and related industries declined is that they could not provide us the information we wanted in an efficient fashion. I could now get my movies via the mail, from a kiosk or through direct Internet downloads. Why would I want to waste precious time and attention driving to a retail store and waiting in line for a movie that I would then have to return in a few days?

In essence, we became more attention-selective because information bombardment forced us in that direction. Simultaneously, technology allowed new distribution networks to form that met these needs. Between these two developments, older versions of informational outlets either fell by the wayside or were forced to change. Having examined information bombardment and the rapid increase in the world's knowledge base, let's now focus on how this information is distributed.

FURTHER READING

Internet statistics: http://www.google.co.uk/intl/en/landing/internetstats/

Human capacity for information: http://www.technewsworld.com/story/Human-Capacity-for-Information-Is-Massive-but-

Finite-68865.html?wlc=1267033841

The Great Wall of China: http://www.journalofoptometry.org/Archive/vol1/pdf/02%20Vol1-n1%20Letter%20to%20the%20Editor.pdf

The data deluge: http://www.economist.com/opinion/displaystory.cfm?story_id=15579717

All too much, monstrous amounts of data: http://www.economist.com/specialreports/displaystory.cfm?story_id=15557421

What is signal and what is noise in the brain?: http://tinyurl.com/2v6zvwd

Most powerful computer: http://en.wikipedia.org/wiki/TOP500

Computer and human capacity: http://www.transhumanist.com/volume1/moravec.htm

Scan QR code for direct link to website, hypertext links and other resources:

CHAPTER 5

The Marginal Cost is Zero

In 1964, singer-songwriter Bob Dylan released his third album, *The Times They Are a-Changin'*. The climactic line of the title track is one of the most memorable phrases of any folk song. Bob Dylan had presciently created an everlasting anthem for change. Without question, one of life's certainties is the presence of change. But I am of the opinion that we have entered an accelerated period of change. The knowledge era in which we now find ourselves has created changes within our world that far exceed the speed of change in generations past.

If technology has provided the means by which the information explosion has occurred and our thirst for knowledge has driven information to be ubiquitous, then changes in distribution networks have been the facilitators. What do I mean by *distribution networks?* Distribution networks are simply paths by which we send products or pieces of information from one place to another.

As technology has advanced, distribution networks have also changed. Even the materials we distribute have changed. As we have demanded information in greater quantities and at faster speeds, our infrastructure has had to keep pace. The ability to distribute information easily and more extensively has become a reality as a result. Today, distribution networks are not only allowing our thirst for information to be quenched but they are actually contributing to the problem of information bombardment. A look back in history can help demonstrate how and why this has occurred.

Product Distribution

Let's go back in time to a few centuries ago, to the agricultural era. There was no such thing as the Internet. In fact, there was no such thing as a telephone. Families would cultivate crops on their farms in order to provide food for their households. Over time, they realized they could earn extra income through selling their surplus of food to other families and markets. Initially, families would take their fruits and vegetables to the local farmers' markets for sale, but as their farms' production increased, a distribution network was needed to reach larger markets. So, families then loaded their wagons and traveled to the nearby towns until all their goods were sold.

Unfortunately, this didn't expand the growth of sales significantly, and the cost over time to travel by wagon failed to make this method of distribution very lucrative. However, this changed in the mid 1800s. Abraham Lincoln signed the Pacific Railway Act, and the railroad bridging the gap between the eastern United States and the western states became a reality. Now agricultural products could be placed in containers and transported across the country for sale. In other words, the railroad allowed a significant increase in the distribution outreach for farmers and other product suppliers.

Despite the progress, the costs of using the railroad were not inexpensive, and the loss of produce in transport was significant. This distribution network was better than what they had previously, but it was far from ideal. Eventually refrigerated railway cars and increased prices for agricultural products offset the inherent disadvantages of railway distribution.

Soon came the Industrial Age. Machine-operated factories and the enhanced use of natural resources created an entirely new demand for product distribution. More and more people were leaving the fields to work on the assembly lines, and mass production of all sorts of products and inventions became the norm. These products needed an even greater outreach to meet market demand. Railroads provided continental distribution, but what about global commerce? How were products and goods supposed to reach markets overseas?

Transatlantic shipping has been present since the first millennium BC, but an efficient way of shipping materials in bulk did not come about until the 1900s. Once the internal combustion engine and gas turbine were designed, large cargo ships could transport large amounts of products and materials between America and Europe as well as to other continents. This dramatic progress in distribution created entirely new markets for many businesses, and at the same time allowed new products to reach a variety of isolated populations. This also allowed many countries, including America, to become extremely wealthy through a healthy export practice.

Though the cost of transatlantic shipping wasn't inexpensive either, the ability to send materials in bulk created economies of scale. Companies could price goods at competitive rates even in foreign markets as a result of these bulk savings. In other words, transatlantic shipping allowed not only a greater outreach but also a more economical way of distribution. With each step we were making the world a smaller place and less expensive to reach. Strong economic momentum allowed us to progress towards a true globalized distribution network.

In 1962 there was a young man who attended Yale University. For his economics class, he decided to write an essay detailing how an overnight delivery service in the Information Age might be implemented. After graduation, he did a tour with the Marines wherein he learned military logistics and aviation systems until 1969. Then, in 1971, Fred Smith founded FedEx Corporation. Building upon his existing knowledge from the Marines and devising a system similar to a bank clearinghouse system, he created the first efficient overnight package shipping company. Literally he became a success overnight because he changed the way products and goods were distributed throughout the world.

In looking at the progress of distribution networks, it is clear that three components are critical. First, distribution must reach a wider market in order to represent an improvement over existing distribution networks. Second, distribution must be of greater efficiency than the existing network. Finally, the cost of distribution must be less than existing options when considering all factors involved. From the wagon to the railroad to transatlantic cargo shipping to overnight air, each of these three factors was addressed in gaining a more comprehensive market outreach.

Communication Distribution

I have talked about the distribution of products and materials, but what about the distribution of communications and information? We know we have been codifying knowledge throughout the centuries, so isn't the distribution of information equally important to product distribution? Definitely! Alphabets and the development of the printing press were not only important for codification but also for distribution. Codified (and later digitized) knowledge could be stored more readily and therefore be distributed more efficiently.

Imagine living in California in the 1860s. You lived in the wild, wild, west. Changes were rapidly occurring in the eastern part of the US, but westerners were cut off from timely information and news. Two or three weeks would pass before news of happenings across the country might reach California. The nation was on the brink of a civil war, yet little news of the rising tensions reached the settlers west of Missouri. Stagecoaches were not a very fast means of information distribution.

Where there's a need, an entrepreneur will find a way to satisfy it—hopefully for a profit. Russell, Majors and Waddell, all owners of a freight company, had the idea that a single horseman could make the trip carrying mail in a much shorter time than a stagecoach. They devised 190 stations each ten miles apart (the average distance a horse could travel at full gallop without stopping) crossing seven states from Missouri to California. In 1860, the Pony Express was open for business. Not only did the Pony Express provide greater incentives for western migration and settlements but it also helped unify many western states with the Union in the fight against slavery.

But progress continued to advance. Within a couple of years the Pony Express went bankrupt and was replaced by the Morse telegraph. The financial expense of horses and riders was sizable, and delays in receiving information were too intolerable. A message received via Western Union telegraph occurred within minutes of sending the telegram. By 1866 transatlantic telegraph cables had even been placed, allowing transcontinental communications to be relayed more rapidly. Not only could products travel easily overseas but information and communications were being distributed more extensively as well.

From the telegraph came the telephone and the postal service. From the postal service and telephone we eventually were introduced to the Internet. With each step information and communication were relayed faster, more directly, more comprehensively and at progressively reduced levels of cost. The distribution network of information for many centuries mirrored the distribution of products, but over the last several decades this has changed. Our desire that information be sent and received almost instantaneously has culminated in an accelerated change in information distribution.

The US mail today can take three or four days to travel across the country to arrive at its destination, but e-mail reaches its target within seconds. I can speak to my cousin in Greece by telephone and talk with her at length, but I can also connect via Skype and not only hear her but see her as we talk. Think about the amount of content all of us receive every day in our inboxes alone! You could likely fill a stagecoach with the equivalent amount of data we now receive in a single day.

Going back to the days of ancient Greece, I envision a messenger carrying a scroll in his pouch by horseback into a field of battle. On the scroll is written a change in battle plans that directs the field general on how to proceed. How is that any different from today, when someone receives an e-mail from his boss outlining a new strategy for his company's division? It's not.

The Greek messenger might get killed in battle on the way to deliver the message. Or he might die of exhaustion upon arrival, as Pheidippides did when he went from Marathon to Athens. My computer might crash, or a server might malfunction, causing the person not to receive the e-mail. The Greek message might become destroyed or illegible in its journey. The e-mail might become contaminated with a computer virus. The field general might choose to ignore the message just as the person might choose to disregard his boss' e-mail. The bottom line is that there is little difference except for the fact that the message is now received more quickly, in more detail and at less cost.

What is truly interesting is that commodities have changed over time. During the agricultural era, crops and produce were the most important items to be distributed. As we entered the Industrial Age, other materials and natural resources became commodities of high importance. But as we have entered the knowledge era, information is the most important commodity. We still need food and products as well as services, but information has surpassed these things in volume. Nothing is more important today than how knowledge is distributed.

The Cost of Distribution

The speed of distribution and its greater outreach are easy aspects to appreciate when talking about the progress of distribution networks over time. Less appreciated is the associated drop in financial cost for distributing items with every stage of advancement. While this has been true for the distribution of products and materials, it has been even more significant for the distribution of information. How much did it cost to send your last e-mail?

If you wish to be thorough, some costs do exist in order to send an e-mail. You need a high-speed Internet connection, a hosting agent for a domain and mail server, and some time to write an e-mail. But these costs, spread over the number of e-mails you send, become increasingly insignificant. For any single e-mail your financial cost is negligible. For all practical purposes, the cost of exchanging information electronically has dropped to zilch. From Internet calls to instant messaging to search options, information in the knowledge era is free. Virtually anyone can access it and send it.

Today we are bombarded with information because there are no disincentives or barriers to sending it. During the days of railroad transport, significant costs existed. These included steam or oil for the engines, labor on the locomotive and maintenance of the railways. The cost of sending something transatlantic included similar costs of maintenance and operation. But what does it cost to keep a server and IP address up and running? Not much at all.

Just imagine what it might have been like if the railways had been free.

"Hey Joe, the four o'clock just pulled into the station. Right on time."

"Good. I'm expecting some packages. Open up that second railway car."

"Holy smokes! Look at all the marketing flyers and promo mailers!"

"Aw, shucks, another car full of spam! Now I have to dig through all of that just to find my packages."

Guess what? That is exactly what we are suffering from

today. We sit down at our desks in the morning when we arrive at work and check our inboxes for all the new messages. *Boom!* Fifty new messages are downloaded from our mail servers. As you look at each subject line, you realize that ninety percent of them are useless messages—junk...trash...spam. You have to weed through the messages you don't want to get to the ones you do. Welcome to the world of free distribution networks.

The only silver lining in this storm cloud is that we have mastered a very useful skill in the process. With increasing amounts of useless information bombarding us we have learned the skills of assess and delete (sounds similar to *seek and destroy*). In less than two seconds we can analyze the sender and the subject line and choose to send the message to the trash forever. For the more clever ones that sneak past this first phase of analysis, we can usually discard them within another couple of seconds of perusing the e-mail bodies themselves. This is not necessarily a bad skill to have.

Spam permeates every part of our lives today. Spam clogs our e-mail accounts and fills our junk mail folders, but have you noticed that spam clogs other areas of our lives also? Despite a higher cost of distribution, postal mail is filled with spam as well. Direct mailers and solicitations via the postal service still have a stronghold over the daily papers that come across our desks. Despite the explosion of television channels, the presence of advertisements and commercials are higher than ever. It is estimated that the average person is exposed to 3,000 advertisements every day. We are all familiar with Google ads and other advertising banners on the Web sites we visit. In order to wade through this sea of distractions, we have had to learn the skill of discernment.

Have you been to a major sporting event lately? The other

week I took my sons to see the Toronto Maple Leafs play at the Air Canada Centre. As we sat cheering along with the Leafs Nation, I looked around the arena. The majority of the surface area accommodated fans, players or media, but a significant amount of visual space remained. Of this remaining space, every single inch was occupied by advertising. Blinking banners, colorful ads, rapidly rotating billboards and sponsor logos covered every otherwise unused piece of real estate. Amazingly, I was so accustomed to such intrusions that I didn't even notice the extent of its presence until well into the second period. If I am that oblivious to it, imagine how my sons will be having grown up in the knowledge era!

This year, the cost of advertising during the Super Bowl was around $2.5 million for a thirty-second slot. The cost of distribution can hardly be described as inexpensive in this light. The number of people reached by this medium is tremendous and has always justified the cost for many advertisers and their corporate clients. But why pay for something if you don't have to? Why not attach your traditional advertising to a more modern and less costly form of distribution?

That is exactly what some of the more innovative companies are doing. GoDaddy.com, during this year's Super Bowl, once again piggybacked its television commercial to several full-length video advertisements on its Web site. In doing so it generated tremendous traffic to its own domain. This awarded it a much greater return on its investment without adding any incremental cost of distribution whatsoever. Expect more of this smart and strategic method of integrated advertising in our lives.

As distribution networks become more extensive, everyone will be competing for that one precious commodity that you alone control: your attention span. No matter how brief, a chance to step into your mental spotlight is their ultimate goal. From companies wanting your business to your own family, everyone is competing for your attention. As distribution costs have fallen to practically zero, we have found that we are being tugged in every direction. We must get better at distinguishing which requests for our attention deserve merit and which ones don't.

Managing Barriers

Predictably, information bombardment will only worsen as we move toward greater Internet penetration and worldwide communication. Currently, 6.8 billion people live in the world and only 1.8 billion are considered Internet users. This results in a penetration rate of approximately twenty-five percent. If you think e-mail spam is bad now, what happens when we approach 100-percent Internet penetration? How much junk will be in your inbox when four times the number of people are trying to get your attention? These are pretty scary figures to consider.

In looking ahead, it might be helpful to look backwards. When the railroad was faced with the costs of railway construction, locomotive fuel, machinery and railroad personnel, a fee was imposed on people who used the railroad for transporting products and goods. When the Pony Express had to purchase numerous horses, hire multiple riders and endure unforeseen obstacles, it sought to increase its fees and to solicit more funds from government grants. When the postal service realized there would be substantial costs in mail delivery, a stamp was introduced (a new form of payment) in order to use their service. In each case, the cost had to be reimbursed in some form or fashion.

But what about today? You are probably saying that there are no costs in sending an e-mail, so how can reimbursement be considered in light of today's free distribution networks? But in reality, costs are indeed present and are much more significant than in generations past. Remember, our attention spans are the scarcest resource in the world today, so the real cost of advancing distribution networks that bombard us with information every waking moment is substantial. We are giving up our attention piece by piece. The only difference between past generations and today is that we are not asking for reimbursement for the cost. But what if we do? How about an e-mail tax? More on that later.

In the Agricultural Age, physical labor was a huge cost. Farming, the development of the railroad and transportation of food products all required human labor in order to accomplish distribution needs. In the Industrial Age, technical abilities and skilled trades became more important as resources. The ability to maintain and repair machinery was important in order for new methods of distribution and manufacturing to be realized. But now we are in the knowledge era. Neither physical labor nor trade skills are as important as intellectual capital. But, in order to tap into intellectual capital, one's attention must be acquired.

Because our attention spans are the gatekeepers to our intellectual capital, each moment of attention we give away has a price. The several seconds a day we delete spam from our inboxes have a price. The time I spend searching for a signal on my BlackBerry has a price. The time I lose with my family because I am surfing the Internet has a price. Because access to our attention has been without significant financial barriers, we tend to think of today's distribution networks as being free. But in reality, their costs are as high as ever.

So what do we do? Much of this will be addressed in later chapters. However, the overall approach needs to be the same as in past generations. We should decide on the costs that each of us experience and should create barriers to offset those costs. For example, my family should have little or no costs to access my attention. But unwanted solicitors should have significant barriers to gaining my focus. Interestingly, many tools exist, which we all currently possess, that can make this a reality, but the majority of us don't use them. Because we have entered the knowledge era so rapidly we have failed to recognize what we have given away freely in the process. It's time to change the way we look at our attention spans and whom we let access them. In some instances, competing interests for our attention will exist, but we have much more control than we think. In order to manage widespread information distribution well, one of the important tasks will be developing wise barriers to unwanted attacks on our attention.

Exploiting Our Hunger

From our conversation in this chapter, you may feel the progress of distribution networks has been a bad thing, but this is not the case. Like most things, progress can be used for everyone's benefit or it can be used in a negative fashion. The villain is not enhanced distribution but instead our inability to manage information bombardment and balance our lives.

We have hungered so much for information that we have allowed many to gain access to our attention spans. In turn, our priorities have become out of whack. We are all trying to get a satellite signal while the most incredible sunset in the world escapes us.

The Internet has enabled the exploitation of our information hunger, but we asked for it. We wanted more and more information. We are the ones who didn't want to be left out of the loop. We are the ones who feared ignorance. In order to get what we craved the most, a better distribution network was needed. Today we have it, and so far we have yet to learn how to discriminate among the different levels of information asking for our attention. This is where we stand right now. But this insatiable desire never ends. We always want it faster, higher, stronger, cheaper. Google is now test piloting a rollout of fiber-optic networks to certain residential communities in America. Wow, I can picture the digital tsunami coming!

FURTHER READING

Pony Express: http://www.xphomestation.com

Story of the railroad: http://www.uprr.com/aboutup/history/hist-ov/index.shtml

Transatlantic cargo ships: http://gcaptain.com/maritime/blog/container-ships-a-brief-history/

Go Daddy ads: http://www.adoperationsonline.com/2010/02/15/super-bowl-web-traffic-converts-for-go-daddy-again-in-2010/

Internet statistics: http://www.internetworldstats.com/stats.htm

Interview with Frederick Smith: http://www.achievement.org/autodoc/page/smi0int-1

Scan QR code for direct link to website,
hypertext links and other resources:

CHAPTER 6

Nobody's Job Is Safe

I am a technophile. I rarely question technology's benefits. For me, all new gadgets are cool! I am the geek who stands in line at the mall in order to purchase the first of this or that before anyone else.

Generally speaking, most of us readily accept that true progress in society is enhanced by technological advancement. Technological developments allow one generation to reach new heights over previous ones. The combustion engine enabled greater travel than horse and buggy. Air travel furthered this ability with more efficient and effective scale and scope. Perhaps space travel will eventually be the answer to saving our planet, which we are rapidly polluting. So technology is definitely a good thing...right? It all depends on your perspective.

Every time a new technology is developed, changes in the world take place accordingly. New behaviors and social interactions occur as a result. Different methods of performing the essential tasks of living evolve. The presumption is that the more efficient, more extensive and less cumbersome a task becomes as a result of technology, the better it is for everyone. But this is often not the case. Just because something can be done faster and easier does not necessarily mean it is better for everyone. These struggles over the benefits of progress have been present since the beginning of time.

Imagine those who first developed the wheel. Instead of requiring four or five men to lift and carry a heavy object, one or two could now roll the object for great distances with the use of the wheel and a cart.Though this technological advancement doesn't seem too impressive, the wheel offered a significant change in the traditional way of life. When new technological advancements occur, the end result is that less human capital is required for each task. This reduction in human capital as a result of greater technology lies at the heart of industry displacement.

From One Era to the Next

Approximately 100 years ago, agricultural development was the focus of one of the largest industries in the world. Farmers and workers labored intensely in their fields, preparing the soil, fertilizing the land, meticulously planting crops in order to maximize yield, and attending to irrigation needs as best they could. Often, entire families and even generations of families would work a single farm simply because the labor-intensive requirement was tremendous to ensure the farm thrived from year to year.

In the US in 1900, the total farming population was approximately thirty million people farming nearly six million farms. The entire US population was seventy-six million. In other words, in 1900 it required thirty-eight percent of the population to feed the entire nation annually. But with time, things changed. By the year 2000 the total farming population had fallen to only three million people while the entire US population had grown to 275 million people. Within 100 hundred years a dramatic change occurred. Less than three percent of the population was now needed to feed the entire country. What caused this change? Technological advancement.

Instead of using oxen, horses and human labor to plow the fields, tractors and heavy farm equipment allowed better soil preparation in much less time. Instead of creatively managing irrigation trenches, advanced mechanical irrigation systems were developed that ensured adequate water supplies to crops. Instead of picking crops by hand, machines rapidly harvested ripe crops in a fraction of the time and with a fraction of the human labor needed. Crops were genetically enhanced to produce greater yields and quality. Sounds pretty great, eh?

What happened to all those farmers over the last century? Obviously they were no longer working the fields with Mom and Pop. Thirty million farmers had dropped to only three million despite the US population more than tripling. Technological advancement dramatically displaced the need for human capital in the agricultural industry. Instead of sons and daughters of farming families choosing to stay on the farms, they decided to seek other industries to earn their livings. From a positive perspective, technology can be viewed as creating new opportunities for these individuals. From a negative view, technology essentially forced them to find other employment. The need for human labor in the agricultural industry had markedly fallen.

The aforementioned changes in the agricultural industry took 100 years, so you might not be too impressed by the degree of industry displacement caused by technology in this setting. But let's consider another example. In the mid 1970s, hundreds of thousands of carburetor manufacturers and mechanics serviced fuel systems on most new and used automobiles. But within a decade carburetor manufacturers and repair services had rapidly fallen in demand. Digital fuel-injection systems, which provided better power, fuel efficiency, performance and reliability, became the gold standard for all vehicles within a very short time period. What happened to these carburetor experts in a span of only ten years?

Like the farmers, these carburetor experts were displaced as technological innovation changed the way cars operated. Carburetors were dying components of the American car, and digital fuel-injection systems were the future. What some thought was a stable and secure talent soon became an obsolete skill. I am sure these guys were singing the praises of technology as they saw their customers slowly dwindling to nothing. People were now able to get around more efficiently and more reliably with better fuel systems, but fewer human beings were needed to provide this service thanks to technology.

Let's jump ahead to 1983. Philips and Sony collaborated on designing the first compact disc. Prior to this, vinyl records had dominated the music industry for years despite the development of the eight-track tape and compact cassettes. More than 50,000 vinyl record manufacturers produced millions of vinyl records each year, but within a couple of years all of this would change. By 1985 Dire Straits became the first musical recording artist to sell over a million copies of an album on CD, and by 1988 over 400 million CDs were being manufactured in over fifty processing plants globally. Do you think CD technology gave the vinyl record stompers the boot? Absolutely.

It logically follows then that on-demand downloads of music and movies, will give the boot to CDs and DVDs.

As a more recent example you can consider the college graduates in the class of 1999. Equipped with degrees in business, software engineering, computer science or marketing, thousands of enthusiastic young men and women set their sights on Silicon Valley. I can hear the comments of my students on stage at graduation in June of that year:

"Hey, Joe. Where are you headed after graduation?"

"I've landed a job with a dot-com in San Jose. I am on my way. How 'bout you, Carl?"

"Me too! The Web is the way to go. Internet business is a sure thing. I am getting paid entirely in stock options. You can't lose."

A few months later, in the fall, Joe and Carl meet again, back home by chance, outside a coffee house.

"Joe, I thought you were in San Jose."

"I was. Things took a dive. What are you doing back home, Carl?"

"Oh. The company disappeared over night. Most of the dot-coms in the area pretty much imploded and all of our stock options became worthless. Heard of any good jobs?"

The farmers were slowly displaced over a century. The carburetor manufacturers were displaced over a decade. The vinyl record manufacturers had to find new jobs in a couple of years. The dot-comers found the harsh reality of industry displacement in less than a year. Internet and communications technologies changed so quickly that these energetic new grads barely got their feet wet before being sent on their way. The need for software personnel, hardware technicians and Internet business development teams was not nearly what was anticipated, and as a result many people found themselves back at the starting block. Technological advancement is truly a wonderful thing. But we must not forget that it ultimately has a serious negative byproduct: industry displacement.

Technology: A Good Thing?

You have heard many experts and proponents talk about how great technology is and how much better we are as a result of it. But this may not necessarily be the case. Certainly, many of the farmers, carburetor manufacturers and vinyl record producers did not feel that technology was their friend. In fact, they lost their jobs as a result of technology. But from a larger perspective, has technology really helped us? In some ways it has, but in others it has not.

Consider medical technology, for instance. Early in the 1980s, a major shift in medical diagnostics took place. Computers played a significant role in this shift but so did specific technological developments in medicine itself. Prior to this, X-rays were the primary mode of radiological diagnosis. But suddenly two new modes of radiological testing became apparent: the CT (computerized tomography) scan and, eventually, MRI (magnetic resonance imaging). These technological advances revolutionized the way medicine was practiced, and the ripples were felt throughout the health-care industry.

Consider a young man presenting to an emergency room after a head injury. On arrival he is alert and awake, with seemingly no complaints or findings. X-rays of the skull show no evident fractures or shifts in the hazy structures. The patient is sent home only to succumb to a progressive intracranial bleed hours later. Now consider the same young man who, instead of an X-ray, receives a CT scan of the head in the emergency room. While the X-ray failed to show any abnormality, the CT clearly shows active bleeding within the skull. The patient is prepped for the operating room, where a neurosurgeon stabilizes the bleeding.

It is hard to argue that technology, in this instance, is not a good thing. A man's life was saved as a result of better technology, and even more examples of such lifesaving circumstances can be shown with MRI scanning. Technology has allowed earlier detection of diseases and more detailed information about overall health in many areas. By looking at quantity of life, these technological tools are clearly beneficial. But what if we look at other issues such as cost and quality of life? There the picture is less clear.

From a cost perspective, the standard for diagnosing patients changed with the advent of CT and MRI technology. Physicians were obligated to order these examinations in an effort to provide patients with the best possible care. Cost was no issue. Instead of a $100 X-ray, people were routinely receiving $1,500 MRI scans. The fact that more than ninety percent of these MRI scans failed to show any abnormalities was inconsequential. People demanded the best care that technology had to offer. Failure to provide this level of care placed physicians in significant positions of liability.

But cost was not the only issue. From a quality of life perspective, some patients did not necessarily receive added benefit from these technologies. Consider a seventy-year-old gentleman who received an MRI scan for headaches, which showed an unrelated cerebral aneurysm. The risk of aneurismal rupture is less than three percent per year, while the surgical treatment to remove the aneurysm might cause illness or death in as many as six percent of cases. Would you take your chances with an aneurysm or would you take your chances with surgery? If you choose the former, how will your life be affected by your knowing that you have an aneurysm in your head? Did the MRI really improve quality of life in this instance?

In the late 1990s my wife was diagnosed with melanoma and had three conspicuous moles removed that were later confirmed as skin cancer. Although we benefitted from universal health-care in Canada and did not have to pay any out-of-pocket expenses throughout the ordeal, the wait time for the initial consult, the surgical procedure and the corresponding confirmation of results was agonizingly slow. Unfortunately, the stress was really just getting started. Given the fact that her grandmother had passed away from melanoma, my wife would have to monitor herself for the rest of her life.

A year later, I came across an advertisement online for body scans in Silicon Valley. Full body MRIs with results in an hour! I happened to be speaking at a conference in San Jose a week later and had the idea to take a small medical vacation at the same time. I took my wife along for the trip, and we ultimately invested in a full body scan while we were there. This was the first time I ever paid out of my own pocket for any health-related issue. It was weird. But the promise of comprehensive and fast diagnostics was too good to pass up. This technological marvel was a sight to behold. This grand machine was one of only a few in the US in private use at the time.

To make a long story short, the medical technician literally took a virtual tour of her entire body and saved it all on DVD. Thankfully, my wife was clean, and the cancer had not spread. We were so elated. Amidst my jubilation I looked over at the technician and said, "Set me up." I hadn't intended to receive a body scan myself, but that was an option private health care offered that the universal system back home did not.

The irony of this story is that although my wife was confirmed healthy, my own DVD scan showed three small kidney stones. Nice—and I'd thought that I was the healthy one! A few weeks later in Toronto, my doctor (who, incidentally, could not find the kidney stones with a traditional ultrasound) literally jumped out of his chair with excitement once he saw the DVD. Before I knew what was happening, he called a team of doctors to come check out my virtual body tour. They looked as if they were salivating as they marveled at the images. Though the stones were too small for any serious intervention, my doctor recommended white cranberry juice three times daily. As a result, I have not passed any stones in the subsequent ten years, which likely means they have disappeared. Technological advancement often works in unanticipated and mysterious ways.

Every technological advancement offers some positives and some negatives. The Industrial Age allowed mass production and greater distribution, but it resulted in environmental pollution, greater segregation of classes and, of course, industry displacement. Similarly, the Information Age has facilitated the rapid transfer of knowledge but has simultaneously resulted in some negative consequences. In addition to stealing our attention spans and free time, it has created a larger digital divide across various regions in the world, and it has resulted in industry displacement for many people as well. Realizing this fact is important as we move forward with the latest and greatest technological achievements. Yes, they offer benefits...but at what cost?

Getting Comfortable With Change

Despite the controversial issues surrounding technological advances, progress and change are inevitable. As you may recall, industry displacement for the farming community took nearly a century. More recently, the dot-comers found themselves displaced within months of starting their jobs. The rate of industry displacement is accelerating at warp speed. It's hard to believe that Twitter has only been around since 2006, yet it has already saturated the social networking market with over fifty million tweets per day. Likewise, video retailers with in-store selections have virtually vanished in the same amount of time. The days of industries being displaced gradually are over. Today, industries can come and go within a span of a few years, if not months. Technology is changing so quickly with the explosion of information that predicting industry longevity is nearly impossible. As the underlying commodity has changed, so has the speed of change. Initially machines replaced the need for physical labor. But as machines have become more advanced, the abilities to replace specific human physical talents and now cognitive talents are occurring at a more rapid rate. This makes the realities of artificial intelligence and its ability to evoke global change on its own more likely.

The bottom line is that we no longer have the luxury of feeling comfortable with our positions in life. I am tenured as a university professor, of which I am extremely proud. It took many years and a great deal of hard work to achieve this level of my academic profession. But while this feather in my cap might have meant stability and longevity for my predecessors, this is no longer the case. Like other industries, education is rapidly evolving, and the methods of how we teach, study and investigate are constantly in a state of flux. Like everyone else, I cannot afford to rest on my past accomplishments. Academic tenure is a figment of a bygone era. I expect it to disappear from universities entirely in the future.

Why do we yearn for stability and resist change so much anyway? One answer might lie within the confines of our own human anatomy. Scientists and researchers have revealed that the way the brain learns is through a repetitive process involving different information pathways. The more you receive the same information, the more likely it is that you can understand and store the information. Likewise, if information is presented in different formats, the ability to consolidate knowledge and learn is much easier.

For example, suppose you are presented with a complex array of written instructions on how to make chicken cacciatore. Visual pathways of the brain distribute the information on the recipe card to different parts of your nervous system. Your memory areas, your language areas, parts of the brain that compare and contrast, and planning areas all have opportunities to analyze and store the list of instructions. If you only see the recipe once you are much less likely to retain all the instructions adequately, compared to seeing the recipe multiple times. Additionally, if you receive the instructions only in the form of a written recipe you are less likely to learn how to make chicken cacciatore well when compared to having the recipe and having someone demonstrate the preparation.

Think of the brain's nerve pathways as paths through a field of wheat. Imagine you are trying to get to a pond in the center of this field, but the wheat is too tall to see the pond. If you travel a single path to the pond on one occasion, you may be able to retrace your steps with great attention if you choose to return to the pond again. But if you frequent this same path over and over, the wheat becomes worn down and the path becomes easier to find. Likewise, if you form multiple paths to the pond from around the perimeter of the field you will be much more likely to reach your destination more quickly from any location. In essence, this is how learning takes place in our brains. The more worn a nerve path becomes, and the more nerve paths present, the better we learn and retain information.

The problem with change is that we like to travel our same old worn paths. Why venture out into the tall wheat when a nice, worn path to the pond already exists? But with technological advancements, the preferred pond keeps moving around. The same old worn path might take us to the pond we know, but everyone else is now going to a bigger and better pond. Unless we accept this fact and learn to accept the change, our old pond will eventually dry up. The difference between today and decades past is that the ponds are drying up much faster.

Much of the research regarding the brain's ability to learn has been elucidated through the discovery of kindling. *Kindling* is a term originally used in regard to patients who suffered from epilepsy. Simplistically, epileptic seizures are short circuits of the brain's electrical pathways. Instead of normal electrical nerve signals traveling from one neuron to another in a controlled fashion, electrical discharges occur uncontrollably, triggering a variety of symptoms depending on which brain pathway is stimulated. *Kindling* refers to a process that facilitates the development of more frequent seizures. The more frequently a seizure path is traveled by an electrical signal, the more difficult it becomes to stop the occurrence of seizures with medication. In other words, seizures beget seizures by creating well-traveled pathways. This is the essence of kindling.

Interestingly, medications to prevent seizures work by reducing the excitability of these nerve pathways. Most anti-seizure medications have side effects that reduce a person's ability to pay attention and concentrate. Just as seizures become more engrained by traveling the same pathways, we learn and retain information the same way. So, when medications inhibit the spread of seizure pathways, the ability to concentrate and learn are often affected as well.

All of these factors highlight how the brain learns and why we are most comfortable with the status quo. Choosing the path less traveled is contrary to what our brains like to do. Like our brains, we like to keep doing the things with which we are familiar. There is security and stability in familiarity. Perhaps this also provides an explanation for why organizational change is so difficult. The collective group of employee brains just wants to travel down the same old paths. But, in order to survive the rapid changes in technology, we must force ourselves to venture into the unknown.

The Power of Re

So how do we handle the accelerating changes associated with technology? What are the solutions to avoid complacency? Just ask the carburetor manufacturers or the vinyl record producers if you want to know the answer. The solution to industry displacement is to harness the skills that allow you to compete, participate and excel in the new market arena. I like to call this phenomenon the *power of re.*

If your skills have fallen out of favor due to technological advancement, then you have one good option. You must retrain yourself to acquire new skills, retool your business with the latest technologies, renew your focus on how your services or products are provided, and recertify to ensure your abilities are competitive. This is the power of re. This is the essential solution to offset the negative risks of industry displacement.

Young people entering the workforce today have already accepted this concept. They have had to relearn, retool and renew repeatedly through years of education just to graduate. Remember, the cumulative codified information base is doubling every eleven hours. What they learned in ninth grade was no longer up-to-date information by the time graduation rolled around. Knowledge had doubled and changed numerous times over the course of their high school years. If they hadn't learned the power of re, then they likely would not have graduated at all.

The same applies to everyone today. Do you think the unionized automotive workers were immune to industry displacement as robotic equipment progressively replaced their positions on the assembly lines? Do you think telephone operators were protected as automated voice data systems took over the telecommunication industry? What about all those X-ray technicians who suddenly saw CT and MRI scans overtaking medical diagnostics? All of these individuals had a choice. They could either do nothing, hoping they would somehow escape the inevitable attrition, or they could relearn, retrain, renew and retool so their skills could keep up with technology.

What are the obstacles that keep us from embracing the power of re? For one, we have already learned that we don't like change. We like what is comfortable, predictable, stable and secure. Additionally, our brains like to process information the same way over and over because this is the path of least resistance. This resistance to change becomes even greater as we get older. The ability to relearn, retrain and retool requires more effort and energy as we age. Medically, this is known by the term *neuroplasticity.*

Neuroplasticity, or simply plasticity, is defined as the brain's ability to reorganize nerve pathways in response to new experiences. In other words, plasticity refers to the brain's ability to change as it learns. Have you wondered why a young child can easily learn two or more languages without difficulty but when an adult tries the same task, the effort seems exponentially harder? The answer is plasticity. The brain's plasticity and capacity to learn peak in childhood and then gradually decline as we advance through adulthood into old age. Therefore, the older we are, the more difficult it becomes to adjust to industry displacement.

What happens in the brain as we learn? For one, we create new pathways of information, as previously described, but our individual brain cells also change. Interestingly, our brains' neurons begin to sprout more connections with other neurons. These increased sprouts connect with other brain cells, forming communications called *synapses.* The more we actively learn, the more synapses we have and the denser the brain's nerve networks become. By using the power of re, we are actually creating more comprehensive hardware for our brain. Learning facilitates the brain's overall capacity to manage information.

But what about the decline in neuroplasticity with age? There is a silver lining here as well. Researchers at the National Institute on Aging have demonstrated that when people perform mental exercises designed to enhance memory, reasoning and learning, it has a positive effect on long-term brain function compared to people who do not participate in mental exercises. In other words, *use it or lose it* clearly applies to neuroplasticity. Not only can the power of re help us offset the negative effects of technological advancement and industry displacement but it can also help us with our brains' health.

Though change is not always welcome and certainly not comfortable, learning new information and skills is becoming increasing important. The best strategy to combat industry displacement is to constantly relearn, retrain, retool and recertify so that your knowledge base is keeping pace with the rest of the world. In the Information Age, knowledge is power, and the power of re is one way to ensure that you are in a strong and secure place no matter what technology may throw at you.

The Invisible Threat of Industry Displacement

Complacency, attrition and being left behind are obvious threats from technological advancement and the resultant industry displacement. However, one of the greatest threats to us from industry displacement goes unrecognized by many companies every day. Even if a company and most of its employees keep pace with progress and change, a significant number of people will still fall by the wayside. Retirement, failure to retrain or relearn, and fear of change are some examples of why some people leave an organization or the mainstream. These individuals represent the greatest potential loss to society as a whole due to industry displacement.

Which individuals most commonly get left behind? Typically, older employees who are more resistant to change are the first to go. Whether they are laid off as technologies replace their skills or whether they voluntarily retire or leave the company, these people have one of the greatest assets a company needs: knowledge. Regardless of whether an employee works in customer service, in the call center or in the mail room, every single person has a unique knowledge base that is valuable to an organization. Every person has at least one tidbit of knowledge that no one else knows. As people leave an organization due to industry displacement, the most unrecognized threat is the drop in the company's cumulative information base. This is a very important component of a firm's intellectual capital.

Several years ago, a longtime employee of one of the major car manufacturers was nearing retirement from his job performing exterior paint applications. He had been with the company for more than twenty years. He received a reasonable pension and, of course, the customary going away party with a chocolate cake in the break room. But no effort was made to acquire this man's vast knowledge from his years of experience. He had accumulated volumes of information about the automotive industry and specifically the paint application process over two decades, but no one bothered to tap into this valuable resource.

The reason for his layoff was technological advancement.

A new robotic machine could now assess and apply the exterior paint to the metal automobile frame in less time and for less cost. But within a week of the man's departure, numerous complaints about the exterior paint were being received from quality assurance inspectors and dealers who had received the vehicles. The paint was chipping in places and appeared to be unevenly distributed. Even after several investigations by numerous people, no one could figure out what was wrong. After another week, one of the supervisors contacted the retiree to come back in order to assess the problem. Within two minutes he noticed that the temperature of the paint being applied was set too high. With a simple readjustment, the temperature was reset and the problem was solved.

What was the cost of this loss of knowledge from the company? In financial terms, hundreds of cars had to be repainted, resulting in an expense of tens of thousands of dollars. But in conceptual costs, the figure is intangible. How can you determine what this employee's knowledge base is worth when no one bothered to take the time to quantify it? At a minimum, an attempt to acquire this knowledge should have been made through an exit interview. Perhaps retraining, retooling, renewing and recertifying this employee would have yielded a better return on the dollar overall. This is the biggest threat to many organizations that stems from industry displacement.

Industry displacement has been occurring throughout history as new technologies cause changes in the way we have lived. But the notable fact is that the speed at which technological changes are occurring has increased significantly in the last several years. What used to take decades now occurs within months. The result is that businesses will come and go rather quickly, as will their employees. In other words, not only will we as individuals suffer from industry displacement but so will small and large organizations. We have to be ready to adapt and change in order to survive. Previous generations were accustomed to working for one employer for their entire careers. Today, university graduates could soon end up working in industries that start and end entirely within a few years.

Part of this process does require a willingness to change and to adapt. This may not come naturally for us unless we have grown up in a culture of constant flux. Finding security and stability in the midst of rapid change can be tough. But all of us are finding it essential to constantly retrain ourselves and learn new information in order to be competitive. We eagerly seek new information so that we can gain greater power in the knowledge era. The important thing is to be sure to acquire knowledge that is necessary without affecting the quality of our lives. What good is it to have pools of knowledge but no time to enjoy the things in life that make us happy?

At the same time, choosing to become obsolete and avoid change is just as harmful. The days of security being attained from a long tenure on a job are over. Unionized laborers, investment banking CEOs and even tenured professors are finding this to be true. In order to enjoy the comforts of security, you now have to become comfortable with constant change. You must retrain, retool, renew and recertify constantly...anything but retire!

As we have entered the Information Age and the knowledge era, most of us have been flying by the seats of our pants. We realize that technology is changing rapidly. We are aware that our attention is being pulled in many directions by a bombardment of information around us. We see that the skills and knowledge needed at our jobs are in a constant state of flux. But few of us have learned the skill of how to manage best this massive increase in information and change. As a result, many of us struggle to cope with the stressful world in which we now live. Industry displacement is just one of the many consequences of the situation in which we now find ourselves.

FURTHER READING

History of agriculture: http://www.agclassroom.org/gan/timeline/farmers_land.htm

Development of the CD: http://news.bbc.co.uk/2/hi/6950933.stm

CT/MRI history: http://www.medical.siemens.com/siemens/zh_CN/gg_ct_FBAs/files/brochures/CT_History_and_Technology.pdf

Aneurysms: http://stroke.ahajournals.org/cgi/content/full/34/8/1857

Brain plasticity: http://faculty.washington.edu/chudler/plast.html

Kindling: http://homepages.nyu.edu/~eh597/kindle.htm

Aging mental exercises: http://www.msnbc.msn.com/id/16284851/

Scan QR code for direct link to website,
hypertext links and other resources:

CHAPTER 7

The Digital Blitzkrieg

"Joe, hit the dirt! Incoming e-mail!"

"I'm gonna try to make it to the rear platoon. Cover me, and update my virus protection," Joe shouts back.

"I can't…I am out of ammunition and I'm wounded. My RAM is low."

"Here, take a couple of rounds of my college-education artillery. It should hold them off for a while. I'll be back with help and update patches."

Joe makes a dash for the rear platoon. With every footstep, blasts of information explode around him, nearly knocking him off balance: news updates, stock tickers, weather forecasts, sports highlights and the tweets just keep coming stronger and stronger from all directions. Somehow he manages to stay upright, but he is bewildered by the onslaught of bits and bytes. The echoes of the blasts and the radiation from his monitor are still ringing in his head. He can barely focus but eventually arrives at his messenger buddies' area in the rear.

"Where's Roger?" someone asks Joe.

"He's back in the trenches. I'm not sure how long he can last there. He has outdated ammunition, buggy software and lots of malware, and there are phishing programs out to get his personal information. He is wounded and his processing power is very slow," Joe replies. "We need to step back and reassess our position. Perhaps we can reboot and try control-alt-delete."

"Reassess our position? There's no time for that! The attack is coming too fast and furious, and it takes forever to reboot the system. That's a luxury we don't have."

"We can't just leave Roger out there in the information abyss."

"Forget about Roger, Joe. Worry about yourself! From the look of things, this ambush is just getting started. It's every person for himself. I am taking cover and turning off my BlackBerry."

Joe ignores the advice and heads back to find Roger. Dodging explosions of attention-seeking missiles, he carefully maneuvers his way back. He arrives at the trench only to find that Roger has succumbed to his wounds.

"Oh, Roger…I guess that old ammunition wasn't powerful enough to ward off the digital blitzkrieg."

In today's knowledge era we are being attacked from every angle. Information bombardment is today's biggest threat. This digital blitzkrieg of bits and bytes is hitting us from all sides as we try to make our ways through our days. E-mails, text messages, tweets, advertising, marketing, video streams, cell phone messages, voicemails and more bombard our attention whether we like it or not. Their increasing volume is frightening, but their enormous influence is even worse. They lure our attention away from more important tasks and activities with ease while we unknowingly pay the price.

Joe was able to ward off the attack, but Roger was not. Today, with information bombardment everywhere, a mentality that every person is out for himself permeates society. In order to survive, everyone must collect as many tidbits of knowledge as possible. Only this strategy seems to guarantee the ability to compete and survive. After all, knowledge is power in the Information Age. As a result, we hoard information for ourselves, hoping to gain an advantage over others in a Darwinian battle where only the fittest survive. Little do we realize the ramifications.

While many people suffer from information bombardment, Roger, on the other hand, suffers a different fate. With an outdated education and inadequate knowledge to compete, he is left behind in this onslaught of information. This is what most of us subconsciously fear the most in today's Information Age, and this fear drives us to cling to every piece of information that comes across our path.

Today, information is attacking us incessantly, and we struggle to survive. On the one side we try to avoid ignorance and industry displacement by retraining, retooling, relearning and recertifying. On the other side we try to discern which information is necessary and which is not so we can maintain some quality of life. When we are unsuccessful in these goals, negative outcomes are bound to happen. Unfortunately, these unpleasant effects are all too common in the world today.

The overall ramifications of information bombardment can be best viewed by analyzing the effects on four different levels. On a personal level consequences can include not only insecurity but also negative health effects. Likewise, effects on group dynamics and function occur when information bombardment interferes with efficient productivity and performance. This is amplified to an even greater extent at the level of larger organizations. Eventually information bombardment can even affect how effectively nations function and communicate with other nations. At each of these levels, information bombardment and poor management cause slightly different consequences. But in every case, stability, security, productivity and performance are at risk.

Individual Ramifications

In preceding chapters, the motivation for craving information has been discussed. Our need for stability and security drive our thirst for knowledge. As information has become more readily accessible and available we have welcomed information bombardment into our lives. No one wants to be ignorant or left out of the loop. But what many of us have forgotten is how to discern which information is worthy of our attention.

I am always keeping my eye out for the distracted driver constantly checking his e-mail in traffic or the disinterested father studying his stock quotes during his son's hockey game. The absolute worst is the constant texting phenomenon, especially amongst my wife's friends. It has gotten to the point where I feel sometimes that I'm living in an instant-messaging casino. Constant beeps, rings, bells and whistles. An individual ramification that you may want to highlight is our advancing ADHD culture. With constant bits of information hitting us, especially at work, we've become unfocused, distracted and disinterested. I see this every day amongst some of my friends, who are unable to focus for more than five minutes at a time.

How many of you tweet? I suspect a good many of you do. I do also (www.twitter.com/NickBontis). But if we really look at Twitter as an information resource, where would you rank its level of importance? In other words, how valuable is the information received on Twitter compared to other information outlets? How much value does it have compared to personal relaxation time? In 2007 Twitter averaged 5,000 messages a day. As of 2010 Twitter averaged fifty million Tweets a day. That is information bombardment! What is troubling to me is that in a race for securing more and more followers, users end up following as many others as possible in a simple dance of "follow me and I will follow you." Ultimately, this reinforcing algorithm pushes the volume of information flow way beyond what is possible to digest.

One choice is to do nothing. In other words, you may just decide to quit trying to keep up with any advancement. Perhaps you turn off your television set, your Internet connection, your cell phone and your social networking accounts. That would be one way to manage information bombardment, and I know many people who have done this and are smiling. But what is the risk of this? Not only are you shutting off unnecessary information but you are also shutting off important communications and data that are vital to your life. These are the tools that provide stability and security. Information helps you maintain employment, earn a living, participate in society and community, and be an active parent and friend. Information is not the problem; it's how we manage it that is the issue.

Shutting off information indiscriminately is dangerous. Without knowledge, you become not only less powerful to influence the world but also less able to influence the direction of your own life. The solutions to information bombardment seek answers that provide better quality of life. Choosing to completely shut yourself off from the world is unlikely to accomplish this goal. Like it or not, we all are in the midst of the Information Age, and acting like an ostriches sticking our heads in the sand is not the best answer.

Alternatively, we might choose to gobble up every piece

of information that comes our way. Every e-mail, every text message and every Web link is given our attention so that we never miss a single tidbit of knowledge. After all, the e-mail promoting the latest clothing sale at your favorite store might come in handy someday. Knowing what Lady Gaga is doing for dinner is also crucial information. Spending a few more minutes looking at a soccer highlights Web site won't affect your time with your family that much, will it?

The opposite extreme to closing the door to any information is opening it widely and taking it off its hinges. Free and unlimited access to our attention spans is available. But there is one significant problem. Attention is a limited resource, if you recall, and ultimately something has to give. When little effort is given to prioritization of information, we eventually pay the price whether it's in our personal relationships or in our own health and well-being.

When we are confronted with information bombardment, what is the most natural response? Typically, we sacrifice those things in our lives that are less demanding for a little more time for absorbing information. Personal time for relaxing, exercise and sleep are the most common things that get sacrificed first. Do you know the secondary effects of neglecting each of these areas? That's correct: poor health. Lack of relaxation can lead to mental stress, anxiety and depression. Lack of exercise can lead to high blood pressure, heart disease, obesity and many other conditions. Lack of sleep is linked to a multitude of disorders, including cancers, and reduced longevity of life.

Interestingly, sleep deprivation is actually counterproductive to learning new information. In a Washington State University report, sleep deprivation was shown to hinder how information is collected and understood by our brains. In essence, we have made more time for information processing through sleep deprivation only to reduce our overall ability to understand it. We sacrifice quantity for quality. Too bad many of my students still prefer to pull all-nighters and cram prior to their final exams.

Information bombardment can alter many chemical processes within the body. Stress hormones and inflammatory proteins are released in greater quantities when we burn the candle at both ends. This is the most likely mechanism by which stress causes so many different physical health conditions. Chronic stimulation of our immune systems due to stress has been linked to cancers, infections, intestinal dysfunctions and other disorders. Recently, obesity has been linked to sleep deprivation effects. Are we willing to gain knowledge at the expense of our own health?

The effects on personal security as well as medical health are major concerns for all of us in the knowledge era. Each of us needs a balance in life between work and leisure. I should know because I have been there. If I am constantly checking e-mails, surfing the Web, answering texts and listening to voicemails, little time is left for the personal relationships in my life or that ever-vanishing time for solitude that gives us real perspective. These are the real threats to us as individuals unless we begin to manage information bombardment more effectively.

Group Ramifications

What are the consequences of information bombardment at a group level? It depends on your perspective, since each of us belongs to different groups. For example, I have a group of students to whom I relate every day. I also belong to a group of professors and other research colleagues. At the same time I am involved in groups within my community, in my children's Greek school, in my soccer league and with other musicians (I play an instrument known as the euphonium). The effects of information bombardment therefore can affect these groups in different ways depending on the point of view.

For example, the most obvious effect is one of absence. As everyone struggles with the same pressures today in managing the onslaught of information, absenteeism is increasing. I might be unable to attend my boys' hockey practice because I have to digest stacks of information for a lecture later in the week. Someone else may have been trading sleep for attention and in the process became ill with the flu, causing absenteeism. While these are effects on group dynamics and function, essentially these show how individual ramifications extend into the group setting.

Other group effects are less obvious. One of the most important aspects is how we share information within a group. Whenever you or I are part of a group, we have a choice to share all, some or none of the information we have. For example, in the workplace we may be asked by a coworker about specific knowledge we have. This knowledge presumably will help them further their own project for the group. Do we relinquish that information to them for free? Do we barter to receive something in return for the information, such as recognition or future favors? Or do we withhold the information because we do not wish to give up our knowledge power to another? In other words, do we share our knowledge or hoard it?

Because knowledge is power, each of us immediately assesses the pros and cons when confronted with a request for information. Our decision to hoard or share occurs as the result of a variety of complex considerations that we make in a matter of microseconds. The dynamics and function of a group can be enhanced or retarded as a result of this behavior. As information bombardment has increased, hoarding has also become more common. After all, if you're the one who sacrificed your time and attention to gain specific information, why give it away for free? The more precious the commodity, the more likely hoarding will become. Two of the most significant ramifications of information bombardment are therefore the inability to share knowledge and the secondary decline in group success.

Like individuals, groups can also be overwhelmed by information. If similar investments in information discrimination do not take place at a group level, productivity declines. Useless information clogs the processes that facilitate efficiency. How many of us have been at town hall meetings where someone has stood up and gone off on a tangent about a story that has little to do with the issue being discussed? In the best-case scenario, a moderator redirected the group discussion, wasting a small amount of time. In the worst-case scenario, the entire group became distracted and lost sight of the main topic. Ever heard of ADHD at a group level?

Different groups will react to information bombardment in different ways. Some proactive groups will embrace information sharing, information discrimination and healthy knowledge management. Others will flounder and suffer as they try to find their way through the maze of constant information. While the ingredients that determine these positive or negative reactions will be discussed in more detail later, generational influences play a big role in predicting group behavior.

Consider the baby boomer generation, for example. Being

born before 1963, this group did not grow up in the Information Age. Baby boomers did not naturally know how to handle an abundance of information, much less manage it well. They learned how to use computers, e-mail and the Internet because their jobs and society demanded they do so. Of all the generations present in today's society, this generation most often struggles with information bombardment. In contrast, Generation X individuals were born between 1960 and 1980, and they adapted to information bombardment more readily. Though computers and the Internet were not necessarily part of their early education, they changed as the world changed. Generation Xers learned to adapt and to absorb information more quickly. The timing was simply right for them to accept information bombardment as a fact of life.

Today, Generation Y individuals are pushing the envelope even further. Not only are they comfortable with multitasking and information bombardment but they are also creating and developing more extensive means of information distribution through innovative networks and distribution systems. But despite their comfort with information bombardment, they still fall into the same pitfalls. They have become information junkies craving knowledge like a drug. In fact, they are the pushers of information in today's knowledge era, and we eagerly gobble it up!

Group effects of information bombardment can reveal several adverse effects and consequences. It is here that micro-effects from too much information evolve into macro-effects. But again, stability, productivity and performance are at stake unless information is managed well. Information affects group health just as much as it affects our personal health.

Organizational Ramifications

The US health-care system is supposedly one of the greatest in the world. From world-renowned medical universities to the latest medical technologies, American health care stands alone at the top, right? According to the 2000 World Health Report, the United States ranked thirty-seventh in the world among other nations in quality of health care. In 2006, American health care ranked thirty-ninth for infant mortality, forty-third for adult female mortality, forty-second for adult male mortality and thirty-sixth for life expectancy. Despite these less than impressive rankings, there was one area where it did rank the highest. The US did rank first in health-care expenditures per capita. Why would a country that spends so much money on health care rank so low in so many important health indicators?

As late as the year 2000, the penetration of electronic medical records in the United States was only five percent among private physicians. This meant that ninety-five percent of physicians kept paper patient charts in their offices. If your records needed to make their way to another physician, specialist or hospital, they had to be copied and mailed or faxed. Unfortunately, this process was extremely inefficient and fraught with errors. In the end, many of the lab tests, X-rays and other studies would be repeated simply to facilitate information gathering. Have you ever heard the following explanation from a physician?

"Mrs. Wilson, we will simply repeat the tests at our facility. We want to be sure the results are accurate."

What he was really saying was:

"Mrs. Wilson, I have very little faith that your records will be faxed or received in a reasonable time, and I have little time to invest in making sure this happens. Therefore, it is easiest if we just repeat the tests here."

See the dollar figures rise? One of the greatest effects of poor information management at an organizational level is duplication costs. We see them everywhere in society. At large insurance corporations, financial institutions, local and state government agencies...the list is endless. When information is not shared effectively, duplication costs are inevitable. With a fragmented pay-for-service health-care system, it's no wonder the US spends the most on health-care yet receives so little in return.

With advancing technology, medical information rose dramatically in a very short time. Not only did physicians have to consider many other additional diagnostic examinations but they also had to interpret and make decisions based on their results. Rather than trying to discern more accurately which information was most valuable, often more information was felt to be the best approach. When tests yielded conflicting reports, the answer was often to repeat the tests or order more tests. This only worsened the information bombardment already present.

Duplication costs negatively affect productivity in any organization. For every dollar spent on duplication costs, a dollar is subtracted from the organization's profits. Quantity of information is not necessarily beneficial, especially if it prevents qualitative information from being recognized. When these practices cost an organization heavily in profits, human efforts or other resources, productivity is squashed. If severe enough, duplication costs can be a terminal disease for an organization.

The underlying relationship between information bombardment and duplication costs is a failure of the right hand to know what the left is doing. So much information is being presented that communication and dissemination of pertinent information throughout the organization fail. As a result you have two or more different groups within the organization investing resources in the same project or problem. But this isn't the only ill effect information bombardment can have on an organization.

Let's look at the O. J. Simpson story. In the hours after Nicole Simpson and Ron Goldman were found murdered, one of the lead detectives discovered several concerning findings at the home of O. J. Simpson. Drops of what appeared to be blood on the driveway, a seemingly matching leather glove to the one found at the murder scene, and red streaks inside the infamous white Ford Bronco comprised a list of concerning evidence. As a result, the detective pursued a search warrant for O. J.'s house through a district judge in Los Angeles.

Unknown to the detective, however, the detective's partner had spoken to O. J. Simpson on the phone; he had agreed to return home on the next flight from Chicago. This omitted piece of information may have resulted in the search warrant being denied. O. J. was not in the house in danger, nor was he being uncooperative with the search of the house. In the trial that followed, presiding judge Ito nearly discredited all evidence found at the Simpson estate because this information was not included in the request of the search warrant. Information bombardment in the midst of all the activity prevented both detectives from having essential pieces of information to perform their jobs effectively.

When information overwhelms an organization without appropriate management, some important facts often escape notice while other unnecessary information filters through. In the end, decisions are based on an array of incomplete data. I think of it as driving through a severe rain storm at night. I strain to see the road illuminated by my car's headlights as large drops of rain pound the windshield, obscuring my view. If my wipers are not working well, I might as well give up on safely arriving at my destination. The same applies to information bombardment. If you don't have effective information management tools in place, the organization is destined to fail in its performance.

The larger the organization, the more profound the effects knowledge management has on productivity and effective operation. Did you realize that as of the year 2005, twenty-five percent of all Fortune 500 companies had chief knowledge officers who directed the corporations' knowledge management strategies? These companies realize the ramifications of improperly dealing with information bombardment. I wonder how many corporations who are not Fortune 500-caliber invest in knowledge management.

Institutional Ramifications

In 2005, the city of New Orleans suffered one of the greatest tragedies in American history. While Hurricane Katrina was one of the most massive and powerful hurricanes in recent times, this alone was not the most concerning problem. The ultimate tragedy stemmed from poor information management and the inability of agencies and administrations to communicate effectively. When the storm had passed, communities were devastated and hundreds had lost their lives.

Exactly one year prior to Hurricane Katrina, the Federal Emergency Management Agency (FEMA) had conducted a mock exercise called *Hurricane Pam* that eerily predicted all of the same events that eventually transpired during Hurricane Katrina. Because of the limitations of the current system, a coordinated effort between federal, state and local agencies was to address several key areas, including evacuation planning, communications among first responders, transportation systems and more. But a month after the exercise the federal administration cut the budget for FEMA's programs significantly, and nothing was accomplished as planned.

When the storm hit, multiple agencies were involved. These included the Army Corps of Engineers, FEMA, the Department of Homeland Security, the National Guard, the mayor of New Orleans and the governor of Louisiana. Each agency had its own information and knowledge of the situation, but none communicated to other groups. In fact, without an emergency communication system, all communication abilities had been destroyed. FEMA accused local and state officials of not providing proper evacuation while everyone looked to FEMA for federal assistance. Rescues were delayed because agencies could not effectively coordinate responses.

A wealth of information was available more than a year before Hurricane Katrina about the need for preparedness, but this information was not shared, not communicated or simply ignored. The result was a major human tragedy—the loss of 1,800 lives—which could have been prevented. These painful realities can occur when information management fails at an institutional level.

What were the main problems? Did institutional agencies hoard information? Did agencies fail to share their information in a timely and efficient manner? Was the amount of information simply too much to integrate in a short amount of time? To answer these questions succinctly…yes. Like the pitfalls of information bombardment at individual, group and organizational levels, institutions risk inefficiency, poor productivity and poor performance when information bombardment occurs. But instead of the costs being quantified in dollar figures, the costs are typically assessed in human lives.

As President Obama stated after an investigation of the 2009 Christmas Day terrorist plot, we "failed to connect the dots," which sometimes happens when multiple agencies in an institution are responsible for different sets of knowledge. This has happened countless times throughout history, but its occurrence is increasing as information bombardment increases. Unfortunately, the stakes appear to be increasing as well. At higher levels of social structure, the ramifications of information bombardment become more and more serious.

The inability to share information and communicate it effectively carries huge risks, but at the same time relinquishing our control over information is just as risky. What happens if artificial intelligence evolves to a point where we take a backseat to information development and control? Who will make decisions for the world then? In whose best interest will these decisions be made? We may not like the answers to these questions. For this reason we need to be involved proactively in information management solutions.

The best solutions lie somewhere in between. In dealing with information bombardment, neither drowning in too much information nor allowing someone (or something) else to manage information for us is a good choice. Instead, we need to adopt ways to share and communicate information effectively while focusing our attention on quality of knowledge rather than quantity. These efforts will not only affect how national institutions successfully operate internally but will also enable nations to work collectively in an ever-shrinking world.

As information continues to advance in the knowledge era, managing what is critical for supporting positive change will become the foremost skill at every level. Attention spans will become the highest-priced commodity. Though information bombardment can be felt in every facet of life, its effects on large social institutions may result in the most profound impacts on our daily lives.

A New Age With New Threats

It is 3:45 p.m. EST and millions of American financial institutions are preparing to close their operations for the day. The New York Stock Exchange is set to close in fifteen minutes. Suddenly, huge fluctuations in stock prices begin affecting thousands of stocks in the domestic market, followed by erratic changes in international stocks. Switchboards light up as thousands of customers call to make sell and purchase requests. Online stock activity bombards the capacity of the servers. Within ten minutes, the entire system comes to a halt as the Federal Reserve chairman announces that a terrorist plot has been effectively launched against five different stock exchanges throughout the world.

In the aftermath, trillions of US dollars are lost in market value as well as lost production, in addition to large amounts of other foreign currencies abroad. Financial markets are shut down for several days while security and technology experts try to eliminate, repair and protect a system that's already felt to be impenetrable. But advancing technologies and expertise have somehow allowed a virus to infect the world's financial database. Unlike a kamikaze pilot or suicide bomber, little traces of evidence remain to help identify which organization or individual is responsible. Welcome to the new age of cyber-terrorism.

Terrorism is attractive to small groups for three main reasons. First, it can be used as a weapon for the weak. Second, it is a means of gaining attention and establishing an identity. Third, it seeks to destroy existing behaviors in the world and replace them with new ones. In the Information Age, physically destroying a town, a building or a group of people is no longer necessary to accomplish these three tasks. All one needs is to influence information and steal the world's attention. Not only is this less cumbersome to accomplish today but, with information bombardment, thousands of creative plots exist by which terrorists can influence large groups of people.

We saw the financial impact of 9/11. Imagine the above scenario and its financial ramifications worldwide. Currency is still a valuable commodity, but as we have ushered in the knowledge era information has become increasingly more important. If knowledge is indeed power, expect terrorist plots to sabotage information databases and our attention spans to a greater extent. Whether this occurs through the use of media or through specific attacks on information systems, we are all at risk for these effects.

Having described how we have arrived at this point in history, and identifying the potential downfalls of information bombardment when not effectively managed, let's now paint a realistic picture of our current information environment. By knowing where we have come from and where we are, we can clearly see which direction we need to move toward in the future.

One of the greatest problems of information bombardment has been the inability to recognize how it is affecting us on a day-to-day basis. We barely have enough time and attention to keep up with the details in our lives, much less step back and see the big picture. In the next section, however, I will take some time to do just that. You might just be surprised by how ubiquitous information has become in our lives and how many times we are faced with information decisions every single day.

FURTHER READING

Tweets per day: http://techcrunchies.com/twitter-tweet-updates/

Sleep deprivation: http://psychcentral.com/news/2010/02/11/new-thoughts-on-sleep-deprivation/11371.html

Losing sleep: http://www.washingtonpost.com/wp-dyn/content/article/2005/10/08/AR2005100801405.html

Health-care rankings: http://healthcarereform.nejm.org/?p=2610

Intellectual capital and organizational knowledge: http://tinyurl.com/2awsv3r

Hurricane Katrina: http://www.pbs.org/wgbh/pages/frontline/storm/view/

Obama outlines anti-terrorism flaws: http://www.cnn.com/2010/POLITICS/01/07/obama.terror.report/index.html

Information-Age Terrorism: http://www.rand.org/pubs/monograph_reports/MR989/MR989.chap3.pdf

Scan QR code for direct link to website, hypertext links and other resources:

CHAPTER 8

Democratization and Super-Penetration

The terms *Information Age, knowledge era* and *social media* have become commonplace to those of us who have witnessed the evolution of the World Wide Web and the Internet firsthand. But despite our physical presence during this evolution, the extent to which the Internet has affected society may not be so obvious. With technological progress advancing so rapidly, having a true grasp of its ramifications may be difficult.

Today we are in the golden age of the Internet. Every new technology has its own golden age, but eventually things change or a new technology comes along. For example, during the 1930s and 1940s radio had its own golden age. Families would huddle around a large RCA radio listening to dramas, world news and variety shows. Everyone wanted a radio in his or her home. But by the 1950s things changed. Television began to replace radio, and progressive regulations and restrictions dictated limitations of radio's use. The Internet age will likely experience the same as we journey through Web 2.0 and beyond.

One day a newer technology will usher in its own golden age, leaving the Internet in its wake. But for now we need to appreciate the current times in which we live. The Internet age has both positive and negative characteristics. In other words, the Internet, like most new technologies, has a dual nature. Greater access to information is a wonderful thing, allowing people around the world to communicate, collaborate and exchange ideas. At the same time information bombardment can hinder efficient growth and productivity and even cause damaging effects. In order to realize the beneficial aspects while minimizing the negative risks, we need to appreciate the Internet age as it exists today.

Democratization of Information

On October 29, 1969, Charley Kline, a UCLA student at the Network Measurement Center, sent the first data message across a local electronic network connected to the Stanford Research Unit a few miles away. He successfully typed in the letters L and O (the first letters of the word *login*) before losing the connection and having the system crash. Despite the inability to complete the task that day, the message sent was the first-ever Internet transmission on a system known as ARPANET.

Though the Internet age was somewhat slow to take off during the first couple of decades, by 1995 the world realized its potential and it soon exploded on computer desktops everywhere. In 1981 there were only a total of 213 computers on the Internet network. By 1995 this figure had risen to more than sixteen million Internet users online. By 2001 the number had grown to an amazing 513 million, and today the estimates are around 1.8 billion. Despite the growth curve for Internet usage being relatively flat for the first twenty-five years since its inception, the last twenty-five years have more than made up for its slow start. Imagine what might happen over the next twenty-five years.

Interestingly, the groups at UCLA and Stanford working on the ARPANET project were funded by the federal government. They were to design a system that would give the US an advantage in the arms race against the Soviet Union. The Russians had just launched their own space program, with the flight of Sputnik taking the US by surprise. As a result, grants were provided to develop more effective communications and enable scientists from different communities to share their data and collaborate more freely. This was the underlying purpose that resulted in the creation of the Internet.

Do you think anyone could have envisioned the degree to which information sharing, collaboration and networking would develop over the next half century? Possibly some visionary did, but most of us in the scientific and academic communities never would have suspected such a revolutionary change. Not only could scientists share their data, experiments and information but anyone with a computer and an Internet service provider could access an abundance of information never before possible. Information was democratized for anyone to enjoy.

Refrigerator-size computers of the 1970s have shrunk to the size of a wallet. A smartphone can accomplish today far more than what a personal computer of the early 1990s could. Text data and basic graphs have been enhanced by video imaging. Layers of location-based data can be mapped on top of digital maps while users continue to mash up disparate informational sources. Your standard route to work from home can now be mapped by satellite with dynamic traffic updates, local shopping, points of interest and even real-estate pricing information all on your smart phone. Innovative software programs provide simple ways to apply information to all sorts of complex situations.

What is the cost of accessing this information over the Internet? Other than hardware and connection costs, access to the majority of the world's information database is free of charge. That's true democracy of information! But is this really free, or is this just an illusion? As more and more of the world jumps onboard the information express, we are beginning to see the real costs that result from ubiquitous information. As Internet penetration expands, these costs have become more evident. To understand this more fully, let's examine Internet penetration more carefully.

Global Internet Penetration

Today, seven billion people live in the world, and approximately 300 million reside in the US. In total, the current estimates of Internet users total two billion worldwide, resulting in an overall Internet penetration rate of twenty-eight percent. Of course, these figures vary by country. Some nations have better telecommunications infrastructures than others, allowing greater penetration to occur. But changes are rapidly occurring as mobile technologies expand to encompass the entire globe. By looking at different statistics we can begin to appreciate these changes and how quickly they are evolving.

For example, countries like the US and Canada have well-established telecommunications infrastructures. Hardwired telephone lines were the first means by which people reached the Internet. Subsequently coaxial cable, and later fiber optics, provided similar hardwired means of accessibility. As mobile technologies began to surface, allowing Wi-Fi and satellite connections, a gradual change within these developed nations in Internet accessibility has occurred.

In contrast, countries like Rwanda and Kenya have little developed infrastructures for telecommunications. The number of hardwired telephone lines is minimal compared to developed nations', yet the ability to access cellular connections to the Internet is rapidly increasing. Nations that were previously hindered from becoming Internet users are now finding fewer barriers to access. Internet penetration is rapidly increasing in this segment of the world's population.

According to the International Telecommunication Union, the ratio of mobile phones to landline phones for individuals in the US in 2008 was 1.7 to 1. In other words, for every landline there were 1.7 cell phones or smartphones. In contrast, the ratio in Kenya in 2008 was 66.9 to 1. The ratio in Rwanda was 78.9 to 1. These ratios reflect the fact that less than one percent of people in these developing nations had landlines for telephone use while nearly fifty percent of the US population had landline access. Extrapolating the data between these two statistical measures supports the notion that mobile-phone penetration is now the same between these three nations despite the US having a clear hard-wire infrastructure advantage.

If mobile technology has enabled telecommunications in developing countries to rival the abilities of the most-developed nations in the world, then it is a small leap of faith to anticipate that Internet penetration will rapidly follow. If a quarter of the world is accessing the Internet currently, what happens when fifty percent or seventy-five percent gains access on a regular basis? You thought information bombardment was overwhelming now! We haven't seen anything yet!

Despite the presumption that the US has the highest number of Internet users, international data actually does not support this. For every 100 people in the US, only seventy-seven people are considered Internet users. In Russia, only forty-three people out of every 100 access the Internet regularly. Even in the United Arab Emirates, which enjoys the best technological infrastructure in the world, Internet penetration is almost seventy-six people out of every 100. If these nations do not represent the highest Internet penetration rates, which countries do?

Consistently, Scandinavian countries have ranked the highest among Internet users. For every 100 people in Sweden in 2010, 92.5 people were Internet users. In Norway, this figure was 94.8. In the Netherlands, the rate was 88.6 percent. In Iceland, the rate was higher than ninety-seven percent. What is it about Scandinavian countries that encourages greater Internet usage? Is it because the climate is so cold, these people have nothing else better to do? Unlikely. The figures for Russia do not support this theory.

The main reasons driving higher Internet usage will be addressed in subsequent chapters, but without question Internet usage is increasing globally at an accelerated rate. If developing nations are able to use mobile technologies to access the Internet more easily, then penetration will soar in a very short time. If characteristics that promote greater Internet use in Scandinavia are adopted by more of the world, then these rates will accelerate even faster. Are we ready for such an increase?

In 1993 the cumulative total number of Web sites on the Internet was only 623. The following year I entered the doctoral program at the Ivey Business School, University of Western Ontario, and created what was affectionately known at the time as *The Official Intellectual Capital Home Page.* It was a single HTML Web page that I coded myself. My objective was to create a worldwide, centralized repository of intellectual capital research, thereby boosting my own reputation as an intellectual capital researcher. First-mover advantage made the site a hit. I had researchers from around the world e-mailing incessantly to be listed in the "who's who" section. I had created a widely respected informational resource that doubled as a reputation builder, all from the basement (or *the dungeon,* as it was known then) of the Ivey Business School.

Today there are more than twenty-five billion web pages within 110 million Web sites where we can surf and extract data. In order for such an explosion of domains to occur, Internet usage figures had to climb significantly and quickly. As Internet penetration continues to rise exponentially, Web sites will concurrently expand, diluting our ability to find the precise information we need. Expect information bombardment only to worsen as a result.

The Phenomenon of Super-Penetration

How many e-mail accounts do you have? In 2006, the average Internet user was estimated to have at least three e-mail accounts to accommodate the thirty-one billion e-mail messages that were sent daily. Yes, I said *billion,* not *million.* What was even more impressive were the statistics on spam. Of all

Internet messages sent, eighty-three percent were considered spam. In other words, only one e-mail out of every six coming to your e-mail accounts was actually information that truly interested you. See why information discernment is needed?

The presence of spam has taught us a few things, however. First, most of us have realized the need for a spam or junk mail filter. Can you imagine trying to filter through all of this ridiculous information without some type of software to screen these messages? We have a hard time handling the e-mail messages that do get through our spam filters, much less the entire batch. This lesson has been very useful and can be applied to other areas of information bombardment, as will be described later. At least from this viewpoint, we now recognize that all information is not good information.

Secondly, as evidenced by e-mail account statistics, we have learned that multiple e-mail accounts are a way around information bombardment to an extent. I personally still have Yahoo!, Hotmail and G-mail e-mail accounts that I set up years ago for different purposes. If I surf the Web on sites that have high spam rates, I use one of these e-mail accounts, if needed, to receive message alerts. In this way I preserve my main e-mail accounts from being targeted by the big spammers of the world.

Avoiding spam is not the only reason to have multiple e-mail accounts. Many people have different e-mail accounts for their business communications and their personal ones. Let's face it: mixing pleasure with business on a corporate e-mail server is an easy way to lose your job in the Information Age. In fact, many people have several different personal e-mail accounts to segregate different parts of their personal lives. This has been a trend for several years, and more than a few public figures have demonstrated this to be true.

The problem is that our strategies to handle spam have fostered even greater information bombardment. Accessing the Internet through different means initially occurred as an effort to avoid spam and to better organize different parts of our lives. Today, with each of us having more than three e-mail accounts, we are finding that we must keep up with three different sources of e-mail correspondence instead of one. Each time we take time to check each e-mail account we give up a small piece of our attention.

The term *super-penetration* refers to the ability to have access to the Internet from multiple sources. Early in the Internet age, an Internet user typically had one personal computer and one e-mail account. But as technology advanced, we increased our accessibility. We began having one computer at home, one at work and one that was portable. We began having multiple e-mail accounts. With advances in cell phone technology we know have pocket-size devices that are Web-enabled twenty-four hours a day. The more access points we carry, the more opportunities exist for information bombardment.

One way to assess the extent of super-penetration is to examine mobile-phone statistics in various countries. Which country do you think has the greatest super-penetration? The US? Certainly the most developed and wealthiest nation in the world would exhibit the greatest information accessibility, right? Wrong. In the US, for every 100 people, there are 86.8 mobile phones. In Greece, my second home nation, the same statistic shows 123.9 mobile phones for every 100 people. Guess which nation has the highest super-penetration? The United Arab Emirates—specifically Dubai. The mobile-phone penetration per 100 people here is 208.7! That means that each person, on average, has more than two mobile phones at any given time!

Why on earth would anyone need more than one mobile phone? Believe it or not, having two mobile phones is not uncommon. I use a BlackBerry as well as an iPhone. Many people have one cell phone for their personal use and one for business. This may occur due to restrictions at work or due to the tax benefits of owning a work-related phone. In essence, this trend is no different from having business and personal e-mail accounts. But did you know that some people have different cell phones for different occasions? One phone may be more practical for daily or outdoor use, but another mobile phone may be selected for an elegant evening affair. Most people simply exchange their SIM card between phones and off they go. Clearly cell phones have become fashion statements in their own right. As accessories, my wife's friend coordinates her mobile phones with her evening wear. I have another friend who uses two phones so he can text on one phone while talking on the other at the same time.

Nearly five billion cell phone subscriptions now serve 6.8 billion people. Even people who have no bank accounts, living in the desert, have cell phones. Technology has created affordability and distribution so that remote areas of the world now have Internet access from mobile devices. Not all of these mobile phones have Internet capability, but as newer generations of devices replace existing ones, devices with Internet capabilities will reach the hands of more and more people. This is how Internet penetration and super-penetration will rapidly spread across the globe.

The noteworthy observation about super-penetration is that it reflects our insatiable appetite for information. From home to car to work to leisure, we want to be connected to information all the time. Having more than one mobile phone, e-mail account, computer or other informational device demonstrates this incessant craving for knowledge. But is this necessary, or is this behavior simply the result of our own insecurities and poor knowledge management?

International Leapfrog

Whether you realize it or not, we are in the midst of a dramatic rise in the world's Internet penetration rate. Mobile technologies are opening doors, allowing developing countries that previously had limited access or no access at all to enter the Internet age. This important fact highlights not only the increased amount of information available to us today but also the degree of information bombardment headed our way.

In the year 2000 countries in the Middle East and Africa had a combined thirteen million Internet users despite their massive populations. In 2008 this figure had jumped dramatically to 108 million people. Predictions for the year 2014 suggest that 208 million Internet users will reside in this region of the world. Within six years the Internet penetration in the Middle East and Africa is expected to double, and over a fifteen-year span it will have increased twentyfold. That is a tremendous increase in Internet penetration.

Which region do you think will lead the world in Internet users in the future? By 2014 the Asia Pacific region will reach a projected total of 1.2 billion Internet users, climbing from a meager 193 million users in 2001. Actually, this region has led the world in Internet usage since 2005. Increasing Internet accessibility and a sizable population base will further this region's ability to stand head and shoulders above every other continent in the world. Nations like India, China and many other small but highly populated countries will undoubtedly dominate the World Wide Web as we move farther into the twenty-first century.

What we are witnessing is a leapfrog effect by underdeveloped nations that are taking advantage of newer technologies and established Internet communications. While the US and other developed nations previously worked through the early struggles of the Internet age, less-developed nations waited patiently until the technology came to them. Mobile connections, satellite networks and a change in the global attitude regarding Internet usage all favored ease of use by less technologically savvy regions of the world. They bypassed the development stage and enjoyed the fruits of other countries' labors. Why invest in hardwired infrastructure when wireless technology is the way of the future?

The practical implication of this leapfrog effect is greater information bombardment for everyone. In a very short amount of time millions more Internet users from around the globe will be creating Web sites, establishing e-mail accounts, publishing online videos and trying to invade your attention with information. This does not take into account the increase in mobile-phone accounts, texts, tweets and other communications that will advance as the Internet age becomes more fully realized. If we are having difficulty with information bombardment and knowledge management today, imagine what the struggles will be in a few short years.

For more than a decade the US and other developed nations have enjoyed technological and informational advantages over many other populations in the world. But this is rapidly changing as the leapfrog effect takes place. Today, access and exposure to information is expanding at a rate never before seen. Most of us who live in countries like the US are not necessarily aware of it. We go about our daily lives with our traditional Internet devices, accessing information as usual. One day, however, it will become obvious that loads of data in different languages and from different cultures will be invading our attention. Based on today's current state of the Internet, that day will be here very soon.

The Good, the Bad and the Ugly of the Internet Age

Imagine the incredible breakthroughs that have occurred in the last twenty years as a result of the Internet age. The mapping of DNA genomes and their association with different diseases was made possible by Internet collaboration among scientists. Space exploration and astronomy research have evolved with greater information networking among the world's brightest astrophysicists. Car safety and transportation systems have been revolutionized as a result of knowledge sharing and standardized communications. The list of benefits the Internet age has brought societies around the world seems endless.

It's never hard to see the positive effects of technological advancement. Even opponents of stem cell research understand the benefits this controversial area may award people suffering from diseases. The difficult task is being aware of what the downside may be when an exciting new discovery is introduced. This certainly applies to the Internet. The amazing access to volumes of information is exciting and oftentimes makes our productivity much greater. We accomplish more at work and in our personal lives as a result of the Internet. But at the same time there are some ugly side effects.

One side effect includes the vanishing ability to keep your private information to yourself. We have quickly moved from a Web of information to a Web of people. In essence, this was the transition from Web 1.0 to Web 2.0. Social networking sites exploded, but with them so did the distribution of personal information. Police routinely monitor Facebook accounts for criminal activity today. Marketing and other information-seeking organizations gather demographic data from personal information spread all over the Web, linking age to geography to consumer preferences and more. The result is that we have less privacy than we used to have.

Additionally, many of you already recognize the increasing amount of time spent online. Perhaps you surf the Web before going to bed each night, or maybe a good portion of your weekend is now spent checking out various Web sites. But not all of us recognize the other small pieces of time in which we give the Internet our attention. Checking our e-mail accounts every five minutes, responding to Facebook messages, sending tweets on Twitter, and other social aspects of the Internet are underappreciated as time spent seeking Internet information. Like most things in life, moderation is the road to better life quality, and the Internet is no different.

As the pool of Internet users continues to grow and grow, certainly wonderful discoveries, inventions and improvements will be realized. Information sharing and collaboration are great tools to achieve a better world and a global society. But everything has a price, even if it isn't monetary. The democratization of information through the Internet age has happened rapidly. There are several examples of firms that have taken advantage of this phenomenon. The community of editors at Wikipedia has democratized the encyclopedia. Video producers on YouTube have democratized the film and television industries. EBay democratized shopping, open-source software democratized software development, and personal blogs democratized news. But if we don't pay attention to the effects of the democratization of information, even bigger troubles lie ahead. For example, true expertise that has been validated through trustworthy peer review is much harder to find. We could also be on a path to democratizing democracy. Think of the implications for representative politics if government could tap into the preferences of the electorate in an instant.

FURTHER READING

Internet and phone statistics: http://www.itu.int/ITU-D/ict/

Cell phone subscriptions: http://reviews.cnet.com/8301-13970_7-10454065-78.html

More than one cell phone: http://www.geeksugar.com/Do-You-Have-More-Than-One-Cell-Phone-3394513

When the Internet age began: http://sky.geocities.jp/enokiec/Nature/N726801.PDF

The Internet age's history: http://www.guardian.co.uk/technology/2009/oct/23/Internet-40-history-arpanet

Internet downsides: http://radar.oreilly.com/2009/11/three-paradoxes-of-the-Internet-age-3.html

The golden age: http://www.pcmag.com/article2/0,2817,1977810,00.asp

Internet forecasts: http://www.etforecasts.com/products/ES_intusersv2.htm

Spam: http://spam-filter-review.toptenreviews.com/what-is-spam.html

Spam statistics: http://www.freeemail.name/Spam_Statistics.html

Scan QR code for direct link to website,
hypertext links and other resources:

CHAPTER 9

Are You Sure You Can Read?

Having talked about the Internet age and rates of penetration, let's talk a little about the tools you need to actively participate in today's world of ubiquitous information. I'm not talking about the need for another computer and a faster Internet connection. Of course you need those things, but the skills a person must have in order to stay competitive in a global market are more important considerations. Without the right personal skills, all the hardware and software on the planet won't help you.

Many of us take these needed skills for granted. If we are healthy we take our sight, our ability to type with our fingers, and our abilities to think and reason as given. We never think twice about our physical and cognitive abilities to move from Web site to Web site or to check our e-mail. We also fail to appreciate our abilities to understand the information presented to us. In order to understand information it must be presented in a type of medium that our brains can comprehend. This medium is language—the ability to use symbols and words to convey meaning and allow information communication.

Even in the most-developed nations of the world, a basic rate of literacy is not guaranteed for all. This fact alone will affect how fast the knowledge era in any given region will progress. Those countries that proactively address basic language limitations will be the ones to succeed more effectively in the Information Age, and those that don't...Well, you get the picture. Therefore, language skills and literacy rates are important subjects when addressing the Internet age and our ability to manage information. As the world rapidly changes around us, we must have the proper skills to handle these changes.

In order to convey information effectively we must have the necessary skills to communicate. As you read this, you may assume this does not apply to you because you live in a region where everyone has those basic skills, or you believe you are already well prepared with the tools needed to succeed in the Internet age. But you might be surprised. The majority of us are far from having the necessary tools for communicating and managing information effectively in the future as the knowledge era evolves. The writing is on the wall. The question is whether we choose to read it or not.

Literacy and the Internet

In the preceding chapter we examined countries of the world that have high Internet penetration rates. Despite the United States' advantages in wealth and technology, several other countries boast higher Internet penetration. Specifically, the Scandinavian countries are included in this category. But what is different about these countries that makes them rank highest among all other nations? What do they have that others don't?

The one common factor these nations share is an extremely

high literacy rate. For example, Finland and Norway are the only two nations in the world listed as having 100-percent literacy rates according to the CIA's *World Factbook*. The Netherlands, Denmark, Iceland, Sweden and Switzerland all are reported as having ninety-nine-percent literacy. In contrast, Greece has a reported literacy rate of ninety-six percent with an Internet penetration rate of less than fifty percent. Rwanda has a literacy rate of seventy percent with an Internet penetration rate of less than one percent.

If you cannot read and write effectively, Internet penetration rates fall rather quickly. In comparing the statistics between literacy and Internet penetration, the curve between the two is not linear by any means. Until literacy rates reach ninety-eight percent or higher, Internet penetration remains less than fifty percent for most nations listed. The curve is parabolic rather than linear, and until this high literacy threshold is reached Internet penetration remains low.

India has a tremendous population but many cannot read and write well. Recent literacy rates in India were estimated at only sixty-one percent. Accordingly, India's Internet penetration rate is only 4.5 percent. China's literacy rate is ninety percent with a concurrent Internet penetration rate of 8.5 percent. Though other language issues and barriers exist in reaching high Internet penetration, literacy is one of the most important tools needed. Until a nation's population reaches a nearly universal ability to read and write well, the ability to use the Internet will remain poor.

How are literacy rates determined? The CIA reports that world literacy is a combined eighty-two percent, but what does this really mean? Unfortunately, the definition of literacy varies between countries. What might be considered being literate in

India may differ significantly from the definition of literacy in Norway. In recording this data from different nations, the CIA acknowledges that the degree of literacy is difficult to compare because of inconsistent definitions among countries. Developed nations view literacy differently from developing nations. This, in part, may account for the parabolic nature of Internet penetration when compared to literacy rates.

As literacy rates exceed ninety-eight percent, two things likely happen within a country. First, basic standards of literacy are increased within that nation in order to accommodate increasing educational demands on the population. As nearly everyone achieves basic reading and writing skills, the degree of literacy begins to climb even higher. As a result national standards are increased for reading and writing, further promoting higher education and Internet usage.

Secondly, the culture of the country changes. As more people become highly literate, daily exposure to more advanced reading and writing occurs for everyone. Not only are standards raised formally within educational systems but informal standards are raised within the social culture as well. Therefore, extremely high literacy rates within a country promote even higher literacy abilities. This is likely the case in the Scandinavian countries.

The bottom line is that literacy is extremely important in the Internet age. As literacy increases among the populations of the world, and as the levels of reading and writing increase, nations will increasingly begin to enjoy higher Internet penetration rates. This is the basic personal infrastructure needed to improve a nation's chances in the Information Age. Without these basic skills, people will inherently be at a disadvantage.

On the other hand, countries that proactively require higher literacy achievements will excel. The choice is ours.

False Assumptions

Assessing the use of language in the Information Age is fraught with misperceptions and false assumptions. We tend to think that things will never change, and this assumption often lies at the heart of doubt, resistance and erroneous opinions. As far as language and literacy pertain to the Internet and the knowledge era, three false assumptions commonly occur. These pitfalls will be discussed further.

False Assumption #1: Everyone Around You Can Read

The United States is one of the wealthiest, most technologically advanced countries in the world. It goes without saying that the literacy rate in the US has to be essentially 100 percent. Well, almost. The same CIA world report described a ninety-nine-percent literacy rate in the US. Therefore, with such a high literacy rate, it is safe to assume that everyone in the US can read and write effectively. Unfortunately, this is not the case.

The problem with measuring world and national literacy rates is the criteria by which literacy is defined. Does completion of elementary school in the US guarantee literacy? It certainly should, but many children don't even have the very basic skills to advance to higher levels of education, much less to succeed in life as adults. Common levels of grade achievement are used to assess a country's literacy abilities; however, this may or may not be an accurate assessment. In the case of the United States, it is not.

In 2003 the National Center for Education Statistics presented a compilation of data collected from most states in the US. The purpose of the report was to determine what percentage of adults had basic prose literacy skills. By definition, those who were not at a basic prose literacy level were unable to read or understand any written information or could only read short segments of common prose but nothing more advanced. The results were pretty impressive as well as quite disconcerting.

The best state scores in the compilation demonstrated literacy rates of ninety-three to ninety-four percent. In other words, six to seven percent of the population in these states could not read at a basic prose level. Many New England states and states throughout the Midwest were included in this group. However, on a less positive note, other states averaged twenty percent of their population who failed to have a basic level of reading ability. Florida, California and New York, notably some of the most-populated states, led the nation in this category. All total, one in every seven people in the US cannot read at a basic prose level.

We do not assume that everyone has the same level of intelligence or can process information the same. Intuitively we know that some people can absorb and retain facts better than others. Some people are more efficient at analyzing data.

Others have better memories, and still others have gifts for deciding which information is important and which is not. In a similar way, people have a wide range of reading skills. Despite the CIA's report and the assumption that everyone in the US has the ability to read well, more detailed assessments show otherwise. A significant part of the population cannot comprehend basic children's reading books, much less information on the Internet.

In practical terms these facts have two implications. First, if we wish to achieve greater success in processing information, improving our reading skills is an important means to this end. Reading more quickly, with greater attention and retention, enhances skills important for the knowledge era. Just as an athlete prepares for a race by training physically, we need to consider similar tasks to prepare for the Information Age. The time has come for all of us to learn better skills for the Information Age.

The second application pertains to information bombardment. Though many people struggle with reading skills in America, eventually they will become more literate. As in Scandinavia, the literacy culture will facilitate greater literacy in the future. In order to survive the knowledge era people will be forced to read and read effectively in all countries of the world. If information bombardment is troublesome now, what will happen when global literacy rates reach the levels currently seen in Scandinavia? This is another reason why one must maximize his or her own personal knowledge absorption rate.

False Assumption #2: English Is the Most Common Language

Remember the statistic that described nearly eighty-five percent of the world's Internet users as residing in the United States in 1990? Even in the year 2000 approximately a third of all Internet users were American. As a result, the World Wide Web has been monopolized by the English language. As the world has shrunk during the dawning of the Information Age, those of us who speak English often assume that the Internet will always be dominated by English content and language. This is what I call *Anglophonic arrogance.*

What language is most commonly used in the world today? Mandarin Chinese is by far the most common, with 874 million people fluent in this language. Is English a close second? Not close and not second. Hindi ranks number two with 366 million people speaking this language fluently. English falls third with 341 million fluent people. But despite its less than top-notch ranking in prevalence, English is the most widely distributed language. English is the primary language in fifty-two countries, and a significant number of Anglophones exist in at least 104 countries. This distribution, along with its early stronghold over the Internet and the world's focus on Hollywood and Wall Street, accounts for a persistence of Anglophonic arrogance.

But what happens when the 1.4 billion Chinese citizens and the 1.2 billion residents of India become fully integrated into the Information Age? If Mandarin and Hindi dominate the planet in number of people, isn't it apparent that these languages will eventually dominate the Internet? Is it practical, or even reasonable, to assume that a combined 2.6 billion people in these two countries will toss aside their primary languages to learn English simply because English-speaking pioneers were the first to arrive on the scene of the Internet?

Certainly translation tools exist that enable Anglophones to understand foreign Web sites. Google translator has been available for years, and Facebook and Twitter allow comments to be posted in multiple languages. Therefore, many of you may wonder whether being multilingual is even necessary. In fact, I expect simultaneous translator technology to be available on cell phones soon. But even with these technological additions, assuming English will forever allow the best opportunities in the knowledge era is naïve. Recent events already highlight this fact.

Google, the Internet giant, in 2010 decided to pull out of China as a result of constant attacks on its infrastructure. Google had identified several cyber-attacks seeking information through the Gmail accounts of Chinese human rights activists, presumably by Chinese officials or related third parties. The battle between two diametrically opposed philosophies of information sharing has resulted in Google's closing its operations within China altogether. Though China appears upset about Google's decision, this does open the door for internal Chinese Internet search companies that are friendly with the government to gain strongholds in the Chinese market. If this happens, one thing is certain: English won't be the primary language.

On a personal note, I have been guilty of my own Anglophonic arrogance. As an active academic researcher I have numerous published articles in peer-reviewed journals all over the world. Articles about intellectual capital, knowledge management, information bombardment and more have circulated through academic and public circles in several countries. In each case, all were published only in English...except for one.

In late 1999 I was invited to write an article for the most prestigious business economics publication in Greece. The editor wanted the article written in English and Greek. I had never done this before, but what did I have to lose? This was the highest-profile issue, which would take a futuristic look into the pending new millennium. I can confidently say that, compared to all the other Anglophonic articles I have ever published, this article alone yielded more comments, more follow-ups, more contacts and more responses than any other. By simply using a different language I had expanded my outreach to an entirely new group of people. All those years I had ignored an entire market opportunity because of my Anglophonic arrogance. This article eventually led to a front-cover profile and a dedicated column. I was soon exposed to hundreds of thousands of Greeks in Greece as well as the diaspora. What did I learn? If you aren't translating your tweets, YouTube videos and written blogs into other languages when you have the chance, you are arrogantly missing the mark.

More than 5,000 languages exist in the world, and of these about 200 have at least a million people who speak them. Up until today English has been the language of choice by which countries most commonly communicate, but this practice could rapidly change overnight. English will likely be a dominant language indefinitely, but the advancement of information globally will empower other countries, like China and India, to exert their own lingual dominance. Recognition that you might also suffer from Anglophonic arrogance is the first step to recovery.

False Assumption #3: Language Skills Don't Require Practice

For most of us, we learned the majority of our language skills in childhood and throughout our educational years. Some of us even majored in a language or several languages. But unless you are a writer, orator or linguist, chances are you dedicate little time to developing new language skills year after year. After all, the language skills you have allowed you to get where you are today. Why should you invest your precious time in a skill that already works?

Other than possibly learning a second or third language, enhancing your primary language skills is something few of us see benefit in doing. But investing in enhanced reading and communication skills is a vital component of success in today's knowledge era. If the new commodity of the twenty-first century is information, then being able to communicate and comprehend information are critical skills. Failing to recognize this and invest in better language skills naturally limits your overall potential.

Why do we assume that we don't need to improve our language skills continually? For one, formal education typically ends somewhere in early adulthood for most of us. As you receive your high school diploma or university or graduate school degree, chances are you won't be signing up for another language class ever again. Like math, social sciences and other basic courses, language skills are assumed to have been mastered well enough to excel in the world. Bigger and better subjects, like business management, financial investments and fashion design, take priority because we have entered a new phase of our lives.

In reality, however, language and communication skills are some of the greatest skills people have in facilitating progress in all areas of their lives. Effective communication in personal relationships has been well described by many experts. Many psychologists are gainfully employed because we seek their guidance in achieving better communication skills with our partners. School communities thrive as families, town administrators and school systems share ideas. Corporations become more efficient and profitable as communications at all levels improve. The better language skills we have, the better off we are.

But greater success in our lives and our jobs is not the only advantage. In a research study published in 2003, more than 400 elderly people were surveyed for information regarding behaviors in the preceding twenty years. Reading, playing board games and playing musical instruments were found to have reduced their risks of developing dementia. The more time people spent in mental activities, the lower the risk of memory loss. For example, individuals who solved crossword puzzles four times weekly had a forty-seven-percent lower risk of dementia than those who solved crossword puzzles once a week. It would appear that performing language exercises and other mental activities may improve our cognitive health as well.

To expand on this, a study out of Wake Forest University studied sixty-six healthy individuals through functional brain MRI exams while they received cognitive training exercises. Functional MRI is able to show areas of the brain that are more active when specific tasks are being performed. After only eight weeks of mental and language exercises, attention, working memory and information processing were all improved in the adults studied. Despite having normal age-related declines in attention at baseline, each of the individuals gained more focus and greater informational skills.

Why does this phenomenon occur? The most likely reason is neuroplasticity. As you may recall, neuroplasticity describes the ability of the brain to adapt to changes as its sensory input changes. If a person loses sight, parts of the brain related to vision shrink in size while areas related to smell, taste and hearing become more active. Nerve cells sprout more connections in growth areas, making a richer network, while other nerve cells, now unused, lose connections. This capacity of the brain's cellular structure to adapt to change is called *neuroplasticity.*

It is interesting that elderly individuals still demonstrate this capacity of plasticity with cognitive training. From neurological literature, plasticity is known to be at its peak in childhood, but subsequently it gradually declines throughout adulthood. The fact that some plasticity is still present in old age highlights the fact that even greater responses to mental exercises can be expected at younger adult ages. Think of all those years after college that were wasted when we could have improved our brains' abilities to process information!

Not only do we need to pay attention to Anglophonic arrogance but we also need to realize that continuing to develop language skills has benefits, such as our brains' abilities to handle information bombardment. Both of these facts suggest that investing in greater language and mental skills can lead to greater personal satisfaction lifelong. Now and into the foreseeable future, language skills are important tools we will require in order to thrive in the Information Age.

Multilingualism

As the knowledge era spreads around the globe and invites many new cultures and languages to come aboard, information will continue to grow at astonishing rates. Today, Internet traffic already doubles every sixty days. This accelerated growth will undoubtedly continue. So what strategies can we consider in order to prepare ourselves? In addition to mental exercises and cognitive skills, learning another language or even several languages makes great sense for reasons already described. This is what is meant by *multilingualism.*

How many multilinguists exist today? Quantifying this figure is difficult as many obscure languages exist and many different cultures populate the earth. However, estimates suggest that globally at least 750 million speak primary non-English languages and English concurrently. The number of people in China and India combined who speak English as a second language is roughly half a billion. Conservative estimates therefore suggest that around a billion multilinguists exist in the world today, and the vast majority do not live in the United States.

In the United States, knowing more than one language is not uncommon due to the number of immigrants who have chosen America as their home. Despite residing in the US for several generations, many ethnic families have a desire to teach their children their family's original language. This has cultural significance for them as a family, highlighting many aspects of their heritage. According to the 2000 US Census, forty-seven million people in the United States, or essentially one in five, spoke languages other than English in their homes. Of this group, thirty-six million spoke English well or very well in addition to the other languages reported. Combining these statistics with the estimated number of multilinguists speaking English at home, we see that roughly a quarter of Americans are capable of speaking more than one language fluently.

I suspect that these figures will be changing rapidly over the next decade. Not only will multilingualism become more common but languages other than English that are being learned will increase in percentage. Mandarin Chinese, Hindi, Spanish and other languages spoken by large communities of people in the global community will drive this trend as more individuals become active on the Internet. This is not a bad thing! There are many advantages to being multilingual.

In addition to the cognitive benefits in attention, memory and information processing, learning different languages opens new worlds to individuals. Despite being of Greek heritage, it was not until I published my article in Greece that this foreign market embraced me as someone knowledgeable in my field. Learning new languages erases a large barrier that keeps you from reaching huge pools of information. Imagine having access to the millions of people in China or India and their information simply by being able to understand their languages.

Like learning in general, our brains are more successful when learning a second or third language at a younger age. At very young ages of development, the brain actually learns languages completely differently than when we are older. All of my children attend Greek school on Saturdays for this reason, just like I and my wife did when we were their ages. During the first five years of language development, children assign words to objects within the language centers of their brains.

For example, a writing tool with lead is labeled *pencil* if the language being learned is English. Then, when that object is seen, the brain retrieves the word *pencil* in order to allow effective understanding and communication. If a second language is being learned at the same time, two words (one in English and one in the other language) are assigned to that object.

Now suppose a twenty-year-old is learning the same second language. Primary language development in English has already been completed. A writing tool with lead is called *pencil* only. A second word for the object does not yet exist. As the person begins to learn the second language, he or she must convert the word *pencil* into another term representative of the new language. Therefore, even after the second language has been mastered, a conversion, although very brief, still takes place. Instead of seeing the object and immediately recalling the word used in the second language, the word *pencil* is recalled and then converted to the alternative word in the second language. It is this extra conversion step that creates difficulty.

Evidently, we are better able to learn second and third languages as young children than we are as older children and adults because the learning pathways are different. If multiple languages can be learned while basic language development is occurring, the process is not only much simpler but also more efficient later. By no means should this deter anyone from learning another language, but it does have implications for our own children's developments and our educational systems in general.

Multilingualism enables one to learn about traditions and cultures of other people around the globe as well. Information is not simply facts and figures conveyed by words and numbers. Emotions, underlying cultural meanings, subtle nuances and jargons all convey important information. Even if your Google translator or simultaneous translation software creates a proper translation, you will miss out on important information these other facets of language contain. As the world shrinks, the prevalence of multilingualism is sure to increase.

Be Proactive by Advancing Your Literacy

If nothing else, in the last decade we have seen the speed with which the world is changing. The Internet and widespread dissemination of information is causing our world to be more intimately connected than ever before. Even with as little as twenty-five percent Internet penetration we are feeling the effects of information bombardment and attention deficit. If we are to survive this onslaught, new skills will be necessary...or, at least, our old skills will need to be improved.

This is where literacy and language skills become important. Though these basic tools of understanding and communication seem quite rudimentary they remain the basis for success in the knowledge era. Why do Scandinavian countries have such high Internet penetration? Because they boast the highest literacy rates in the world. But basic literacy is just a start—advanced literacy and multilingualism will be the basic tools needed to navigate the information highways of the future. If you want to be in the fast lane you had better learn the tools of the trade.

As you ponder the information in this chapter, two important recommendations should be clear. First, a dedication to improving language and communication skills should be a lifelong journey. Not only do these skills provide the basis for success at all levels of life, but they also promote a healthy brain. Second, we must be on guard against Anglophonic arrogance. English may be the most popular and most widespread language in the world today, but numbers suggest this will not always be the case. As the Internet is shared among all nations of the world, multilinguistic information will become the norm and not the exception.

Specific prescriptions for these potential problems will be discussed in later chapters, but the most important thing is to be proactive. Don't wait to invest in a new language skill. Don't procrastinate when it comes to enhancing your abilities to comprehend new information and to communicate more effectively. Information bombardment is already here, and each day it chips away at your attention a little more. By learning new skills and enhancing your language abilities you can stay in charge of your attention span and your life. These are some of the most important tools to help you manage information in the knowledge era.

FURTHER READING

Literacy rates: https://www.cia.gov/library/publications/the-world-factbook/fields/2103.html

Internet penetration map: http://www.kwintessential.co.uk/map/Internet-penetration.html

Basic prose skills in the US: http://nces.ed.gov/naal/estimates/StateEstimates.aspx

Most common languages: http://anthro.palomar.edu/language/language_1.htm

Google China: http://www.nytimes.com/2010/03/25/technology/25google.html

Study of elderly and language: http://www.time.com/time/magazine/article/0,9171,1147142-3,00.html

Wake Forest MRI study: http://www.agingwellmag.com/archive/071708p16.shtml

2000 Census brief: http://tinyurl.com/2wky7x7

Speaking multiple languages: http://www2.scholastic.com/browse/article.jsp?id=920

Scan QR code for direct link to website,
hypertext links and other resources:

CHAPTER 10

My Home Is My Castle

When I was a kid, my family's home was much different from my home today. On weekends or after school I spent a great deal of time playing soccer or riding my BMX bike with my friends in the neighborhood. My family and I would watch television shows together and go to the movies occasionally. Our favorites were *Three's Company* and *Little House on the Prairie*. We also played board games and cards for fun. More than anything, time didn't seem as pressured compared to the homes of today.

Today my three children have a smorgasbord of activities from the moment they wake to the time they fall asleep. Children's television programming has increased tremendously since my childhood. Video games and interactive electronics abound. Between these advances and what seems to be a marked increase in extracurricular activities, my children are constantly immersed mentally in some activity. They are experiencing information bombardment at a very early age. They are so used to the frenetic pace of their lives that they get bored very easily.

The rapid changes in global telecommunications manifest themselves in our own homes. We experience information bombardment at work nearly every day, but few of us realize the extent of information bombardment in our homes. Yet this is one area where we have the greatest degree of control in our lives. From television to computers to progressive integration technologies, changes have occurred so rapidly that they have affected our professional environments as well as our personal time almost without us knowing it.

While it is important to realize the current state of our world from all perspectives, appreciating the current state of the home environment may be the most important. Home is our safe haven. This is where we unwind and relax. Home is the place where we have our most important relationships. Our homes are where we have complete control over determining our own priorities in life. Therefore, in this chapter, we will define the current home environment and explore the changes occurring as we move toward the future.

The Role of Television in the Home

Today, having televisions in our homes is taken for granted. The Nielsen Company reports that ninety-nine percent of American households have at least one television set. This statistic comes as no surprise to any of us. However, the degree to which television permeates our lives is worth noting. In a life span of sixty-five years, the cumulative total time spent watching television is estimated to be nine years. To put it another way, our children average 900 hours in school each year, yet they average 1,700 hours of television watching over the same length of time. How much impact do you think this information medium has on us?

Despite its astounding presence, television has been relatively slow in securing this stronghold over our attention spans. Television was not available commercially until the late 1930s, and a home option was not truly accessible until the 1950s due to cost and the lack of programming. In 1945 fewer than 7,000 television sets existed in homes in the US, and only nine stations scattered throughout the country existed. By 1960 only 500,000 color television sets were in use. Hardly a rapid growth phase compared to today's standards.

Overall, two factors influenced the pace at which televisions became a part of the standard home environment. These were limitations in technology and limits imposed through regulations that significantly hindered advances in the television industry. These same factors were not present during the Computer Age, which differed dramatically in its permeation of society. In many ways the television actually paved the way for the computer and the Internet in our homes, as will be described later.

Technological limits for the television industry consisted of a few obstacles. For one, wireless technologies were nonexistent, and even satellite technology was not available until the mid-1980s. Cable systems had been developing as early 1948 in a few states, but as of 1964 only one million homes were hardwired for cable. By 1987 this figure had only climbed to fifty percent of US homes. Establishing widespread cable connections was expensive and cumbersome, and the more-rural areas that benefitted the most from these systems often posed the greatest challenges.

The second major obstacle was the Federal Communications Commission, or the FCC. Despite the ability to receive distant cable communications, the federal government froze the cable industry from doing so until the 1970s. Concern over the ability of local markets to survive was a big reason for these restrictions, but eventually things changed. Deregulation of the industry expanded the television market for new content and also opened the door for private capital investments.

With new content, ample funds and a captive market, the marriage between advertising and television was established. Television enjoyed the revenue and advertisers realized they could sell their products and services much more efficiently by gaining access to people's homes. By the late 1970s television was generating $7.5 billion in advertising revenues, accounting for twenty percent of all advertising dollars spent in the US.

Since then advertising has become so commonplace, we celebrate commercials almost as much as we do television programming itself. Year after year many people tune in to the Super Bowl simply to see the new advertisements being released. Some television programs have awards shows for the world's funniest or most clever commercials. In other words, advertising invades our attention spans almost as much as the TV shows we choose to watch. Until pay-per-view television and TiVo options became available, we had no control over which messages we saw and heard.

By the twenty-first century cable television industries began experimenting with video on demand, subscription video and interactive television, which continues today. With greater control over programming and with the lower cost of digital video recorders, television has continued to maintain a strong presence in our homes. In 2007 only 20,000 people used devices like DVR and TiVo, but by the end of 2008 nearly seventy-four million people used them. Think about it: these devices allow you to pick and choose what you want to see when you have time. What could be more attractive in the age of information bombardment with the objective of optimal time allocation?

Today the number of televisions in the average US household exceeds the number of people living in the household. In other words, we crave information through the television so badly that we need not only one television set per person but nearly one for every room of the house. Even so, it took nearly sixty years for the television industry to get to this point. By the time the personal computer was available for home use, televisions had taught us that technology wasn't so bad after all. As a result, the invasion of the computer industry in our homes occurred much more quickly.

The Role of Computers in the Home

Amazingly, hardly anyone had a computer in his or her home twenty-five years ago. By the mid-1980s Steve Jobs and Bill Gates were just beginning to envision their empires in the computer world. Less than three percent of the US population had computers in 1984, and these models were such dinosaurs that many of us would not recognize them as computers.

Within a decade ten percent of the US population would have personal computers, and by the year 2000 computers were present in more than half the US households. Since then this figure has grown to eighty percent of US homes now having computers. Given the time it took television to make comparable degrees of penetration, the growth of the home personal computer has been impressive. What took the television industry more than thirty years to accomplish took the computer industry less than fifteen years. The speed of change had basically doubled.

Why did the computer take over our home environments so much faster than television? Primarily, the obstacles that hindered television's growth were not significant barriers to the expansion of the Internet age. Technological advancements in computers occurred much faster, and because of this regulations were not able to keep up with the pace. Control over content, significant censorship, limitations on expansion and taxation on Internet access have not been issues as they were for the television industry…so far.

The development of wireless technologies, broadband access, satellite connections, cellular networks and high-speed processors allowed information to spread among Internet networks to a variety of computer devices. This developed faster than regulators or advertisers could figure out how best to manage this new wave of information dissemination. In essence it was the speed of technological advances that facilitated the growth of both the computer and the Internet. Bill Gates' vision of having a computer on every desk in every home was not so far from being a reality as the twenty-first century ushered in the knowledge era.

From another perspective, television aided the rapid growth of computers in our homes by establishing precedents. Cable companies and other telecommunication companies had already learned how to bring information from all over the world into our homes through the television set. Accomplishing this with the computer and the Internet was much easier the second time around. In addition we were already accustomed to having an electronic device as a centerpiece in our everyday lives. Adding a second major electronic informational device was less of a social change for most Americans.

The television cracked the door open for information from around the nation and around the world to come into our homes. The computer then opened the door all the way. Between both media, we now had information access anytime we wanted it. No longer did we have to wait for the evening news to hear the weather report. We could simply dial it up on the Internet. The greater amount of information access and control lured us into creating today's home-computer environments.

Integration Systems

Does anyone remember the 1975 film *Rollerball?* In the film, actor James Caan portrayed a sports legend playing a brutal game designed to show the futility of individual efforts in a world run by corporations. But in the film the corporate leaders of the world communicated by video conferencing, and Caan's character walked through his ranch home as images of his former wife appeared on television monitors in every room. At the time of this film, this level of integration was futuristic and viewed as a technology that was several decades away at least. But in just a few short years fellow employees in multinational corporations were routinely communicating through similar technological means.

In essence, this combination of real-time video and telecommunications was the first major step in what is known as *computerized telephonic integration*. This simply combines multiple media, enabling our ability to see, hear, speak and access other people or information sources remotely. It is a means by which we collaborate and communicate efficiently with people who may be in a distant location or in the next room. Computer telephony integration, or CTI, is already here today, and even bigger changes are soon headed our way.

One of the most important developments facilitating CTI was the development of broadband Internet. Many of us remember the days of dial-up connections that downloaded information over what seemed like an eternity. Then IDSL connections came along but with a price tag that many of us couldn't afford. Finally cable and broadband DSL connections became available, and our ability to communicate hasn't been the same since. It's hard to believe this ability has only been present for the last ten years.

We can now access video and photographs within seconds. Voice over Internet Protocol (VoIP) communications are now possible. The integration of video, voice and data revolutionized the way many people communicated. Products like Vonage and Skype enabled long-distance video communications for pennies a minute. YouTube became a popular sensation almost overnight. Social networking sites were able to usher in Web 2.0 with broadband and greater integration systems.

The ability to integrate different information systems affects everything we now do and will continue to do so as these systems rapidly progress. What does this have to do with our home environments? Certainly corporations and businesses need video and telecommunication systems, and personally we all enjoy the integration of systems on our personal computers and smart phones. But this won't primarily affect our home environments…or will it?

I had a friend who, in the late 1990s, was awake in the middle of the night, feeding his newborn daughter. As he sluggishly sat on the couch with his newborn he turned on the television and found an infomercial that caught his attention. Philips TV was introducing a new product called Web TV. The device allowed the television to integrate with the World Wide Web. You could check and send e-mail from your TV by using a wireless keyboard and, of course, surf the Web.

Needless to say, my friend pulled out his credit card and bought the device. Infomercials work best when you are sleep-deprived, I guess. In a couple of months my friend and his wife were accustomed to navigating their television-Internet from the comfort of the couch. But after a few months of use and some very large credit card bills from Internet shopping, they stopped the WebTV service. The home environment had been affected by this simple integration between computer and television. They were no longer spending time together doing anything except watching each other move from Web site to Web site.

Today, Apple TV has been developing a more advanced version of a similar product to integrate the computer and the television. More noteworthy is Google's current collaboration with Intel and Sony TV to develop a fully integrated Internet computer television that uses its newly developed Android operating system. By combining television touch screens, video streaming, Internet search abilities, VoIP systems and more, full integration among all potential sources of information media will be brought into one device. My bet is that this device will be located in the middle of your home. Where will that be? Your liquid-cooled secure server in the basement.

Considering that Americans watch between four and five hours of television a day and use computers two to three hours a day at home, a fully integrated home system allows advertisers to again find a captive audience more easily. Add radio and phone to the integrated system and these numbers climb even higher. It's one-stop shopping! This is how information will bombard our homes in the future. The illusion is that we have more control over the information and an easier way to access it. However, unless we manage the information well, it will consume more of our personal time than we can afford.

Microsoft predicts that more than a billion people will be using VoIP telephones, messaging and video conferencing within the next three years. Likewise, the business telephony integration market is expected to expand fivefold in the next five years. Extrapolate these statistics to our personal lives and the rapid changes in infiltration of information into our homes is clear. Even our cell phones will be integrated into the home system as well. Imagine a time when a single tool can collect e-mails, messages and tweets from all of our online accounts as well as digitized voicemails and video messages from work, home and your car all in one unified inbox. We are already there.

No matter where we go, we will be connected…It will be inescapable.

Say Hello to Nancy

Michelle is a fourteen–year-old girl living in the year 2015. She comes home from school with a social sciences assignment due the following day. As she climbs the stairs and enters her room, she is greeted by Nancy—her personal computer.

"Good afternoon, Michelle. How was your day at school?" Nancy asks in her soothing, feminine voice. A high-definition flat screen displays an image Michelle chose specifically for Nancy's appearance.

"I have an assignment due tomorrow," Michelle replies. "I need to write an essay about a prior president who got into some trouble with an intern."

"You mean the former president Bill Clinton, Michelle?"

"Yeah, that's him. What do you have on him?"

"Which medium of information would you prefer, Michelle?"

"Video, of course!"

A projection hologram appears in front of Michelle, accompanied by 9.1 digital surround sound emanating from miniature speakers embedded throughout her room. Images of the former president speaking his address to the nation play for Michelle as she absorbs the information.

"I did not have sexual relations with that woman," the hologram says.

After several video clips and sound bites, Michelle pauses the video presentation.

"Is there any other media you would like to examine, Michelle?" Nancy asks, detecting the pause.

"Yes. I need text transcripts and summaries about the president as well as full-color images to pick from," Michelle replies.

Nancy obliges and displays detailed holographic photographs for Michelle to examine. With a touch of her finger, Michelle chooses some and deletes others. Then she briefly examines the written transcripts.

"OK, Nancy. I have some questions."

"Yes, Michelle."

"What happened to him? Is the dog still alive? Is Chelsea married? Is Monica still selling purses? Why did Hillary stick around?"

Nancy and Michelle share a back-and-forth dialogue for another fifteen minutes with additional video, text and images providing the answers to her questions in detail.

"OK, well, I guess I am done. Nancy, please paraphrase everything we talked about into a two-hundred-word essay using proper grammar, with the selected images, and fire it off to my teacher's e-mail account by tomorrow morning," Michelle states before video calling her friend next door.

You might think this is an exaggerated scenario, but all of this aforementioned technology is available today. Computer telephonic integration, holographic images, interactive voice data systems and more could make such an interaction a reality. Just think how much more efficient and effective learning could be! The agony of trying to find the right piece of information would be markedly reduced.

Many aspects of information technology are wonderful. Michelle benefits immensely from the use of such integration and learns within minutes what would take hours for most children. This does not make her any less knowledgeable than some who spend four times the amount of time extracting the information from textbooks and Web sites, but it does allow her to have more free time.While the integration of systems today poses threats to our attention spans and our personal lives, it also provides better ways of learning. Instead of reading, copying and memorizing, students can apply higher-order learning skills to information. Application, discovery, innovation and improvisation are the characteristics of higher-order learning. Michelle was able to do this rather quickly by receiving the information about former president Bill Clinton through multiple forms of media and then using higher-order skills in her dialogue with Nancy, her home computer, with the latest artificial-intelligence algorithm aiding and anticipating Michelle's requests. The data was received efficiently, leaving more time for analysis and interpretation.

Search Costs

One of the greatest benefits information technologies have brought into our lives has been improved efficiency. Consider Michelle from the above example doing the same homework assignment thirty years ago instead. Computers didn't exist, nor did the Internet. Most homes did not have the resources to allow a research paper to be written. Michelle would have needed to go the local community library in order to research her topic (of course, she would have been barefoot, trudging in snow, uphill both ways for miles!).

Once she arrived at the library all the information about

available books was stored in one efficient location: the card catalog. (Think about the time it took to maintain this dinosaur of an organizer.) Michelle would locate the letter C for Clinton and then identify a book or two that seemed to have the information she wanted. After reading the location of the book off the card and writing it down on a scrap piece of paper, she would walk up a couple flights of stairs and peruse the many shelves until she came to that location. Hopefully the book was not checked out!

For the next several hours Michelle would hand copy the information onto some paper without necessarily absorbing any of the data on the page. With a little luck she would finish this task before the library closed for the evening. Otherwise she would return to do the same task again on another day. Once the information is copied, Michelle would finally read and study it before organizing it into a thoughtful essay. Out of the time spent on her assignment more than ninety percent would be spent on search costs—finding the right information. A tiny fraction would be spent on actual learning, and even a smaller fraction on higher-order learning.

As a university professor I evaluate student essays regularly. Unlike the days of the card catalog, today students have a new research friend called Google. After I assign a topic for a paper, some of my students dial up the Internet and begin their searches. They type in a few search words and then click, peruse and repeat until they find a site containing the information for which they are searching. From there it is a quick copy and paste into a Word document with some slight alterations and voila! Their essays are complete. I call them the *Ctrl-C, Ctrl-V generation.*

But what has improved? From one perspective, the search

costs are less. Instead of spending hours in a library copying text they can now copy and paste. However, they still must spend time searching pages of Web information in order to find the right data. The more complex the topic, the more search time is required. Most importantly, their analytical skills are not being enhanced. The information is simply being regurgitated without any higher-order learning involved…and, of course, the grade I award the essay will reflect that.

Our brains process information in different ways. For example, direct memorization can be accomplished without ever activating our higher-learning centers. An image or set of words seen with our eyes can be transferred to our memory centers without any thought regarding its meaning. Similarly, copying text by hand only involves seeing the words and transferring the images to the motor areas of the brain, which then activates our hands to write. Visual areas, language areas, motor areas and memory circuits are active but higher-brain regions are not being stimulated.

In contrast, the frontal parts of our brains and upper brain cortex is where analytical skills reside. Applications of what we are seeing and hearing to past memories, learned information and conceptual ideas occur in these regions of the brain. In fact, these regions are often called the *association cortex* because they link several areas of the brain together, allowing in-depth interpretation and analysis. This is higher-order learning, which distinguishes our abilities as human beings from other animals'.

If we simply spend our time searching for information and then regurgitating it without invoking our brains' powers to analyze and interpret, we fail to reach our potential in creativity and informational learning. Integration systems of today and in the future will allow us to reduce these unnecessary search costs and let us spend more time using the advanced areas of our brains. In other words, we can work smarter and not harder.

Eventually the world's data will be better organized and consolidated, and the ability to refine search tools will continue to improve. We are on a threshold today where integrated systems are allowing more-efficient and better learning. This is occurring in our homes, our schools, our places of business and even on the run through mobile technologies. From a positive perspective, the time wasted on searching for information (and, therefore, the attention we have wasted) will be markedly reduced. But potentially, we risk even greater information bombardment unless we proactively choose to manage this data well.

Home: A Sanctuary or a Thoroughfare

During the release of Web 1.0, a natural migration from physical and social interaction occurred. Salespeople were working from home a few days a week. Home offices and businesses became more popular as means to save overhead costs. Kids and adults spent greater amounts of time in front of computers, playing video games, surfing Web sites and much more. The world was becoming small islands interconnected through the Internet. Many people were concerned that social skills would regress as a result.

But with Web 2.0 and social networking sites, the opposite seems to have occurred. People who are Internet-active are more connected than ever. Friends from the past now regularly keep up with each other through Facebook. Artists promote their music and visual arts through MySpace. Business acquaintances maintain professional relationships through LinkedIn. Advertisers scour the universe of tweets for brand evaluation. Despite our attention being focused on miniature screens, our ability to socially connect has actually increased as system integrations have occurred.

With the changes in computerized telephony integration, all phases of our lives will continue to change. Our homes will become hubs for centralized information. Television, Internet, telephone, music, movies and all types of media will converge there. All members of the family will be able to access whatever information they want in the particular mediums they want at any time of the day. Ubiquitous information at our fingertips 24/7. We asked for it, and now we will have it. But how will we manage it?

There was a farmer who grew crops and sold them at a farm stand on a small, rural road adjacent to his farm. He had an abundance of crops, and each harvest season he would sell to the few people who traveled by his stand. Every year he hoped for more traffic so he could sell more of his crops. Slowly the population grew around his farm, and the road was developed into a four-lane highway. The farmer's sales increased significantly. But even then he wished for even greater traffic because he had so many crops to sell.

Eventually the state received funds to place a major interstate highway and exit adjacent to his farm stand. Almost overnight the number of people stopping at his stand tripled, but so did many other businesses. In fact, the region was seen to be desirable by many other industrial plants and farms. Despite having an ample number of customers, the farmer noticed that his crop yield began to decline rapidly each year. Between air pollution and toxic waste from some of the industrial plants, his farm was no longer as healthy as before. After much soul searching he finally sold the farm and moved away, seeking the rural peacefulness his family had taken for granted.

Having our homes accessible to an abundance of information can be wonderful. But we should not sacrifice our personal health and the health of our families in an effort to satisfy our knowledge craving. While information at school and at work is an expected part of each environment, our homes should be our personal sanctuaries. Only the information we want to receive should access our homes, and maintaining boundaries and priorities is important for a healthy lifestyle. The goal is to embrace the efficiency and control that new technologies award us without polluting our homes with information bombardment.

FURTHER READING

TV in every home: http://thetechedition.com/a-television-in-every-home

History of TV: http://www.high-techproductions.com/historyoftelevision.htm

TV viewing: http://www.cnn.com/2009/SHOWBIZ/TV/02/24/us.video.nielsen/

Computer and Internet stats: http://www.census.gov/prod/2001pubs/p23-207.pdf

Computer timeline: http://www.computer.org/cms/Computer.org/Publications/timeline.pdf

Business telephony: http://digitalmedia.strategyeye.com/article/db6OrzJnFY/2010/03/25/microsoft_forecasts_explosion_in_business_telephony/

Google TV: http://www.google.com/tv/

34 GB a day: http://bits.blogs.nytimes.com/2009/12/09/the-american-diet-34-gigabytes-a-day/

Scan QR code for direct link to website, hypertext links and other resources:

CHAPTER 11

What Did My Toilet Just Say?

It is eleven o'clock? Do you know where your BlackBerry is? (Typically this announcement was done by local news stations at 10:00 p.m. or 11:00 p.m.). This is an odd question, but it would be even more unusual if your BlackBerry began asking where you were. In the 1970s local television stations would broadcast the question "do you know where your children are?" to American families late in the evening as a means to promote child safety and responsible parenting. The key word in the question was *where*. The assumption was that if you knew where your children were, then you had more complete information about their activities and well-being.

Jumping ahead to the twenty-first century, our need to know the whereabouts of not only people but also places and things has skyrocketed. GPS devices permeate our society, and many of us cannot even navigate through a small town without their assistance. IP addresses easily identify the locations of users across the world, making surveillance and networking easy. RFID (radio frequency identification) tags track inventory from Arkansas to Zimbabwe and will soon be providing other information about each of us to a variety of entities. As the traditional real estate adage states, it's all about location, location, location.

What happens when devices, machines and even ordinary household items begin tracking our whereabouts in order to keep us constantly informed of remote happenings? If you think information bombardment from your e-mail, voicemail and electronic communications is overwhelming now, just wait until you start receiving data from your car, home and other nonhuman objects. How will we filter what is important then, and how will we be able to focus our attention on anything for longer than a few minutes without being interrupted?

If we are going to be able to manage information effectively, then we will need to anticipate the progressive changes in information headed our way. Currently people are the ones who initiate and respond to information every day, but these days are limited. The amount of information requests and notifications will rise exponentially as technological advancements continue. We are only just seeing the tip of the information iceberg presently.

Location, Location, Location

Ahhh, do you remember the good ol' days with handwritten letters, single telephone lines, phone numbers in yellow pages and white pages? Things move so rapidly that we tend to forget how different they were only twenty years ago. In some parts of the world they still haven't changed.

Decades ago people knew how to reach you by way of your address. A letter was composed, and your mailing address was placed on an envelope along with a stamp. A few days later you would receive the letter. If a more rapid means of communication were needed, the person would call you. In order to place the phone call, the area code identifying the state region, the prefix code identifying the city region and the line number identifying your exact phone line would be dialed, allowing direct access. Even if you wish to speak to someone face to face you need to be sure he or she is in close enough proximity to hear your voice. Communication and the exchange of information have always required knowledge of location.

In the digital age this requirement is no different. Instead of home addresses and phone numbers, we now depend on a new set of location identifiers. IP addresses, RFID tags and GPS devices are the locator tools of the Information Age. These nifty tools allow people, as well as other items, to participate in the exchange of information throughout the world by providing the necessary location and identifier data. Understanding how these tools work and how they will change in the future is important in anticipating changes in information bombardment.

IP Addresses

All computers and many electronic devices that access the Internet have unique location identifying numbers that are called *IP addresses.* The *IP* portion stands for Internet protocol, and in the current IP address system these addresses are composed of four groups of numbers called *octets,* with an example of a typical IP address today being 66.249.64.123. The system currently in use is the IPv4 system, which stands for *Internet protocol version 4.* Each number of the octet can range from 0 to 255, so the total number of IP addresses possible in the IPv4 system is 4.3 billion. In other words, 4.3 billion different nodes or locations can exist representing different Internet access points for computers, printers, smartphones or other Internet devices.

Four point three billion IP addresses seems like a staggering figure but, if you recall, seven billion people currently occupy our planet. What happens when the twenty-five percent of the population that is Internet active expands to fifty percent or more? Since the 1980s the knowledge that a shortage of IP addresses would eventually occur has been appreciated. In fact, all the current available IP addresses in the IPv4 system are expected to be used by end of 2011. Through the use of increasing numbers of Internet-active devices, these available IP addresses are rapidly vanishing.

To understand this trend, consider the current US population of 300 million people. Out of the 4.3 billion total IP addresses currently available, we use 1.5 billion IP addresses ourselves in the US. That means that for every person in America, each averages around five IP addresses! Can you imagine living in five different locations and having five different mailing addresses? While physically this would be difficult to manage, digitally we do this with ease by having different IP addresses for our home computers, our work computers, our digital phones, our printers and more.

If Americans average five IP addresses each, there is little question that a tremendous mismatch between global supply and demand is upon us. To compare, the average number of IP addresses per capita in China is only 0.2. The same figure applies to India. In my native country of Greece, this figure is only 0.385 IP addresses per person. As Internet penetration increases, a new system to accommodate demand must be devised.

Indeed, a new Internet protocol system has been devised and has already begun to be installed in newer electronic devices. Known as IPv6 (Internet protocol version 6), this new IP address system has sixteen octets instead of four octets and has 128 bits of data instead of thirty-two bits in its addresses. The capacity for this new version to accommodate a greater demand is tremendous. IPv6 can provide an estimated 3.4×10^{38} of IP addresses compared to the measly 4.3×10^{9} IP addresses with IPv4. This allows every single person on the planet to have up to 5×10^{28} IP addresses...Do you think that might hold us over for a while?

Unfortunately, the penetration of IPv6 is far from adequate to prevent the coming IP address shortage. A 2008 Google research study demonstrated that the IPv6 system had less than a one-percent presence among currently used computers and Internet-active devices, despite having been available since 1998. New smartphones currently being produced require IPv6 as part of their platforms, as do most computers, but most currently used computers and devices in operation must be either replaced or adapted to allow communication with devices using IPv6 addresses. Certainly there will be some growing pains over the next few years associated with this transition.

Just how large is a number like 3.4×10^{38}? If you consider that billion has nine zeros in it (10^{9}), then you begin to grasp the enormity of the number of IP addresses we will soon have available to us. Let me put it in more concrete terms. Scientists estimate that if all the deserts and beaches of the world and the ocean floor were combined, and if all the grains of sand were counted, there would be roughly 7×10^{20} grains of sand in total. This is slightly more than half of the IP addresses that IPv6 will allow. That is impressive!

But why would we need so many IP addresses? Each person can only have so many Internet-connected devices, right? But what if every single item you owned suddenly had an embedded nanochip that had its own IP address? Your blue shirt has a chip that can detect a lack of starch in its material, so it notifies you via the Internet that it needs to go to the cleaners'. Your carton of milk in the refrigerator nearing its expiration date sends you a text via its embedded chip, making you aware that a new carton is needed. Are you beginning to see the possibilities?

Of course, who would ever place a chip in a milk carton or a shirt? That seems ridiculous. Just imagine the television commercial promoting the product.

"Tired of milk going sour in your fridge? Frustrated by arriving home and finding spoiled milk after you just left the store? Sweet Cow Creations is the only brand with the ability to tell you when it is about to expire! Innovative technologies allow the carton to notify you in advance of a pending expiration date! For pennies more, you never have to cry over spoiled milk again!"

On second thought, this doesn't sound so bad, huh? With an explosion of Internet penetration and IP addresses just around the corner, don't be surprised to find this a reality in the very near future. Imagine the amount of information you will be bombarded with then!

Radio Frequency Identification Tags (RFID Tags)

Unlike IP addresses, which require connections to the Internet, RFID tags provide identification and locator functions for a variety of things, ranging from products to people. Honestly, their presence is now so ubiquitous, you may not even realize them when you see them. If you have ever used a fast-pass system on a highway or swiped a badge to gain access to protected areas at work, you have used an RFID tag. Even clothing retailers routinely place these devices in their items as antitheft measures.

RFID tags are composed of two parts. One is an integrated circuit that stores identification information and other data and allows a radio-frequency signal to be modified upon interaction with a tag reader. The other component consists of an antenna that receives and transmits a signal. Active RFID tags have batteries, enabling them to activate their own radio-frequency signals, while passive ones have no batteries and require external sources of activation.

So what are the advantages of RFID tag devices? First of all, they can encode a significant amount of information. Once the tag is close enough to a reader, this information can be transferred to a database system that is much larger. No Internet connection is needed, and the tag devices are small enough to be hardly noticed. Even passive RFID tags can hold 256 bits of information, making them much more attractive when compared to other currently used systems.

Consider UPC bar codes, for example. These codes require lines of sight to be scanned, and only one code can be scanned at a time. UPC codes also provide a limited amount of information about a product or item. Alternatively, RFID tags can be read from a distance, can be read through clothing and other thin materials, and can be read along with multiple other RFID tags simultaneously. It won't be long before the UPC code will be a thing of the past.

Imagine going to the grocery store and collecting your food items for the week. As you go down the aisles you select items and pack them into shopping bags. After you are finished, you stroll past an RFID tag reader with your entire grocery cart filled with bagged items. But instead of having to take each item and place it on a conveyor belt, the reader records all items while still in the bags, tallying up your entire order within a couple of seconds. Though these processes are not quite in place, their development is currently in progress for stores to begin implementing soon.

Wal-Mart has used RFID tags for several years, tracking large pallets of materials as they move from one inventory warehouse to another. Likewise, these tags are used to determine when a reordering of inventory is needed. This not only facilitates efficiency but reduces the amount of human capital needed in their daily processes. While the use of RFID tags to replace human labor may not be attractive to many, utilizing people for higher-level skills only makes sense. Industry displacement due to technological advancement is inevitable. The real question to be asked is whether or not these electronic communications could one day facilitate artificial intelligence and enable technological singularity. In other words, the ability of RFID tags and other identifiers could provide an automated platform upon which higher-level decisions could be made without the need of human input.

From an alternative retail perspective, RFID devices have great marketing potential as well. Today, when a person accesses the Internet from an IP address, data is constantly being acquired about the types of Web sites, the types of products and the time spent on each Web page as they surf the Web. For a retailer this information is being collected as soon as an IP address user enters their Web site domain. By collecting this data they can identify shopping trends and demographics of their consumers. Unfortunately, when consumers choose to go to a physical location, marketers and retailers lose this ability.

But imagine shopping in a department store in the near future. As you walk around with your bag or cart that contains an RFID tag, information is constantly being collected about which departments you enter, how long you spend in each department and which items you actually purchase. As you leave the store, the cart RFID tag is matched to your credit card information and purchases in the store's database. In essence, the RFID tag has allowed consumer information to be collected in a brick-and-mortar store the same way it is collected on the Internet.

Another use of RFID tags today includes tagging different animals for different purposes. Lost pets can be tagged in order to facilitate return to their owners. Female boa constrictors can be captured, sterilized, tagged and again released to enable localization of other boa constrictors that are damaging the natural ecosystem in the Everglades. Cattle and sheep are being tagged so that individual livestock can be better managed and inventoried for economic prosperity in the farming industry. In fact, one RFID tag that's been developed is small enough to be placed onto an ant in order to study insect behaviors by entomologists!

Even tagging humans with RFID devices is being explored for various purposes. The Food and Drug Administration recently approved the implantation of RFID devices in human beings as being safe. Encased in a glass container with a curled antenna, the small tag is placed subcutaneously, usually in an individual's arm. The device is then loaded with information about the individual that is stored and easily read if the information is needed. Should a person arrive at a hospital unconscious or severely injured, a quick swipe of a reader across the implanted tag would enable access to an entire information database detailing the patient's medical conditions and history. Other human uses now being considered include RFID tags for infants and children to help with identification in abduction cases. Is this the new digital leash for children for the future? How long will it be before implanted RFID tags are standard for everyday transactions in order to avoid identity fraud?

Though privacy and security issues lie at the heart of more-aggressive use of RFID devices, without question such technologies are enabling greater amounts of information to be available to us from a variety of animate and inanimate entities. Information may be simply a multi-number digit linked to an identification database, or it may contain volumes of detailed data specific to the item or person possessing the tag. Not only is information around us increasing, but it is coming at us fast and furious.

GPS (Global Positioning System) Devices

IP addresses provide location information for Internet access points, and RFID tags allow identification of items when located within reasonable proximity of a reader. But GPS devices provide the most detailed information about geographic locales. The US' space-based navigational satellite system has revolutionized the way many industries and individuals go about their daily routines. Paper maps are almost a thing of the past, and many of us would not even consider traveling to a new city without GPS assistance.

But what is GPS? Despite the complexities of space-orbiting satellites and precision atomic clocks, the basic concept of the GPS is quite simple. The entire system is composed of twenty-four medium-orbit satellites that provide information to ground receivers throughout the world. By triangulating various distances between an object and at least four satellites, the precise location can be pinpointed anywhere in the world. With additional safeguards in place to ensure constant accuracy of time calibrations and measurements, GPS provides geographic information down to nearly every single meter of the globe.

The information GPS provides is quite extensive. It is most commonly used for location and navigation needs, but GPS is also commonly used for tracking, precision mapping detail and for time calibrations. Of these, I would like to focus on its tracking and locating abilities. While GPS awards us significant information in many areas of our lives, it is its tracking and locator abilities that have the potential to affect us the most in terms of information bombardment.

Decades ago people would travel to a new city and look for a nice restaurant in which to dine. They might ask some locals, check the Yellow Pages or maybe check with a concierge if one were available. In the worst-case scenario they would take a leisurely drive and simply peruse the town for a place that looked appealing. That rarely happens for most of us today. We don't have time to waste on taking a leisurely drive or asking around. What are the Yellow Pages, anyway? Instead we pull out our iPhones, go to Google Maps and search for any

Mediterranean restaurants within a three-mile radius of our location. Within a minute (or less) we have a list of restaurants from which to choose. In the process we may have also located a dry cleaner, a post office, a theatre, a park and several other points of interest without investing much time at all.

These location tools are wonderful, and we have GPS to thank for such technology. But while the convenience of such information is apparent, the negative aspects of this smorgasbord of data may not be. Before, when you took that leisurely drive, you might have found a couple of places that appealed to you. The decision could have been made easily since the choices were few. With GPS the choices have expanded significantly. Every decision is more complex because you have greater amounts of information to decipher. Instead of one Italian café there may be five. You may then feel the need to look at each one's menu (online of course) and perhaps read a few customer reviews from earlier in the evening before making the decision. Without question, your eventual decision will be more informed, but was all that information truly necessary? After all, it's just a meal.

Many of you are aware of the Google application called Google Latitude. It's one of my favorites. This cool little application allows you to give permission to friends and family to know your whereabouts at all times. It utilizes the GPS aspect of Google Maps, and, when enabled on your smartphone, locator services broadcast your location to whomever you wish. Initially Google Latitude was mostly used as a social networking tool among colleagues and friends. People could see if someone they knew was in close proximity. If so, they might have had time to meet for a cup of coffee or a quick chat.

But more and more such locator applications are being promoted for other purposes. In the post-9/11 era, when fear and insecurity are everywhere, GPS mobile-tracking services are providing information to parents about where their children are, to men and women trying to keep up with their partners, and to law enforcement to keep track of registered criminal offenders. None of these uses are necessarily bad unless it is taken to an extreme. The purpose in each case is to ensure greater safety. But when might the benefits of these tools in alleviating worry and stress slide into feelings of paranoia and mistrust?

Several years ago a friend of mine was about to turn thirty years of age. His girlfriend thought it would be a great idea to throw him a surprise birthday party at his favorite restaurant. She contacted all their friends, made arrangements with the restaurant and did her best to throw him off track so it would indeed be a surprise. But near the time of his planned party, my friend paged his girlfriend to find out where she was. Being at the restaurant, preparing the final details for the event, she made the mistake of calling from that location. His caller ID provided him with the information of her whereabouts, but when he asked where she was she gave a false location in order not to give away the surprise. He immediately became suspicious.

As a result my friend jumped in a cab and headed for the restaurant, hoping to catch her in her lie. But when he walked through the doors of the restaurant and saw the room half decorated for his own birthday, he felt like the biggest fool. The information he had received unintentionally ruined his own surprise and created mistrust for no reason. He left the restaurant and returned an hour later, pretending to be surprised, but needless to say the impact was somewhat anticlimactic. Sometimes too much information can be detrimental.

Google Latitude does allow users to put in false addresses

and even to hide their locations when they do not wish to be located, and this is helpful in protecting security and privacy, which is important. But don't be surprised if you have to explain to those accustomed to knowing your whereabouts why you were hiding or why you input a false address. Once information is made available, it is hard to take it away without justification. This is where GPS devices pose a risk for us in the Information Age. Knowing the locations of more and more people, places and things not only causes a greater complexity in our decision making, but it also creates greater expectations for available information on an ongoing basis.

The real power of location-based services like these occurs when they are mashed up together with other databases. The best example is real estate. Digital maps can be navigated with GPS gadgets while various properties have satellite pictures as well historical market value data and local municipal tax information. All from the comfort of your mobile phone.

Wearing a Suit of Information

In the 2001 film *A Beautiful Mind,* Russell Crowe portrayed mathematics and economics genius John Forbes Nash, Jr. In a very vivid scene, suffering from schizophrenic delusions and hallucinations, Nash mutilated his arm trying to remove an assumed listening chip installed by the Department of Defense. Though the chip was part of his psychotic delusions, today's technology indeed makes this scenario a potential reality. We all might be swiping our forearms as we pass through airport security.

Locators and identifiers are expanding in number at remarkable rates. Within a few years the number of IP addresses available will be enormous. The use of RFID devices will increase beyond their already-ubiquitous presence and they will continue to shrink in size and cost. GPS tools will continue to create progressively more detailed maps of information for us to use when navigating through our daily lives. All three of these tools are already being integrated to provide comprehensive databases of information about people and places as well as things. What happens if such an integrated system becomes truly unified? Can you conceive of the amount of information this would provide on a continual basis?

Today the requests for information we experience predominantly come from other people. You receive an e-mail from your boss requesting a presentation. Your spouse sends you a text asking you about the plans for the weekend. Your buddies send you tweets and messages about their moment-to-moment happenings and ask for an update from you. With smartphones, computers and many other devices we are already being overwhelmed by information every single moment. Soon, however, people won't be the only sources of informational updates and requests.

Your car will notify you of a needed oil change and tune-up. Your home will notify you that its air conditioning unit needs its annual maintenance and filter change. Your bathroom scales will request your range of desired weights so it can coordinate with the refrigerator and your shopping orders in devising a menu and an eating schedule for you. All of these enhance the quality of life potentially, but imagine the amount of attention that will be awarded to all of this informational input. Imagine when GPS, RFID and IP addresses get hacked by spammers who target you with pinpoint marketing communications! When does the quantity of information destroy the quality of life instead of enhancing it?Today we have the ability to control information more easily. We can choose to isolate ourselves from our computers, e-mail accounts and cell phones and spend time with our families and friends. Perhaps we even spend some time in solitude. But more and more we are being followed by requests for information no matter where we are. Most of us are constantly connected to information in some way or another, whether we are at home, at work or in between. Information is becoming increasing portable and mobile. Where we go, so goes information. The tools detailed in this chapter are only making this phenomenon more comprehensive.

We wake up and put on suits of information, and we rarely take them off until we go to bed at night. In fact, many of us put on the suits even if we get up in the middle of night to use the restroom. We do quick checks of our e-mail or phone messages before taking off the suits and crawling back into bed. Over time, our suits have become thicker and more cumbersome. Simple shirts and pants have become three-piece suits with hats and ties. The heat outside is getting hotter and hotter. Beads of sweat are pouring off us as the rays of information beat down upon us in our wardrobes of ever-increasing data.

Understanding the direction where current technologies are headed can help paint a picture of the near future. Information bombardment is already being felt by most of us whether we realize it or not. But, more importantly, the onslaught of information is just beginning. In the subsequent chapter I will take you on a journey into the future. Applying what we have learned about IP addresses, RFID tags and GPS abilities, you can envision a world that is not too far away. If we don't take active roles in managing information bombardment in our own lives now, we just might drown when the flood gates open wider.

FURTHER READING

What is an IP address?: http://computer.howstuffworks.com/Internet/basics/question549.htm

IP addresses by country: http://www.bgpexpert.com/addresses-percountry.php

Grains and atoms: http://www.thenakedscientists.com/forum/index.php?topic=19016

Introduction to RFID: http://www.rfident.org/#RFID%20Today

RFID tags: http://www.information-management.com/news/7096-1.html

Implantable RFID: http://www.aimglobal.org/members/news/templates/template.aspx?articleid=243&zoneid=24

Sheep and RFID tags: http://www.rfidjournal.com/article/view/4203

GPS and timing: http://www.trimble.com/gps/gpswork-timing.shtml

Google Latitude: http://techcrunch.com/2009/02/04/broadcast-your-location-to-friends-with-google-latitude/

Scan QR code for direct link to website, hypertext links and other resources:

CHAPTER 12

Car Accident (A Fable)

"Nine one one. What's your emergency?" the digital operator spoke in an eerily natural voice.

"This is BlackBerry device PIN one seven N B six nine two seven calling in reference to Chris Pappas. Shock impact sensors suggest a vehicular accident. GPS data identifies current point of location as three forty-five West Farmland Road, approximately twenty-five meters west of the paved roadway. Request emergency services."

"Please verify authenticity code," the digital operator stated calmly.

Chris' BlackBerry proceeded to send encoded information identifying its authenticity to the dispatcher. Its IP address was matched against a database of registered IP addresses, which listed the 2,342 IP addresses belonging to Chris. Upon a successful match, a series of encrypted codes were transmitted back and forth and within a matter of seconds, the operator was able to proceed.

"Emergency services have been dispatched. Device, please upload all relevant medical data, demographic information and recent historical data related to Chris Pappas."

"Permitted data upload initiated," the BlackBerry replied over its voice over IP connection. Chris had previously selected what data and information could and could not be transmitted in case of emergency. These were the parameters in which the BlackBerry had to operate. In another few seconds, the operator had all the pertinent information, which was instantaneously transmitted to the ambulance and emergency vehicles en route.

"Time transpired since accident twenty seconds and counting," the BlackBerry recorded. "Temperature readings suggest human viability and radial pulse is detected at one hundred twenty beats per minute. Respiration present, but depth too shallow to record breaths per minute. Motion sensors fail to detect any other movement in the vicinity."

"Noted," stated the digital operator, documenting receipt of the information. "Estimated arrival of emergency services between sixty and one hundred twenty seconds."

"Technical analysis of vehicular computer operations indicates a primary failure. Proceeding to commence notification of family members and home unit," the BlackBerry continued.

"Proceed. Emergency services will contact as well."

In the wreckage, Chris lay unconscious in the driver's seat, still strapped to his seat by the harness and pinned in place from the deployed airbag. The 2016 Ford Focus lay upside down in a field, a notable distance from the rural country road. A small stream of steam escaped into the cool night air, rising from the undersurface of the car's engine. The quiet was only interrupted by the interchange between the 911 operator and the BlackBerry device.

■ ■ ■

Miles away, Maria Pappas was helping their oldest child with her homework assignment. Multimedia holographic illustrations, videos and auditory content were streaming on the child's iPad. They were studying the 2008 election campaign of America's first African-American president. Despite the fact that Anastasia was only eight years old, a complex discussion between liberalism and conservatism had begun. Suddenly, the contents of the hologram paused as an emergency message alert was displayed. Simultaneously, Maria's BlackBerry, which was about the size of a quarter, vibrated on her wrist. A small Bluetooth earpiece receiving communications wirelessly from the wrist device began to detail the contents of the emergency message in her ear.

"Emergency message for Maria Pappas," the BlackBerry stated.

"Proceed with message," she quickly replied and listened intently as her BlackBerry relayed the information regarding her husband's apparent accident. Before Maria could talk to her two children, another call interrupted the emergency message transmission. With another glance at her wrist, Maria saw it was emergency services.

"Hello, this is Maria Pappas. What is going on?"

"Mrs. Pappas, this is EMT Johnson en route to three forty-five West Farmland Road, from where we received device notification of an accident. The limited information we have right now indicates that your husband has a pulse and is breathing, but he is presumed to be unconscious based on lack of movement noted in the vehicle by his communications device."

"Oh my god!"

"Has your husband's RFID tag been recently updated with all his pertinent health and personal information?"

"Um, yes…He uploads it faithfully every month. How far away are you?"

"We'll be arriving in less than thirty seconds. The doctor will contact you as we know more."

"Yes, please! I'm on my way, but I am several minutes away. Where will he be going?"

"Western Regional is the closest hospital."

The ambulance's voice-activated computer had already verified the IP address of Maria's Blackberry, which was listed in a medical database as Chris' emergency contact. As EMT Johnson ended the transmission with Maria's BlackBerry, the ambulance arrived at the scene of the accident. In the background, additional sirens from police and fire vehicles were quickly increasing in volume as they also approached.

The EMTs found Chris in an unconscious state, but indeed he did still have a strong pulse and was breathing shallowly. The vehicle appeared stable though incredibly mangled from what appeared to have been repeated rollovers through the peaceful meadow.

Johnson, after assessing Chris' vital signs, swiped a small wand over Chris' right wrist to verify his identity and enable a recent upload of all of his medical and personal information. The data was then transmitted to the Western Regional ER, enabled by the wireless equipment on the ambulance that maintained a constant Internet connection with the hospital. The other EMT, Jasper, quickly reviewed the information while paging through a series of hologram images locally displayed by the ambulance, detailing the entire medical history of Mr. Pappas.

A few miles away, at Western Regional Hospital, Dr. Goode viewed Chris' information as well as a direct, real-time video of the accident scene being transmitted via Skype Platinum programs through wireless technology. Step by step, Goode was able to assist Johnson and Jasper in assessing Chris' condition.

"Get the C-collar on him. Any external injuries noted?" Goode asked.

"Blood pressure one hundred palpable. Pulse one thirty and climbing. Respirations shallow. Abrasions to the left face and chest. Right leg looks to be injured and lacerated. Deep laceration to left brachium. Unconscious with no response to deep pain."

"Get him on a board after the collar, place some EKG leads and run normal saline in two IV lines wide open," Goode stated. "I want an electrolyte and blood-gas scan on the way in. Let's move, guys."

■ ■ ■

Maria made arrangements for her mother to stay with the kids, and within a couple of minutes she was on her way to the emergency room.

"Items added to your list for the market include a gallon of organic milk, a dozen omega-enriched eggs and a loaf of whole-wheat bread. These items are deficient and ready to expire," her BlackBerry device spoke in her ear. The refrigerator was equipped with an RFID reader that enabled its contents to communicate volume information and expiration dates to the refrigerator, which then relayed the information nightly to Maria's personal communications device as requested.

"Weather for tomorrow is sunny with a ten-percent chance of afternoon showers. Highs in the low seventies. Air-quality index excellent, cloud coverage intermittent, winds light from the east," the device continued.

"Cancel scheduled routine communications for twenty-four hours," Maria barked into her BlackBerry and then swiped her wrist to unlock her car, which was sitting in the driveway. Her Lincoln Transporter recognized her identity through her RFID tag. This and the voice- recognition software built into the car's computer were standard features.

"Start engine and navigate to Western Regional Hospital—fastest route."

The car engine started, and Maria followed the GPS instructions to navigate her way to the hospital. Her Lincoln was equipped with dynamic traffic-flow updates and also featured automatic lane scanning. Music began to play from a predetermined song list Maria had selected.

"Music off. Locate Chris' BlackBerry for tracking and display," she said nervously, hoping her husband's device could still be detected.

Within a few seconds, Chris' BlackBerry was located en route to Western Regional as well. She could see on her GPS screen his familiar icon moving along the interstate approaching the hospital. Maria felt relieved that the EMTs had arrived and were caring for him, but she knew that seeing his GPS icon meant absolutely nothing. She called his BlackBerry but received no answer. Why hadn't the EMTs called her yet? She barked out another command:

"Turn on video camera for device PIN one seven N B six nine two seven." Both Chris and Maria had previously preauthorized full functionality of each other's devices. Immediately, a high-definition video signal displayed on her Lincoln's navigation system, showing both EMTs taking vitals and caring for her husband. Audio filled the speakers of her vehicle as she calmly spoke.

"Thank you for taking care of my husband. I am several miles behind you." A few second passed.

"Regional traffic system reports traffic delay due to construction along I-20. Suggest an alternate route to facilitate travel-time efficiency," the car's computer stated.

"Proceed," Maria replied.

"False entry detected at home," her BlackBerry then reported in her ear. "Request to call nine one one."

Maria realized she had set the home alarm out of habit and forgot her mother was coming over to watch the kids. Her mother didn't know the security code, and likely she had falsely set off the alarm.

"Request denied. Scan RFID tags in home for new people," Maria said thinking quickly on her feet.

"New person identified. Effi Markou."

"Deactivate alarm and secure door and window locks. Raise AC to afternoon room temperature, turn on kitchen lights and preheat oven," Maria stated.

"Commands confirmed, house secured."

"Can everything please just shut up!" Maria whispered to herself, afraid to say it loudly, fearing some device may actually react to her voice. She was tired of the distractions, but she didn't feel safe any longer without her constant informational updates.

■ ■ ■

"Dr. Goode, electrolyte scan and blood gases are completed. You have the results," Johnson stated.

Chris lay stabilized on an EMT board and in a neck collar. A large IV had been placed in each arm, but his vitals were declining. Johnson had placed a cuff over Chris' wrist that displayed constant electrolyte, oxygen and blood-cell information by a transcutaneous infrared transmitter. The different molecules had different spectroscopy patterns, which allowed results to be shown without taking blood samples. A constant Internet connection between the ambulance's equipment and the ER provided this data immediately for Goode to interpret.

"His hematocrit is low and his blood pressure is dropping. I suspect we have some internal bleeding," Goode stated. "Nurse, notify radiology that we need a stat MRI on this patient on arrival—full-body."

"Doctor, patient's records indicate he is a metal artist."

"Damn. That means metal fragments. Alright, change MRI to a full-body CT. They had better be ready. Get me the on-call general surgeon and neurosurgeon. They're gonna need to prep the OR if these scans show bleeding."

Goode continued to look over Chris' records, noting that he was not only a metal artist but also married with two kids. He was forty-two years old and otherwise healthy except for a history of intermittent headaches. After receiving a negative CT of his head six months ago, he had been treated for migraines. He had no allergies and took only a migraine preventative. Goode then expanded the database to include all genetic relatives based on the recent implementation of universal DNA identification requirements in the country. Within seconds, Goode could see fifteen of Roger's blood relatives and their medical illnesses in a holographic family tree image. No other red flags in Roger's history appeared to be present.

While Goode was reviewing Chris' medical history, administrative staff at the hospital had already downloaded all of his medical insurance and demographic information into their database. Chris had never been a patient at Western Regional, but once ambulance care had been initiated the hospital was permitted to access all relevant information that would pay for their services. The RFID scan in the field by the EMTs had been transmitted not only to the ER but also to the admissions department. Insurance approval had been verified before Chris had even been loaded into the ambulance.

"His oxygen is dropping," Goode reported. "Check his intubation and ventilator settings."

Jasper verified with his stethoscope that Chris was receiving air flow into both lungs while Johnson verified the portable ventilator settings.

"Placement appears good. Settings at forty-percent oxygen," Johnson stated.

"Let's move it to fifty percent."

"Done. We're pulling into the hospital now."

■ ■ ■

"Fuel is below ten-percent capacity," Maria's car stated. "Recommend refueling. Fueling station around next corner. Tire pressure at front driver's location is five percent below optimal. Seventy-five percent tread still available."

"Cancel vehicle notifications," Maria said in an irritated and frantic voice. She was about ten minutes away from Western Regional.

"Update on Chris' GPS location," she continued.

Maria could now see that Chris had arrived at Western Regional. The video feed from his BlackBerry showed that he had just been wheeled into the building. But the lack of medical information was killing her. It had been nearly fifteen minutes since she had spoken to the EMTs. What was going on? She made a mental note to complain to the hospital administrator about the tremendous delay in information communication. Maria pushed harder on the accelerator and ran a traffic light that had just turned red.

"Photographic image of license tag taken," Maria's car reported, indicating that the automated cameras at the intersection had captured her violation. "You have two options, immediate payment of fine from PayPal account on file or scheduled in-person trial on May 17 at nine o'clock in the morning."

"Ugh, just pay it," Maria shouted into the air.

"Financial information access notification. Western Regional Hospital administrative department has viewed health insurance and public financial documents on Chris Pappas and family," Maria's BlackBerry reported.

Maria thought that surely this was a good sign. Why would they be accessing financial information unless Chris was indeed alive and being treated? She held on to her optimism as she neared the hospital entrance.

Maria pulled into the emergency room parking lot. The lot had been equipped with parking space identifier tags that communicated to her car which spaces were vacant.

"Three parking spaces available. Select closest space or manual selection?" her car inquired.

"Enough already!" Maria exclaimed as she slammed the

car into park just outside the ER door, ignoring the sign that read "NO PARKING."

"Alert. Unauthorized parking location. Suggest alternative space."

Maria could no longer hear the barrage of updates coming from her automobile as she rushed through the ER doors and into the triage lobby. She thought she had escaped, but before she could begin speaking with the triage attendant, her BlackBerry beckoned her.

"Automobile notification message. Illegal parking space violation reported. Suggest relocating automobile to approved space."

Maria reached down and silenced her BlackBerry. It was something she rarely did, but given the situation she didn't want any more ridiculous interruptions.

"I'm Maria Pappas," she blurted out to the desk attendant. "Chris Pappas is my husband. He was brought here by ambulance. I need to know what is going on!"

"Yes, Mrs. Pappas," the attendant acknowledged. "Please swipe your arm for identification purposes. I will get Dr. Goode."

Maria swiped her wrist across the counter and heard the attendant's computer say, "Maria Anastasia Pappas , DOB March 29, 1982." The attendant stood and walked into the back, leaving Maria alone at the counter. She looked around the lobby and saw a young child who looked to be suffering from the flu, and then she thought of her own children. What if Chris didn't make it? What were the kids thinking right now, after she left in such a rush? Maria reached down and turned her Blackberry volume back on. She couldn't risk not being connected.

"Mrs. Pappas, I am Dr. Goode."

"Hello, Doctor. Please, how is Chris?"

Goode paused, making sure he chose his words well.

"Chris is unconscious at the moment. I did a cursory exam, and he looks to have an injured right leg and some bruising. But my biggest concerns are his low blood pressure and low red blood cells. I think we may have some internal bleeding. He is in the CT scanner right now, and I have surgeons ready to take him into the OR if it shows bleeding."

"Oh my god," Maria gasped. "What happened?"

"I'm not sure. His car was the only vehicle involved. We did pull the car's computer recorders. The external camera recording from the vehicle shows nothing that triggered the accident, but the internal camera may be more revealing," Goode replied. "Your husband's face seemed to contort immediately before he lost control of the car. Does he have any history of seizures?"

"Seizures?" Maria asked, surprised. "No. Never. He is as healthy as can be."

"I have seen his medical records. What about these headaches he has been having recently?"

"Oh, yes. He has been having headaches for about a year off and on. We were told they were migraines. Is that not correct?"

"They may be migraines. I'm just trying to get all the information I can."

"Dr. Goode, the CT results are ready," a nurse reported, interrupting their conversation.

"Come with me, Mrs. Pappas."

Goode stepped around a corner and into a small room with

a computer the size of a wallet lying on a small desk. With a swipe of his wrist across the tiny device, the hospital's radiology department's interface appeared by hologram in front of Dr. Goode and Maria. Goode then entered some additional identifiers, and Chris' full-body CT scan appeared for review. Goode reviewed the images section by section until something caught his attention.

"Mrs. Pappas, excuse me just for a moment."

Goode called Dr. Victor, the staff neurosurgeon, on his wrist phone.

"Dr. Victor, are you looking at the scan?" Goode asked.

"I am. Looks like we have a bleed. He's rolling into the operating room as we speak," Victor replied.

"Any thoughts based on the scan?"

"The location is unusual for trauma. I am suspicious about an aneurismal rupture, but I won't know for sure until I get into surgery."

"I'll speak with his wife. She is here with me now."

Goode proceeded to explain to Maria that Chris had an intracranial bleed. The bleeding could have been the result of the accident, but at the same time it could have occurred from the rupture of an aneurysm. If this were the case, the rupture could have also caused a seizure and have been the real cause of the accident.

"Doctor, what are his chances? Is he going to be OK?" Maria asked.

"The area of bleeding is significant, but it's too soon for any of us to tell. We'll know more after Dr. Victor is able to examine the area in surgery."

"Reminder of unauthorized parking location," Maria's

BlackBerry stated at what seemed to be the most inappropriate time. "Parking attendant approaching, live video feed available."

"Look, he's gonna be in a surgery a little while. You can wait in the OR waiting area. As soon as I know something, I will let you know," Goode said as he led Maria down the corridor.

"Thank you, Doctor."

■ ■ ■

"Nurse, please hand me the saw," Victor demanded as he prepared to cut a burr hole in the frontal area of Chris' skull.

"Yes, Doctor," she replied.

"Dr. Victor, I have cannulated the patient's right subclavian vein. Ready to release the wireless capsulated vascular camera when you are," the invasive radiologist reported.

"Go ahead and proceed if we have the digital imagery in place."

"It's ready," the radiologist replied as he injected the dust-sized camera through the large IV.

In a couple of seconds, the complete outline of the subclavian veins, the chambers of the heart and Chris' aorta appeared on the digital screen. The tiny camera was sending continuous video imagery in high definition to the screen, which occupied nearly half a wall in the OR suite. Victor watched as images on one side recreated Chris' vascular tree of blood vessels in a three-dimensional pattern while on the other side a detailed view of the insides of the vessel walls was shown.

"Alright, it appears the patient has some minor atherosclerotic plaque along the left and right carotid arteries, less than twenty percent," Victor stated for the OR recorder. "Anatomy otherwise within normal limits. Intracranial vasculature now appearing."

The entire room watched as the tiny camera began to reveal the cause of Chris' condition. As the images unfolded, an abrupt spasm of one of the major arteries on the left side of his brain was apparent. This indicated an aneurismal rupture rather than a traumatic injury to the brain. Undoubtedly, the rupture had been the reason Chris had lost consciousness.

"Alright, people, we have an aneurismal rupture," Victor barked. "Let's rock and roll. Open the aneurysm tray and infuse one point five grams of Dilantin."

Victor began sawing a quarter-sized hole in the left frontal skull region. The increased pressure from inside the skull was released as the opening was made, and Victor worked feverishly to clamp the end of the ruptured cerebral artery.

"Blood pressure dropping to one hundred systolic," the nurse reported.

"Begin pressors," Victor ordered speaking to the anesthesiologist, then asked, "OR computer, what is the elapsed time?"

"Time since anesthesia began twenty-three minutes fifteen seconds. Time since ER arrival thirty-five minutes fifty-two seconds. Time since estimated patient event forty-nine minutes twenty seconds," the automated OR computer responded.

"Alright, clamp is in place, bleeding appears stabilized," Victor stated. "Please re-administer an encapsulated camera."

The tiny camera was specially designed so that after several seconds, the biodegradable device decomposed and was eliminated through the urine. The device was also inexpensive; it could be re-administered at minimal cost.

Again the entire staff watched the screen in the OR suite,

and within seconds it again displayed a detailed view of Roger's blood vessels. While the spasm and rupture were still evident, the inside view of his left anterior cerebral artery demonstrated successful closure and stabilization.

"Blood pressure increasing and stable," the nurse reported.

"OR computer, link Dr. Goode into the OR suite, please. Auditory only," Victor ordered.

A minute later, Dr. Goode announced his virtual arrival at the OR suite. His voice was evident over the OR speaker, but his video image was suppressed so that the radiology data could still be seen on the digital screen. Goode, on the other hand, had video access to the OR suite from his computer and could see what was transpiring in the room.

"Dr. Goode, can you see the encapsulated vascular camera images?" Victor inquired.

"I can. Tell me what I am seeing," Goode continued.

"We have a left frontal ACA aneurysm rupture as evidenced by the spasm here," Victor explained, pointing the shadow of his scalpel onto the image. "We have clamped and attained stability. Patient has stable vitals. We should be done soon, with the patient transferred to recovery within thirty minutes. He will move into neuro-ICU after that."

"Excellent," Goode replied. "I will let his wife know."

■ ■ ■

Maria was sitting in the lobby outside the operating room. She had contacted her mother to bring the kids to the hospital and had spoken with Chris' family, who lived out of town. Though she wanted to talk in person with the kids about their dad, she didn't want them to have to ride all the way to Western Regional without knowing some details. Therefore, she had talked with them via Skype Platinum, through which she connected using her BlackBerry. Her wrist device not only had a microphone with noise cancellation but also a high-definition camera. She conferenced in Chris' parents and his sister. They all listened intently as Maria gently explained that Chris had been in a severe accident.

Just as she had finished talking with them, Dr. Goode rounded the corner and came into the lobby area.

"Mrs. Pappas, I just spoke with Dr. Victor in the operating room," Goode began. "Chris is stable right now and they are finishing up, but he is still unconscious. It looks like he has suffered a ruptured brain aneurysm. That's why he lost consciousness and had an accident. He may have even had a seizure because of it."

"A brain aneurysm! Is he going to be OK? Can I see him?"

"You can't see him just yet, but he will be going to—"

"Incoming call from Effi Markou," Maria's BlackBerry interrupted. Maria pushed a button, sending her mother to voicemail.

"Sorry," Maria apologized.

"That's alright. He will be going to neuro-ICU probably within a half hour. You can see him then."

"What does this mean? Is he going to be alright?"

"I wish I could tell you, Mrs. Pappas, but it's very early. Predicting things like this is nearly impossible at this stage. We should know—"

"Notification message. Dog failed to receive food and water this evening," the BlackBerry reported, having received its own notification from the home computer. The dog bowls, like the refrigerator contents, had RFID tags that monitored volume levels and reported their status to the home computer several times a day. Maria finally silenced her BlackBerry for good.

"I am so sorry, Doctor. What were you saying?"

"We should know more in a couple of days about his condition. Right now he remains critical."

■ ■ ■

Over the course of the next several days, Chris regained consciousness and was able to be moved out of the neuro-ICU. His repeated head scans showed a progressively shrinking area of blood in the brain, but he had suffered some brain injury and a stroke from the aneurismal rupture. His right leg and arm were slightly weak as a result, and he would remain on seizure medications as a precaution. But all in all, he was very fortunate to be alive. Months later, after a long course of rehabilitation, Chris was finally able to resume his normal life, as was everyone else. He was well again.

"Maria, I am heading to the store," Chris said.

"Don't forget to download the list from the refrigerator," Maria said as she walked into the kitchen.

"Already did it," he replied. "When are you going to realize I am one-hundred-percent back to normal, including my memory?"

But just as Maria had spoken, his BlackBerry announced an alert.

"Urgent notification message. Morning dose of Dilantin medication past due."

"You were saying?" Maria said with a playful smirk.

"Never mind. Would you please hand me my pills?" He popped them down his throat and within seconds the powder had dissolved to a molecular level. Microscopic imagery on his BlackBerry showed that the medicine was targeting the right area and that his whole body was responding favorably.

■ ■ ■

The above story is, of course, fictitious and envisages technological advancements in the future. But the reality is that this type of future is only a few short years away. With the explosion of IP addresses, the development of nanochip technology and RFID tag abilities, GPS locator and tracking services and a slew of other computer-related advancements, all of these depictions are not only possible but likely within the decade. Information will be coming at us from all directions. Are we ready?

As demonstrated, Chris' survival and favorable outcome was made possible by the enhanced information and communications enabled by technological advancements. Treatments and assessments were conducted faster, more complete information was available, and communications were more thorough and efficient. All of these resulted in a life-saving intervention when truly every second counted. This is where information technology can be of great benefit.

But at the same time, Maria shows the importance of proactive management of information. Alerts and notification messages will bombard us constantly. Requests for decisions and our attention will seem endless. Not only will other people solicit our time and attention but so will the personal items in our lives. Perhaps the best thing may be simply to disconnect from this information, but like Maria we become dependent on having this knowledge. The fear of being disconnected keeps us from effectively managing information bombardment in our lives. Even with an emergency at hand, Maria finds it difficult to cut the umbilical cord of her familiar source of information nourishment. Ultimately she manages to balance the critical updates with the nagging alerts, albeit within a very stressful situation.

Having seen where we currently are in the knowledge era with information bombardment and the future direction of technological advancement, it is now time to explore what these things mean at different levels of our society. Regardless of whether you approach these analyses from an individual, group, organizational or institutional perspective, information bombardment is important to understand. At each level, different insights can be gained, and they will highlight the types of solutions that can be explored. This will be the next step in our journey toward understanding how information should be best managed as we move into the future.

Scan QR code for direct link to website,
hypertext links and other resources:

CHAPTER 13

Impact at the Individual Level

There I sat, bathing in the warm rays of a midday sun. I could hear the kids playing off in the distance along the shoreline, and my wife was sitting in her beach chair next to me, enjoying some much-deserved leisurely reading. I, on the other hand, lay comfortably reclined in a state somewhere between conscious relaxation and light sleep…or so I thought.

Suddenly I felt a buzzing on my right thigh. Was I dreaming? I could have sworn I felt my BlackBerry vibrating in my right front pocket. But how could this be? I had on swim trunks, and I had purposefully left my phone back in my room. Sluggishly I opened my eyes and lifted my head off the chair. It was just as I'd thought: there was nothing on my leg. Just a tactile hallucination…one I call a *phantom vibration*.

Guess what? I am not the only person who has experienced phantom vibrations. When I came back from vacation, I asked several of my friends and colleagues if they had ever experienced anything similar. Believe it or not, they had. Some had felt vibrations in the middle of lectures. Others described having them in their sleep or while driving. At first I was surprised that such a phenomenon was so common, but after a little reflection, it made perfect sense. This was yet another manifestation of information bombardment.

The combination of our need to be constantly connected to sources of information and the fear of possibly missing a juicy piece of data drives our anxieties. As a result, we become overly vigilant and sensitized to the slightest hint of new communications. Have you ever had your stereo too loud and thought you heard your cell phone ring when it didn't? Do you falsely hear e-mail alerts as you drift off the sleep? These are all the same phenomena as phantom vibrations, and they all demonstrate how information bombardment can affect us on a personal level.

This chapter deals with the effects that information bombardment has on you as an individual. The effects are quite widespread and can affect many things, from personal relationships to your own health. Unless we can appreciate the negative effects information bombardment has on us individually, we will unknowingly become victims of its influence. This in turn will result in less productivity on one hand and an unhappy lifestyle on the other. Therefore, understanding is important so we can begin to take control over the information we receive.

Relationships

As human beings, we are social creatures. We thrive socially through friendships, intimate partnerships, parenting, business relationships and relationships with our extended families. Without relationships, most people would agree, life would lose a great deal of meaning. Personal relationships let us express ourselves, love others, understand the complexities of life, mentor our children and so much more. While much can be gained from books, the Internet and other sources of information, nothing can replace time spent with other people in our lives. Let's face it: relationships are time-intensive and require constant nurturing.

The way we behave might persuade you differently, however. As our love affairs with smartphones, iPods, computers and other information devices have increased, the time we commit to social relationships has fallen. It's interesting that beginning in the 1970s and 1980s, the divorce rate in America climbed significantly, to nearly fifty percent. Guess what...It hasn't returned to preexisting levels since. Many factors played roles in this major social shift, including women's rights, multiculturalism and more. But it is interesting that the increase in divorces occurred during a period when the Information Age was gearing up. How much of a role do you think information bombardment had on these failing relationships?

Let's apply some numbers to the situation. In the year 2000, a survey assessed the amount of time dads spent with their children. Notably, fathers have been participating much more in parenting over the last several decades, but even so the figures may surprise you. On weekdays, fathers averaged 2.5 hours a day with their children and on weekends 6.2 hours. This may not seem so alarming, but in reading the fine print, dads were only directly interacting with their children half of this time. The other half of the time they were simply available in the house somewhere (probably checking e-mail or surfing the Web).

The other interesting statistics were the information gathered about income and education. While increased education correlated with increased time spent with one's children on average, increased income had the opposite effect. In fact, for every additional $10,000 in annual income received, there was a reduction of five minutes of father-child time spent per day on average. The old saying "time is money" certainly applies here.

The more time each of us spends giving our attention to various outlets of information, the less attention we have for the important relationships in our lives. Often we negotiate tiny moments every day and every week so that we can check our e-mail one more time, download new software or watch the latest YouTube video clip. Every time this happens we choose to divert our attention from our spouses, families and friends. This is how problems arise and how we eventually suffer as a result.

I imagine that some of you might disagree. You might say that the increase in social networking technologies has reversed the initial trends of social isolation. The argument might be that people are actually better connected today through technology. Without question, social networking has facilitated communications between many people. But the relationships I am speaking about are not the ones that can survive on frequent tweets about what you're doing at the moment. Real social relationships require face-to-face time. This includes using two senses that are still foreign to the Internet: touch and smell. You still can't hug your children from afar, and you still can't smell the fragrance of your spouse from a different city. For these gifts, you have to be there.

I have colleagues who unfortunately have long-distance relationships with their children because of divorce. Each of them makes attempts to call and talk on the phone as often as possible. Some use Skype to interact through video with their children. Others have instant messaging and e-mail communications regularly. But no matter how effective these technological tools become, they do not replace direct, in-person time spent together. Kids aren't the only ones who need this; we all do. Nevertheless, my colleagues often express a lack of real, deep connections with their children and often describe how exasperated they feel by the limitations of technology.

Your spouse doesn't need just to get an e-mail update about your personal thoughts or to check in with you by phone to hear about the latest events in your day. Your partner needs to see, feel, smell and hear you in person. These social contacts reveal so much more than information. They provide personal memories upon which a life is built. Who wants to build a life on tweets and e-mails? Not me. You shouldn't either. In order to make the most out of your relationships (and your life), you must guard your attention against assaults from information bombardment.

Personal Security

Much of human behavior is geared toward creating a safe and secure environment while still meeting our basic needs. In this way we are much like any other animal species. But our world is much more complex than any other animal's. Terrorism, identity theft, oil spills and airplane crashes are some examples of complexities that are specific to humankind. These unforeseen and sometimes intangible threats affect our feelings of security much more than physical threats. But exactly how risky are these imagined scenarios?

Herein lies the problem with personal security. In essence, security can be defined according to two parameters. One is based on reality while the other is based on psychological or "gut" feelings. Both can result in the same assessments of threat versus security, but often they don't. This is where we get into trouble. When facts and feelings disagree, we tend to go with our feelings.

Assessments of our personal security, when based on reality, are firmly anchored in information. Data, statistics and probabilities are objective facts that provide knowledgeable input when determining whether a situation is threatening or not. In other words, real security assessment is based on mathematical principles and weighs true risk against the effectiveness of prevention. This is our logical side and the basis of rational thinking.

In contrast, security assessments based on our feelings are far from objective analyses. These subjective assessments are based on past experiences, public perception and deep emotions that might come from a variety of sources. Many times these psychological assessments are not supported by real information about risk but by projections about what might happen. In some instances, despite the facts saying otherwise, we still perceive a lack of security because our emotions get the best of us.

Let's take a common example. How many of you have a fear of flying? Throughout the world every year, airplanes take at the most the lives of hundreds of people on average. In contrast, automobile accidents kill thousands during the same period. The security analysis based on facts and figures demonstrates clearly that we should feel less secure in our cars than we do on airplanes, but for many this is not the case. Why? The answer is our psychological analysis of security. A forty-ton plane floating thousands of feet in the air at 500 miles per hour just doesn't feel as safe as a half-ton car with four tires on the ground.

Our brains have essentially two systems that work together in assessing threats. One part—the upper brain, called the *cortex*—is responsible for the logical processing of information. This area does its best to assess situations as closely to reality as possible. It uses objective data received from the body's senses and analyzes this data into logical constructs predicting risk. Our cortexes provide us with rational understandings of how we should behave.

The other part of the brain that is important in assessing threats is the limbic system. This region of the brain lies closer to the brainstem and is much older, in evolutionary terms, than the cortex. The limbic system is the part of the brain that tells us whether we are the hunter or the hunted—whether we should run or fight. It bases its assessments on emotions rather than logic. If something looks or feels insecure, it isn't safe. If something looks new and strange, it's risky. When the limbic system disagrees with the cortex in the assessment of a situation, the limbic system usually wins.

This is all good to know, but what does this have to do with information bombardment? Quite a bit, actually. As we get bombarded by e-mails, instant messages, voicemails, texts, tweets, Skype calls and more, our rational cortexes tell us that we are being overwhelmed by information. But despite this, we keep on plugging away. Why don't we stop? The reason is that our limbic systems do not yet feel secure. Without information constantly coming into our lives, we still feel uneasy. We become too scared to disconnect from our information lifelines because we emotionally perceive some threat—the threat of ignorance and being left behind. For example, if the lights on our phones are flashing or we have e-mail notification icons showing on our desktops, we tend to get feelings of anxiousness. How about that really strong feeling we get when returning from somewhere that had no Internet access? We anticipate our fixes so intensely that we must check our inboxes immediately upon return. A stampede of raging elephants could never stop this urge.

If we were to step back and rationalize our real insecurities, we would understand that we could disconnect for hours and maybe even days at a time without any significant threats to our livelihood. When you reconnect again, you will realize that you still have your job, your spouse, your home and everything else. In fact, your relationships, as already pointed out, may be improved. But for most of us, our emotions and worries drive our actions, and we continue to let information bombardment affect our lives despite this understanding.

Job security is one aspect of personal security. Having a job means an income that will allow you to provide food, shelter and support. Therefore, job security is a big part of personal security. It is safe to say that most people would rationally choose to create stable work environments in order to maximize this area of security in their lives. If income is secure, then we have fewer threats against many aspects of our lives.

However, in a recent survey by Soft Panorama, two-thirds of business managers described tension with work colleagues and unpleasant work environments as a result of information bombardment. The amount of data and information that had to be consumed created decreased productivity instead of enhanced performance. Employees felt overwhelmed, professional relationships became increasingly strained and job security became more risky as a result. Instead of adding security, information was undermining it.

Despite information providing a means to enhance personal security through better risk assessments, our emotional attachment to information leads us even further toward informational bombardment. We are data junkies; we just cannot help ourselves. The more we connect to our electronic devices for our fixes, the more we believe we can make better decisions and feel more secure. But if we take on more than we can handle, the same information that we think will help us can actually hurt us.

Mental Health

That information bombardment can cause stress isn't really earth-shattering news. But what do we mean by the term *stress?* Stress is used so commonly in our everyday language that its clinical definition may be unclear. One basic definition of stress is a heightened sense of concern and awareness due to a real or imagined threat of some kind. For example, you might be stressed because of an upcoming presentation at work. Or you might be stressed because you have to undergo surgery. These are different situations, but stress is evoked because you sense some form of danger.

When we feel stressed, our bodies react accordingly. Our hearts race, our blood pressures rise, our pupils dilate and our thoughts become focused. This reaction, called the *fight or flight response,* is triggered by the release of adrenaline in our bodies. This powerful hormone regulates almost every organ in the body to be ready to react in an instant. The stress response is therefore a protective response for us (as well as animals) to help us be prepared and to anticipate dangerous situations.

Imagine for the moment that you are traveling through

New York City and suddenly find yourself lost in a rough part of town. Your GPS isn't working, your cell phone battery is dead, your car is almost out of gas and you haven't a clue which direction to turn to get back to the interstate. This is acute stress. You immediately sense danger and your body reacts accordingly. Now imagine you are fighting the war in Afghanistan on the front lines. Instead of experiencing the same sense of danger on a one-time basis, you must live with this sensation for weeks and months at a time. This is chronic stress. When we use the term *stress* in everyday life, we generally are referring to chronic stress.

Though these are intense examples of stress, similar comparisons can be drawn to less-intense events in our lives. Having to present to the board with only an hour's notice will likely provoke acute stress, but if this occurred week after week, chronic stress would soon develop. In both situations our bodies react and release adrenaline and other stress hormones in response to the stress. But chronic stress is what leads to a condition I refer to as *adrenalization*. This is where the body must continuously react to stressful situations without the opportunity to recover, and ultimately this is what leads to negative health effects.

Though mental and physical health effects from information bombardment and stress can occur, mental health effects are more common and better appreciated. Of the various mental health disorders, depression and anxiety are by far the most common chronic stress disorders. In fact, one in five Americans suffers from some type of mental health condition, resulting in $16 billion worth of lost work time annually. Of these people, half suffer from depression, which has been labeled the leading cause of disability in the United States.

While more than twenty million Americans experience depression, almost seven million suffer from anxiety, which is also a leading cause of disability. If you have any doubt about this claim, recent statistics support that forty-three percent of Americans take prescription medications for mood disorders like depression or anxiety. While antidepressants routinely rank among the top three medications prescribed, anxiety drugs ranked seventh and eighth in recent polls. It is no coincidence that these disorders have become more prevalent in our society over the last three decades.

When chronically stressed and adrenalized, we can react one of two ways. Some people react by becoming agitated or angry at the increased demands in their lives. They become overly emotional, irritable and agitated. If this persists, these individuals may develop chronic anxiety. The other group of people responds by withdrawing from responsibilities and demands. In other words, they shut down. They begin to show less and less emotion in their daily activities, and their energy levels decline. This may eventually lead to overt depression. Interestingly, some people fluctuate between the two conditions, exhibiting features of both depression and anxiety.

But how does information bombardment cause depression or anxiety? As we continue to take on increasing amounts of information in both our personal and professional lives, the demands on our attention and time slowly begin to erode our mental capacities to function in a healthy manner. We try to make time for family relationships, sleep and work as well as the constant stream of data we believe we need, and in the process important things are sacrificed. Most commonly, personal time and time for self-reflection are the first to go. Sleep is usually next. These sacrifices make it more difficult for us to rationalize that the real root of our problem is information bombardment.

The more demands we feel, the more frustrated and angry we become. As a result, we become depressed, anxious or both. Our abilities to function well and our relationships, job performances and other areas of our lives begin to deteriorate. This further increases our stress, leading to a seemingly never-ending vicious cycle. But there is hope for breaking this downward spiral. The key is to establish control over information bombardment.

Physical Health

Under the prior category of mental health effects, mood disorders were predominantly addressed in relation to information bombardment. In this section, we will talk about all the other effects on our bodies (and minds) that result from a state of chronic stress and information bombardment. Being in a state of chronic stress causes the continuous release of stress hormones and chemicals, and these substances affect nearly every organ in the body. It's no surprise that chronic adrenalization thus results in a variety of health problems over time.

Let's talk just for a moment about adrenaline. This substance is responsible for revving our bodies up for perceived stress, and it is produced by two small structures in the body called the *adrenal glands,* located in the abdomen. But adrenaline is not the only hormone the adrenal glands produce. These glands are also responsible for producing sexual hormones and precursor hormones that keep our bodies' abilities to function well balanced.

In situations of long-term stress, adrenaline is constantly being produced and released by the adrenal glands. Without time to regroup, the adrenal glands eventually become exhausted. They cannot keep up with adequate adrenaline production; they also fail to maintain the needed balance of other hormones throughout the body. This is how a chronic state of adrenalization can result in a variety of physical health problems. If we allow information bombardment to create this chronic stress state, we are putting ourselves at risk for significant medical illnesses.

Some studies have shown that thirty-three percent of all business managers suffer ill health effects as a result of information bombardment. This statistic climbs to forty-three percent for senior managers. The nervous system, intestinal function, the skeletal system and even the heart are among the common targets of chronic stress. Consider the following health disorders that are most commonly described when considering stress-related conditions:

- The nervous system—memory loss, loss of concentration, ADD, migraines, insomnia
- The skeletal system—joint pains, fibromyalgia, connective tissue disease
- Cardiovascular—high blood pressure, atherosclerosis, heart disease
- The intestinal system—ulcer disease, irritable bowel syndrome, weight gain
- The immune system—greater sensitivity to infections and cancers
- General—chronic fatigue syndrome

The most common mechanism for developing the conditions listed is, indeed, chronic stress. However, one disorder likely has a different mechanism, which is even more closely related to information bombardment. Attention deficit hyperactivity disorder, or ADHD, describes a condition wherein individuals experience an inability to stay on task and focus their attention for long periods of time. Between 1997 and 2006, the number of individuals diagnosed with ADHD rose three percent each year. That means that within a decade, there was a thirty-percent increase in the number of people diagnosed with this condition! That is an impressive increase.

The reasons given for the increase in ADHD diagnoses have been numerous. Some claim that better awareness now exists among diagnosticians. Others have attributed the increase to a greater appreciation that adults may also have the disorder. Still others feel that workplaces have made the detection of ADHD easier due to increased attention demands. But what I find interesting is that few people are attributing information bombardment to the actual cause of this disorder.

In my opinion, it is not the atmosphere of information bombardment that is exposing ADHD tendencies among our children and even adults. Instead, I believe that the environment of information bombardment is creating ADHD itself. In order to absorb the multitude of data streams coming at us from all angles, we must have quick, brief attention spans that can jump from one item to the next. The onslaught of information demands this type of strategy so we can focus on moment-to-moment events.

From frequent interruptions of television programming by thirty-second commercials to multitasking between six or seven different devices at a time, we are being socialized into having shorter attention spans. I must juggle my BlackBerry, iPod, Outlook, Internet browser, telephone and computer hard drive all at once while still maintaining my social relationships. If I don't have the ability to shift my attention from one task to another within seconds, life is hopeless...or so I may think. It's no surprise that the number of people labeled with ADHD has risen so much in such a short time.

The link between information bombardment and your physical health is quite clear. When we burn the candle at both ends by spreading our attention too thin, our bodies begin to be affected. Just as we feel overwhelmed in general, each one of our bodily systems is being overwhelmed as well. As a result, the likelihood that we may develop a variety of medical illnesses increases steadily. It's time to take better care of ourselves by learning to manage information bombardment better.

The Push and Pull of Information

Since the days of the card catalog in the public library, we have progressively reduced the time it takes to search for desired information. For example, when our parents were in school and were required to prepare research projects for class assignments, they would spend on average ninety percent of their overall efforts searching for the information. Today, it is exactly the opposite: Google has provided a reallocation of time and effort so that it now takes roughly ten percent of your overall project time to find the information you need.

What is exciting is that the industry of search is still only in its infancy. Today we use keywords to identify subjects in which we are interested. We input our best guesses into a search engine query box and a list of images, videos, books, articles, sites maps and news stories is provided, trying to match information to our chosen keywords. Inherently, we have progressively gotten better at selecting keywords, and search engines have improved in trying to meet our requests for knowledge. But the cost of search (in terms of the overall time required to find what we need) still represents about ten percent of the overall work.

In the future, search engines will likely incorporate many other useful tools to reduce our search costs even further. Increased mobility of search by wearable devices that provide information immediately, voice recognition tools that allow verbal requests instead of typed ones, personalization that may match specific aspects known about us to our search, and the use of natural language instead of keywords are all real possibilities. Instead of remembering to search for information later via text, you instead can simply say out loud, "Why is the sky blue?" and the voice recognition search device attached to you will provide you with the exact answer.

With search tools, we are naturally pulling information to ourselves. We have to initiate the searches in order to get the answers we want. With less search costs, fewer pieces of information that we do not care about will reach our attention. In essence this is a positive thing. However, what if we could not only pull select information to us but also restrict which information was pushed at us? In other words, what if we could establish filters that allowed only information we wanted to reach us? This would be a great way to get a handle on information bombardment.

As stated many times in this book, information is not necessarily a bad thing. Like many things, it becomes negative only if used in excess. Therefore, information bombardment is the villain, not information itself. Understanding this, it is important to realize that one of the most positive things about the Information Age is the ability to acquire knowledge easily. In turn, the ability for lifelong learning is tremendously enhanced with greater access to information. The critical step for us as individuals is simply to determine how to receive only the information we want and need. In essence, we need to refine the amount and type of information pulled to us and pushed toward us at every instance.

Believe it or not, you have more control than you think. Even today, tools exist that enable you to filter which data bombards you. Like search engine tools, these will continue to improve over time. But you as an individual have the power to implement these tools to your benefit. Choosing which information arrives at your mental desktop is a conscious choice. Making these choices may be difficult as you cut the cord to some information, but ultimately the rewards in health, relationships, security and life quality will be well worth it.

FURTHER READING

Effects of information overload: http://www.softpanorama.org/Social/Bombardment/information_bombardment.shtml

Kids spending time with dad: http://findarticles.com/p/articles/mi_m1272/is_2663_129/ai_63986720/

Psychology of security: http://www.schneier.com/essay-155.html

Depression facts: http://www.depressionperception.com/depression/depression_facts_and_statistics.asp

Anxiety statistics: http://www.anxietycentre.com/anxiety-statistics-information.shtml

Understanding stress: http://helpguide.org/mental/stress_signs.htm

Recognizing signs and symptoms of stress: http://my.clevelandclinic.org/healthy_living/stress_management/hic_recognizing_signs_and_symptoms_of_stress.aspx

Attention deficit hyperactivity disorder (ADHD): http://www.healthcentral.com/adhd/c/1443/71959/diagnosis-explained/2

Future of push-pull search: http://googleblog.blogspot.com/2008/09/future-of-search.html

Scan QR code for direct link to website,
hypertext links and other resources:

CHAPTER 14

Impact at the Group Level

As an individual, I have enjoyed many personal and professional achievements in my life. I am happily married with three healthy, wonderful children. I am an avid soccer player, coach and enthusiast. I attained a doctorate degree in strategic management and I am a business professor at McMaster University. My individual achievements are things of which I am very proud and for which I am very thankful. However, I continue to have an indefatigable desire to do more. In order to balance these areas of my life, I must manage information well—how to get it, use it and make more as fast as possible.

In this chapter as well as subsequent chapters, I would like to shift gears a bit. Instead of simply identifying information bombardment in our current spheres of life, I would like to focus on information as capital. *Capital* is anything that is considered an asset or investment, and information is the new capital of the Information Age. It is an intangible commodity that is often impossible to quantify. In fact, much of the information we will talk about at an organizational level is actually embedded within the intangible culture, policies and procedures of the organization. This is also referred to as the *intellectual capital* of the firm.

Intellectual capital starts with the individual. Take me, for example. I have knowledge that I pass along to my students in the form of lectures, notes, assignments and tests. I have tangible knowledge that I am conveying to you in the form of this book. I have knowledge of soccer strategies, tactics and skills that I teach other players as well as my sons. However, I also have loads of intangible knowledge that I intuitively know but can only communicate through example or demonstration.

Let's first take a look at social groups and the concept of intellectual capital. How is information used in a group? How is it distributed among team members? Is it done so willingly or with some resistance? What influences whether information is shared or not among colleagues? The reason this is important in a group setting is that it will affect how information is distributed and shared in a larger setting. The goal is to maintain ample intellectual capital and to get the most out of this asset whether you are an individual, a group, an organization or even a larger social institution. The group setting is our first opportunity to understand how we communicate and distribute knowledge in this evolving Information Age.

From a sociological perspective, a group is two or more people who share common characteristics. While this broad definition defines some basic features of a group, it is too limited. Most groups are considered to be relatively small in size. Common characteristics within a group usually involve a fairly focused range of interests and values. In addition, a degree of social interaction must take place. These criteria eliminate larger collections of people from being considered as groups.

For example, the American people as a society could, in theory, be considered a group. However, I don't socially interact with every American. We do share some interests and values, but the scope of a large society extends beyond what we consider a group to be. Groups are narrower in scope and as a result provide better reflections of how individuals interact in close social settings. These interactions provide our first insights into how we approach group-level knowledge.

Which groups do you belong to? You belong to your family and extended family as groups. You likely belong to a group of colleagues at work. You may belong to a sports team or other groups that reflect your personal interests. In each of these groups, a narrow level of interests is involved, and individual social interactions exist. Groups that are more intimate, like your family and close friends, are usually referred to as *primary groups* while formal and less-personal groups are referred to as *secondary groups.*

Each of us has both types of groups in our lives, and we manage information differently depending on whether a group is primary or secondary. For example, I will share my feelings, thoughts and worries about most everything with my wife. Information about my work, my health and my insecurities is easily volunteered to my wife because she is part of the intimate group of my family. But I am not likely to share this information with a colleague at work. Suppose I share with a colleague that my health is poor. That information is private and may be uncomfortable for me to share with someone who is less close. Even worse, it could be used to limit my advancement in my career.

Whether talking about a primary or a secondary group setting, the same dynamics of how knowledge is handled apply, but the level of trust and transparency in the group relationship influences the extent to which information is exchanged. By viewing groups according to these characteristics, changes can be made either to encourage or to discourage the transfer of knowledge within these settings.

Knowledge Is Power

Another way to express intellectual capital is by using the term *collective brainpower.* Let's face it: that's what information ultimately is. Information has been codified over the centuries through a variety of tools, including the Internet, but all of it reflects the collective brainpower of billions and billions of people since the beginning of time. The invention of the wheel led to the invention of the cart. The invention of the microscope led to the discovery of bacteria and the ability to make antibiotics. Each piece of data is a stepping stone to an even greater piece of knowledge.

The term *brainpower* wasn't just coined because it sounded cool. The output of the brain indeed awards each of us a degree of power. Whether it is the output of your brain or the output of someone else's, knowledge is a desired commodity because it provides us with advantages. The more information we acquire, the more powerful we become. Of course, not all knowledge awards significant increases in power, and some may offer very little if any. But knowing something that someone else doesn't always confers a degree of advantage regardless of how slight.

In this regard, knowledge does not follow the standard rules of economics. Typically, with increased supply comes a declining level of demand. However, in the case of knowledge, more is always better because knowledge's value is ever-increasing. The ability of greater knowledge to build on previous information allows intellectual capital to break the rules of traditional economics. No matter how much information is attained, more can always provide greater opportunities and value to a person, group, organization or institution. Of course, this is also the reason why information bombardment is a real problem.

If knowledge is power, then knowledge affects how we interact in a group setting. When an increasing number of Americans became Internet-savvy, one of the greatest areas of change was health care. The inventions of WebMD, Medscape and many other health information sites gave people the power of medical knowledge, which had been nearly nonexistent previously. Individuals actually understood what effects diseases had on their bodies, the risk factors associated with them, the diagnostic tests likely to be performed as well as treatment options.

This little shift in knowledge dramatically changed the way doctors and patients interacted. Patients would go in for their medical appointments armed with printouts of data they obtained from the Web along with lists of informed questions. In other words, patients became empowered through knowledge and could gain greater understanding from the group interaction. Doctors, on the other hand, had greater obligations to share more knowledge in greater detail because of this power shift. Ultimately, the overall increase in knowledge enhanced the quality of health care. It also showed how increasing knowledge furthered an even-greater increase in informational demand.

The example above between the doctor and the patient shows what can happen when positive collaboration and sharing of information occurs. But in many situations we may not wish to provide the information we have to another. Perhaps a real risk is present, where that knowledge will be used to our disadvantage, or maybe we perceive a risk, whether real or not, that we are unwilling to take. Many factors influence whether we choose to relay information to other individuals. However, the main underlying reason is simply based on the fact that knowledge is power, and none of us freely gives away our power without thoroughly analyzing the costs, risks and benefits involved.

Sharing Versus Hoarding

"Joe, this is Roger from the West Coast sales office."

"Hey, Roger. How is it going?"

"Pretty well. Are you going to be attending the sales meeting in Chicago for our department next week?"

"I am."

"Great, then you probably have already collected some of the industry's data for your region's sales presentation."

"Yeah, I have collected the majority of it. Why do you ask?"

"Well, as you know, we have had power outages all week from the quake. I was hoping you might be willing to share your industry data with me to save me some time."

"I see."

"Look, I know it's my responsibility, but I am in a bit of a time crunch. I'll return the favor next time, Joe. I would definitely owe you."

Sound familiar? At some time or another we all have been in situations like this. Someone we are associated with wants us to share some information. Whether it is because of his or her lack of effort or opportunity, or whether he or she simply does not have access to the same knowledge, a request for us to share information is made. How do you respond? What factors influence your decision? What would you do if you were Joe?

Because knowledge is power and the information you possess is one of your greatest assets, we either consciously or subconsciously decide whether or not we will relinquish our knowledge on a moment-by-moment basis. Sometimes the decision is obvious. Someone asking for an assignment for work or school that he or she has failed to complete usually involves a conscious awareness of what we are giving away. But even then, some subtle aspects of our analyses are not clear-cut. Some of our risk-benefit assessments fall beneath the surface of our conscious beings.

Consider Joe for a moment. In the flash of an instant he must make a decision as to whether he will provide Roger with the industry data needed for his department's presentation. Here is a list of some of the questions that may pop into Joe's head:

- What has Roger done for me lately?
- Do I owe Roger?
- Is the quake the real reason for Roger's unpreparedness?
- Will the data give Roger an advantage over me?
- Can I take advantage of Roger's lack of preparedness?
- Is it ethical to help Roger given his situation?
- What favor might I gain in return in the future?
- What is Roger's past history in asking for information?

- Is Roger's balance sheet of knowledge, compared to mine, positive or negative?
- Can I leverage my position with Roger to gain other advantages?

The list of topics and questions considered in this brief instance is both complex and comprehensive. It is an advanced algorithm. The aggregate calculation of pros and cons is completed within seconds. Whether Roger's request comes via e-mail, phone call, text or other means of communication, the same task of analyzing risks and benefits occur. We do not give away power without gaining something in return that we feel is at least proportional to the price of the information we are sharing. That something may be a future favor, an immediate trade, the building of our own brand, a benevolent feeling or any of a number of other commodities. Ultimately, if the price exceeds any foreseen benefit, we will choose not to share the knowledge. Our rational minds will tell us to hoard instead.

It is human nature to seek security and safety, and power awards these things. Therefore, acquiring knowledge is a natural way of ensuring these feelings. But because of this, we also negotiate whether information is shared or hoarded. At a very individual level we must determine to our best abilities whether information is best leveraged through sharing it with others or through keeping it to ourselves. This perspective varies depending on the values of an individual, and these values can be influenced by the dynamics of the group.

Some groups promote hoarding while others promote sharing. The nature of the individuals in the group, the incentive structure in the group, the position of individuals in the group and other factors affect the knowledge-sharing environment. To some extent, even the overriding culture of society may influence this behavior. Though all of these aspects are important and offer avenues through which to promote informational collaboration, the final decision whether to share knowledge or not boils down to a knowledge-power analysis by the individual holding the informational asset.

Culture's Influence Over Knowledge Sharing

Without question, specific individual characteristics influence whether a person chooses to share or hoard knowledge. Depending on which factors the person feels are most important, the decision may swing either way. But from a global perspective, knowledge sharing clearly has greater benefits to mankind. The collaboration of knowledge between groups facilitates greater efficiency and progress within an organization. Sharing knowledge among organizations creates greater achievements within a society. Improved information sharing between nations creates better cultural understanding, tolerance and peace. The bottom line is that dispersion of information is the means by which productive innovation and progress are realized.

So how can we as individuals in group interactions create environments conducive to knowledge sharing? Interestingly, many of our natural reactions are defined by our own social culture. Around the world, societies can be characterized as either individualistic or collectivistic. By definition, *individualism* describes decisions and behaviors that are primarily governed by the needs of the individual. Individualists believe that following the pursuits of self-interest is the best way to promote greater quality of life for all of society. This perspective, to a great extent, is held by most Western cultures and tends to favor knowledge hoarding rather than knowledge sharing.

On the other hand, *collectivism* refers to a belief that the interests of the group are more important than the interests of the individual. By promoting a collection of individual assets, benefits for everyone can be achieved to a much greater extent than if everyone pursued his or her own individual interests. In other words, the sum is greater than its parts. This view tends to be consistent with most Eastern philosophies and, of course, it favors greater knowledge sharing than hoarding.

Which one is correct may be a matter of perspective and philosophical opinion. If you recall, however, knowledge is power, and greater knowledge is achieved through a stepping-stone type of progress. Greater supply of knowledge facilitates innovation and creativity, and thus informational progress is best achieved when individuals share knowledge within a teamwork structure. Unfortunately, sharing information does not come naturally for Americans. As individuals, we are each seeking to attain the American dream, and the common mentality embedded within our culture teaches us that uniqueness, individuality and self-interest are the traits most admired. This hardly encourages knowledge sharing.

In a study of forty-eight management trainees, half from Western societies and the other from Eastern societies, tasks were given to each group to complete. Some trainees in each group were assigned tasks designed for individualistic efforts while the others were assigned group-focused tasks. As expected, the Eastern-society group of managers flourished in group activities while the Western-society group did better in individualistic assignments. But which one is better or worse in terms of information growth and progress?

The "I" societies of the world are touted as being more creative and innovative simply by nature of their individualism. The inherent conformity of the "we" societies to promoting group goals is assumed to suppress creativity and uniqueness. But in relation to information sharing, "I" societies must barter and negotiate information amongst themselves while information flows more freely within "we" societies. Ultimately, the question remains unanswered as to whether one social culture favors progress and growth more than another because of this.

In considering the ideal society, perhaps a culture that encourages the best of both worlds would be ideal. An individualistic society that also participates in groups and organizations designed to promote information sharing may indeed offer the best chances of creativity, innovation and progress. We will explore some of these considerations, but it is important to realize that social barriers exist in our culture in cultivating such a climate. Group dynamics need to be powerful in their ability to encourage information sharing in order to overcome individualistic tendencies.

Factors Encouraging Knowledge Sharing

Establishing group dynamics that promote informational sharing is not as difficult as it may sound. However, it does take a conscious decision to promote such behaviors. If we do not, the tendency is for group members simply to convert to their individualistic ways and hoard information in order to gain more power. The following are some areas to consider when assessing group dynamics of knowledge sharing.

Incentive Structures

How a group defines incentives can be overt or occult. For example, a group that awards a title or prize to the most-productive individual is offering an overt incentive for individual production. Conversely, assumed social favor among group leaders and members for being the most productive may be an occult incentive for individual achievement. Both are powerful, and both influence people's behaviors within a group setting. The challenge is defining existing group incentives and altering them to achieve desired behaviors that favor knowledge sharing.

In designing incentive structures that favor collectivism while still encouraging individualism, it pays to stay open-minded. One method may be to mix both individual and group incentives together. For example, one could encourage creative efforts among group members to promote individualism but only award success at the group level. In this way, knowledge hoarding on the part of one person would promote the individual's success at the expense of the group. As a result, other group members would frown upon this behavior, causing an occult disincentive, and the group would fail to receive its overt collective reward.

Unfortunately, this does not always go as planned. Unanticipated group incentives for knowledge hoarding can still develop. Increased popularity within the group because of a person's greater knowledge (and power) can sometimes occur despite group incentives. But if the incentives for group success are powerful enough, these tendencies can remain minor and encourage some degree of individual creativity and innovation. This combination often creates a good structure for success.

The Inherent Natures of Group Members

The decision to share or hoard information even in collectivist societies is determined by individuals. As a result, the nature of an individual within the group is a significant component of whether knowledge is shared or not. But how can groups encourage knowledge sharing when the beliefs, values and attitudes of the individuals are the key determinants? The answer involves an attempt to align the individuals' beliefs, values and attitudes with those of the group.

In addition to group culture, the feeling of trust is significant in encouraging knowledge sharing. If a person does not feel that he or she can trust information with another group member, then a natural barrier to knowledge sharing will occur. For example, my willingness to share all of my personal feelings with my wife is based on a complete level of trust with her that is not evident with any other person. In order to promote trust, group values should be defined and practiced on a constant basis. Consistency and the passage of time are essential ingredients in developing trust among group members, and without trust, the group culture is unlikely to foster collaborative efforts.

Other values and attitudes that encourage knowledge sharing include respect, honesty, candidness, charity and the sharing of other commodities besides knowledge. When these are fostered in the group setting, the entire environment becomes less antagonistic and more cooperative. Likewise, group members begin to adopt the same values and attitudes as the collective group. The more these values, attitudes and behaviors are facilitated, the more likely a collaborative informational environment will develop.

Members' Feelings of Security

While this may be a more powerful factor in work-related groups, an underlying feeling of security has a direct impact on whether knowledge is shared in any group setting. For example, if an employee feels that cutbacks are around the corner and that some of the team may lose their jobs, then the employee may hoard information to make himself or herself appear more powerful and useful to the team and the organization. In turn, this can be detrimental to the team's efforts in an environment wherein things are already strained.

By promoting group incentives and positive group values, this tendency can be minimized. However, human nature, especially in Western cultures, will tend to shift the balance toward knowledge hoarding when situations of threatened security exist. Therefore, additional measures to offset these tendencies may be required in order to best encourage group collaboration.

Depending on the situation, reassurances may or may not be possible. If job loss is inevitable for some members of the group, then transparency and information provided to the entire group about the situation are often the best actions. Knowing what is happening and what factors will determine job loss or security allows group members to plan for their own individual situations. However, this may cause premature loss of members or employees. The risks and benefits of this transparency in preserving open communication and informational sharing have to be considered.

In contrast, transparency is always encouraged if reassurances can be given. A lack of information about what might be happening will always promote feelings of insecurity and paranoia. These feelings can be quickly dissolved by providing favorable knowledge about the group situation. When information does not flow freely into the group, then information sharing within the group is less likely as well. Knowledge, as always, is power, and more power given to a person will allow him or her to feel more secure.

The External Environment

The environment outside of the group can also influence tendencies toward informational collaboration and sharing. These may or may not be susceptible to influence, but in some organizations these external dynamics offer other opportunities to foster knowledge sharing and growth. Competition among groups, organizational cultures and group opportunities are just a few of the important aspects exerting external influences.

Let's take competition, for example. If several groups are competing for results in similar tasks, the competition itself can serve as a unifying force within the group. In other words, the group has not only a common goal but also a common competitor. This tends to draw members of a group closer together and to encourage shared knowledge in order to successfully meet the group's goals and overcome group competitors in the process.

The downside of such competition is the hindrance of shared knowledge among groups from a larger perspective. When groups compete, a natural tendency to hoard knowledge within groups develops. Just as knowledge hoarding by the individual limits group success, the same process among groups limits an organization's success. This will be discussed in more detail in the next chapter. The challenge is to create a healthy environment of competition among groups within the organization while still defining a common goal for everyone.

Organizational cultures tend to have trickle-down effects. If organizations tend to be secretive and nontransparent, then groups within the organization will be less likely to act in a cooperative and collaborative fashion when it comes to information. In other words, as the upper level "suits" behave, so will the employees. Senior management tends to be a microcosm of the rest of the organization. The overriding culture has to support the subculture. To expect a group to embrace consistently healthy knowledge sharing practices when the external environment does not is unrealistic.

Consistency in promoting knowledge sharing and collaboration is the important ingredient in this recipe. By fostering incentives, encouraging group success and creating positive cultures for knowledge sharing, groups will naturally migrate toward a collaborative and cooperative style of interaction among their members. By maintaining some degree of individualism within the group and enhancing the growth of intellectual capital, creativity and innovation will be more readily apparent.

IGO Learning

Much of the individual creativity that democratic societies encourage stems from the belief that power is distributed equally among all people. In other words, the freedoms of speech and expression and the right to be counted in society through our right to vote empower each person to pursue their dreams with their unique talents. This cultivates innovation to a great degree.

If knowledge is power and the dissemination of power encourages this same innovation, then knowledge sharing works toward the same goal as individualism. But as we have discussed, collectivism fosters knowledge sharing to a greater extent than individualism. The ultimate goal is therefore to create a process by which individual knowledge and creativity are converted into group knowledge and, eventually, organizational learning. This gives us the best of all worlds.

IGO learning (I=individual, G=group, O=organizational) is simply the means by which systematic processes allow the knowledge of the individual to be transferred to the group and, subsequently, the organization. The learning dynamics and processes of a group have been discussed in this chapter, and in the next we will address the same at an organizational level. As you might imagine, these become progressively more complex. For the individual, the problem was information bombardment. For the group, the dilemma can be information hoarding. But at the organizational level, it is the loss of intellectual capital that poses the biggest threat.

FURTHER READING

Managing organizational knowledge: http://www.Bontis.com/ic/publications/IJTMBontis.pdf

Intellectual capital models: http://www.Bontis.com/ic/publications/MDBontis.pdf

Knowledge economics: http://www.Bontis.com/ic/publications/KnowledgeEconomicsBontisHartBeat.pdf

Individualism vs. collectivism: http://www.via-web.de/individualism-versus-collectivism

Scan QR code for direct link to website, hypertext links and other resources:

CHAPTER 15

Impact at the Organizational Level

When I first graduated from university, I went back home to live with my parents in Scarborough, Ontario. My first job was working for one of Canada's largest banks. Every day I would struggle amidst a mass of humanity on the train toward downtown before finally arriving at the tall skyscraper where I worked. It was there that I gained my first experiences in how large organizations functioned.

Working as a mutual fund analyst, I began to hone my skills in corporate valuation. Despite my business school education and the ever-present GAAP (generally accepted accounting principles), it soon became clear that an organization's value was more than simply the bottom line of assets minus liabilities on the balance sheet.

If you took all of Microsoft's assets and liabilities, you would be able to create a balance sheet that defined the actual book value of the company. But the value of Microsoft's stock on Wall Street would not come anywhere close to this figure. At one point, Microsoft traded at $25 per share with nine billion shares outstanding. This gave the company a market value of $225 billion. However, the book value of the company as quantified by generally accepted accounting principles was only $45 billion. What was the difference between the two values? I soon came to realize that the gap between the two figures was attributable to intellectual capital.

Nobel Prize winner James Tobin is responsible for developing the Tobin's Q ratio, which compares market value to the actual replacement value of a company's assets. The higher the ratio, the greater amount of intangible assets a company possesses. For the above Microsoft example, the Tobin's Q ratio was 5.0 (225 divided by 45), indicating that its market value was five times greater than its book value. While growth potential, competitive advantage and a firm's patent portfolio all play roles in its value, intellectual capital is increasingly the main explanation for why so many firms have high Tobin's Q ratios today.

Let's not forget that Tobin envisioned that the Q ratio would tend toward a value of one in the long run. That in fact the market value of a firm (what we pay for a stock on the exchange) would be equal to what the accountants say the firm is worth (the book value as presented within the financial statements). However, as we accelerate into the information era with knowledge-intensive organizations such as Google, Microsoft, RIM and Apple leading the way, I don't see many firms approaching the Tobin Q level of one any time soon.

Intellectual capital is the most important asset of today's era. It is intangible, elusive and poorly quantified in most settings. Plus, it does not adhere to the basic economic principles of supply and demand. Demand never ceases and often accelerates as supply rises. Intellectual capital hides in individuals' brains, group dynamics, organizational processes and the firm's brand within the marketplace. Despite valid attempts to devise methods for quantifying it, codifying intellectual capital remains a challenge.

In 1991, Leif Edvinsson of Sweden was the first to develop a measurement framework of a company's intellectual capital. Working for an insurance organization called Skandia, Edvinsson and his colleagues included a measurement of intellectual capital in their annual report alongside the other traditional assets of the corporation. Measurement items were developed as proxies of intellectual capital and included investments in employee training, new technologies being used, computer literacy, employee turnover rates and the number of new business ideas being implemented. As it turned out, the intellectual capital report was a strong indicator of whether the organization enjoyed future success or not.

What Leif Edvinsson soon figured out was that whereas traditional financial statements were accurate depictions of past economic activity, intellectual capital reports were strong leading indicators of future performance. While analyzing financial statements and potential mutual fund transactions, I knew that this was a huge revelation. But it would take a journalist to bring the field of intellectual capital to the masses.

In June 1991, Tom Stewart was on the board of editors of *Fortune* magazine. After assessing various methods of evaluating intellectual capital, he determined that one thing became evident. Intellectual capital was composed of three key sub-units: human capital, structural capital and relational capital. Tom Stewart wrote a poignant cover story in *Fortune* outlining the prominent role that these units of intellectual capital played in the context of firm innovation, competitiveness and market position. As soon as I read the article, my jaw dropped. I was in awe. This was exactly what I was looking for. This magazine issue changed my life. Just as the cover story's title exclaimed, "Brainpower is a company's most valuable asset."

This was the inciting event that changed my career direction from financial analyst to academic researcher. I spent the next several years back in school, conducting research around the world for my doctoral studies. I further developed the initial conceptualizations and measures introduced by Tom Stewart. Two decades later, these terms are now commonplace, with rich descriptions and a significant following within academic research and professional practice.

Human capital is the stock of knowledge that exists at the individual level in an organization. Since this knowledge resides primarily in the minds of employees, it is often thought of as tacit and thus difficult to codify and transfer. Some would argue that all of an organization's knowledge exists only in the minds of employees. However, it is not that simple, since organizational knowledge also exists in other forms. For example, in structural capital, which is the knowledge left behind when employees go home for the evening.

An organization with strong structural capital offers a supportive culture that allows individuals to try, fail, learn and try again. The essence of structural capital is the knowledge embedded in the routines of an organization. It is external to the employee but internal to the firm. Structural capital deals with the mechanisms and structures of the organization that can help to support employees in their quests for optimum performance. An employee can have a high level of intellect, but if the organization provides poor systems and procedures, its overall intellectual capital will not reach its fullest potential. Organizing intellectual assets with information systems can turn individual know-how into group knowledge.

Relational capital is comprised of customer and supplier relationships, knowledge of market channels and an understanding of the impact of governmental or industry associations. Although many managers recognize the importance of relational capital, they often have a difficult time tapping into the wealth of knowledge that exists in their clients and suppliers. The knowledge embedded in an organization's network of relationships is a powerful vehicle for success. Understanding what customers want can be the difference between a leader and a follower.

Being able to estimate and quantify each of these important elements in an organization is critical to the overall management of its intangible assets. In essence, a firm's intellectual capital defines whether it is growing or declining in value.

While intellectual capital is the brainpower of an organization, knowledge management is the learning ability and the flow of information that enables a company to increase its intellectual capital stock. An organization can have a significant degree of intellectual capital under its roof, but if efforts are not taken to protect it, value can precipitously drop. Like any asset, intellectual capital must be utilized in order for an organization to thrive. Despite this realization, many CEOs estimate that only twenty percent of all corporate knowledge is actually being used within their companies.

As of 2005, approximately twenty-five percent of the nation's top Fortune 500 companies had appointed chief knowledge officers (CKOs) for the purpose of protecting and growing the intellectual capital within their organizations. This figure has since remained steady. However, in Canada, CKOs are only evident in approximately five percent of the largest corporations. Indeed, the responsibility of measuring, managing and developing intellectual capital must go beyond the role of a senior executive who sits at the mahogany table. Intellectual capital management is the responsibility of all employees in the firm.

Human Capital

The most important component of intellectual capital is human capital. This is the knowledge that lies within the minds of the employees or members of an organization. Unfortunately, this knowledge is not easily transferred, nor is it easily codified. Human capital not only includes explicit knowledge but also tacit knowledge within skills, expertise and behaviors necessary to perform various tasks. Because of the intangible nature of such knowledge, human capital is difficult to quantify and capture.

Some examples of tacit knowledge include decision-making skills, innovative creativity and improvisation. These qualities comprise a large part of human capital within an organization and cannot easily be bottled and packaged for the organization to put on a shelf and reuse when necessary. It is very important to try nonetheless. If this component of intellectual capital is lost because an employee walks out the door, then the organization's overall stock value drops accordingly. This decline in value would be no different from an employee leaving with an expensive piece of equipment.

For example, consider a surgical nurse who has been with a hospital organization for twenty years. She knows all the surgeons, their skill levels, their instrument preferences and their idiosyncrasies, as well as many shortcuts around much of the operating room's bureaucracy. Because of her knowledge, the operating room runs efficiently, smoothly and consistently. This equates to higher performance and better profits for the hospital directly but also better patient outcomes and greater job satisfaction for the surgeons.

But what happens if she suddenly leaves? Has her tacit expertise been codified and measured? Has it been passed on to another surgical nurse? Then, there are further implications. Do patients receive poorer care? Do the surgeons become more stressed? Are complications more likely to arise, thereby delaying recovery?

Education makes up a significant component of human capital within an organization, but experience, attitude and even genetics play significant roles as well. We are all aware (even though it may not be said out loud) that different individuals have different genetic abilities to acquire and process knowledge. Likewise, we all have different life and job experiences that award us different skills. Even our personalities create different individual approaches to various tasks that either increase or decrease our potentials to acquire knowledge. All of this comprises the human capital of an organization.

In essence, human capital is the collection of individuals' intellects within the organization, and the scope of human capital is only limited by the capacity of the organization's members to acquire and possess knowledge in all its forms. It is the ultimate source of innovation and strategic renewal within an organization. As a result, the failure to attempt its identification, codification and measurement serves as a significant disservice to the organization as a whole.

Structural Capital

Understanding the importance of human capital in assessing an organization's intellectual capital is straightforward. After all, human beings possess knowledge. So, human capital is an essential part of an organization's knowledge stock. But what about the policies, procedures and systems an organization has in place? These also contain a great deal of inherent information and knowledge. At first glance, this may not be obvious.

Several weeks ago, I had lunch with an old friend. He is a physician who initially began as a private practitioner in the community. Now he is one of the leaders of a regional healthcare system and manages the clinical administrative division. When he first completed medical residency, he made the decision to join a group practice of five physicians. Their ages were quite varied, and the two oldest were nearing the ends of their careers. Through the years, the group had seen many changes in health care, and they also had adopted many processes and practices to adjust to each wave of change.

Admittedly, my friend received no formal education or training in the business of medicine. He was exceptional in his clinical skills, but overhead, profits, balance sheets and economies of scale meant nothing to him. In the midst of managed-care reform, he found himself lost in a quagmire of administrative bureaucracy. Had it not been for the practical processes and procedures in place at his new practice, he would have suffered many pains through trial and error.

Fortunately, the practice he joined provided him with the knowledge needed to operate an effective medical business. This knowledge is part of what has made him an expert in medical administration today.

While the physicians in the practice had a great deal knowledge regarding medical administration, none of them directly provided him with their knowledge. Instead, he acquired the knowledge simply from the systems already in place. This reflects the organization's structural capital, which is a critical component of intellectual capital that is often overlooked. Because this knowledge is embedded within daily routines, its presence may not be readily apparent. But without it, an organization's ability to function and flourish would be significantly diminished.

The elements of structural capital are many. They involve an organization's efficiency, procedural innovations, access to information and ability to codify information for easy storage and transfer. These intangible aspects of an organization's operational flow can be just as hard to quantify as an individual's tacit knowledge. But capturing and codifying these components are good places to start and provide the means for organizational learning.

Structural capital is everything left in the organization after all the employees leave for the day. Policies, procedures, methods and systems that remain provide the foundations of structural capital. Structural capital can be divided into technological components and architectural components. Technological components are the basic abilities of an organization to function. In contrast, architectural components are how these abilities can be integrated and provide a means for developing new abilities.

Basic technological components might include how an organization communicates, how it assesses risk, how it manages sales and how consumer databases are maintained. These are fundamental parts of an organization, and within them an abundance of knowledge exists. This knowledge was created for the organization by numerous individuals over years of existence. Many of the individuals and their human capital may be gone, but some of their human capital was transferred into the structural capital of the organization.

Architectural components allow these technological components to be integrated and quantified. When this fails, a loss of knowledge can occur. For example, communication methods may be adequate for sales procedures but not for codifying information databases. Risk assessment methods may favor greater organizational profits, but they may offer little when developing a creative environment for employees. An organization's architectural function provides a larger view of efficiency, productivity and growth and promotes organizational learning.

When an organization does not pay attention to structural capital, many threats to success can develop. These will be covered shortly. Organizations that support strong structural capital assets are those that foster experimentation and tolerate some degree of failure. Creativity and innovation is encouraged through this type of environment. As a result, the structural capital stock of the organization grows, and so does its value.

Relational Capital

My first-ever summer job was as a bylaw enforcement clerk at the local city hall. I sat in a five-foot-square cubicle where I answered a phone all day long. From nine o'clock in the morning until five in the evening I received various calls from individuals who were seeking information about city bylaws. For example, people wanted to know about the rules related to how often the grass needed to be cut on their front lawns, what sort of pets were prohibited, how loud a stereo could be played in a house and the exact location and dimensions of a property line so that a fence could be erected.

By the end of the summer, I knew the city's bylaws by heart! I had become an expert. Indeed, I was one of the city's most valuable human capital assets. I also understood the procedures and systems that were required to dispatch a city inspector, and I had a full understanding of the penalties that could be imposed if a bylaw infraction was confirmed. Almost all of the city maps and housing blueprints were housed in the basement warehouse at city hall (we didn't have digital copies or Google Maps back then). By the end of the summer, I could find any property's description, full specifications and dimensions faster than anyone.

Also by the end of the summer I had fielded hundreds and hundreds of bylaw enforcement requests. I had looked up hundreds of property maps and dispatched the appropriate information to homeowners and building contractors. It didn't take long for me to figure out where the inefficiencies in the system were. But was anyone willing to listen to me? Not a chance. After all, I was just the summer employee.

Indeed I possessed a great deal of human capital and was cognizant of the organization's structural capital strengths and weaknesses. But the real important asset was my full appreciation of the city's relational capital. I knew intimately the sources of information that were embedded within building contractors, homeowners, city inspectors, architects and urban planners. In short, relational capital represented the knowledge I had gained within the relationships that I had developed. Of course, all of this wonderful value went up in smoke after I returned to school that fall.

Of the three components of intellectual capital, relational capital is perhaps the most difficult to codify and measure. By nature, relational capital lies outside an organization, making it harder to collect and control. In addition, relationships are constantly changing. Customers come and go, contacts in the industry vary, regulations change, new technologies are developed and market conditions fluctuate. With the occurrence of each of these variables, relational capital changes from one day to the next. This inherent limitation on its longevity makes it all the more important to try to capture relational capital not only consistently but frequently.

For business organizations, knowing what a customer wants or doesn't want can make the difference between being a market leader and a market follower. Knowing the anticipated future technologies of vendors, partners and suppliers can provide a company with a strong competitive edge. Understanding how the market and industry will change from industry professionals and regulators enables timely development of better strategies. This is the relational capital component of intellectual capital, and like human capital and structural capital, it enables an organization to learn and grow effectively.

Threats to Organizational Learning

An organization's intellectual capital is its brainpower, and because of this I like to view an organization as a large brain. The human capital of the brain is each individual brain cell that provides key knowledge to the entire organ. The structural capital is the connection each brain cell has with other brain cells when establishing systems and networks. Finally, relational capital is the interactions these brain cells have with the body and the environment through numerous sensory receptors. In order for the brain to flourish, all of these components need to be active. But what happens when they aren't?

Suppose a stroke occurs and brain cells die, reducing the amount of cellular knowledge. Perhaps a lack of proper nutrition prevents a rich network of brain cell connections from forming. Or maybe we choose to ignore information we receive through our senses that would encourage new patterns of thinking. In a similar fashion, all of these same considerations can affect the intellectual capital of an organization. In this section, we consider the major threats to intellectual capital that are constantly present.

Attrition

Suppose you have become an expert in your field. You have gone to school and attained degrees, gaining competency in a certain domain. You have worked under the tutelage of other experts and conducted research leading to a great deal of experience. After years of demonstrating your expertise, you now sit among the leading experts in the world on your subject.

What happens now? You can just kick back and relax because you've made it to the top, right?

Wrong...unless, of course, you don't want to stay at the top. In the information era, knowledge is always growing and expanding. The amount of intellectual capital present today may enable an organization to be the top dog, but unless the organization continues to grow, its intellectual stock will be worth less and less as time passes. The organization will suffer from one of the greatest threats to intellectual capital, which is attrition.

Since information is constantly growing, an organization must keep pace, maintaining its level of intellectual capital. Even if the maximum capacity of intellectual capital is achieved, it will not stay maximized unless proactive steps are taken to replenish the organization's ever-declining level of knowledge. This is the external pressure on an organization resulting in attrition. Using the brain as an analogy again, the same process applies. Our brains never stand still but instead are constantly adjusting to a changing environment.

From a human resource perspective, attrition occurs in other ways. Illnesses, deaths and retirements cause a natural attrition of human capital and intellectual capital in an organization over time. There's no way around it. Employees will come and go and with them goes intellectual capital, unless preventative steps are taken. In contrast to the evolving external information environment, the natural loss of human capital reflects the internal forces of attrition.

No matter how smart the current people in the organization are, at some point they will depart, whether it's in a month or in thirty years. No matter how high the intellectual capital stock is today, there is no guarantee it will remain high in the future compared to others in your industry. Indeed, attrition is inevitable, but with the right strategies an organization's knowledge can be preserved.

Turnover

Like internal attrition, turnover reflects a loss of human capital in an organization and a drop in the overall level of intellectual capital. But unlike attrition, which is the natural loss of employees, turnover results when employees choose to leave or are forced to leave an organization. Layoffs, terminations and suspensions are examples in which organizations find themselves responsible for turnover. This is termed *involuntary turnover.* Other times, people may simply choose to leave on their own due to life circumstances or better opportunities. This is termed *voluntary turnover.*

The difference between internal attrition and turnover is simply whether or not the loss of human capital can be anticipated. Organizations can project retirements and a certain degree of sickness among their members, but predicting involuntary and voluntary turnover is tricky. Both attrition and turnover have the same effect on an organization's intellectual capital in the short term, and both cause the knowledge capacity to decline. But long term, turnover has a greater potential to cause harm to an organization because of competitive forces. Departing employees are likely to join competitors. Therefore, not only will your organization be losing intellectual capital but another organization will be gaining what was initially your knowledge stock.

In some industries, turnover rates are incredibly high. For

example, the health-care industry averages a twenty-percent turnover rate. In other words, one in every five individuals annually leaves his or her job to find other employment. This figure reflects a huge loss of intellectual capital every year that must be addressed. If an organization fails to pay attention to these losses, undoubtedly the overall value of the firm in terms of intellectual capital will fall. Unfortunately, in difficult economic times, many industries other than health care experience similarly high rates of turnover and are faced with these challenges.

Opportunity Costs

With both attrition and turnover, significant costs are involved. Direct costs are involved in hiring a temporary employee to fill a vacant job in the short term. Additionally, other subsequent costs are substantial and include recruiting, hiring and training a new employee for the long term. Conservative estimates project the cost of replacing an employee due to attrition or turnover as equivalent to the salary of the person leaving. If the US health-care industry payroll is believed to be approximately $250 billion, and twenty-percent turnover is expected each year, then the immediate costs of turnover are $50 billion per year. Wow!

Opportunity costs are the costs to an organization that occur as a result of a deficiency of intellectual capital. In other words, because an organization's knowledge stock has dropped, opportunities in the market and industry are lost.

Suppose your organization is a hospital system in a small community. You have a rival hospital in your catchment area, but overall you are performing well. As CEO, you arrive at work on a Monday morning to find the town's only neurosurgeon in your office. He has decided to leave your hospital. Even worse, he is considering transferring his staff privileges to your competitor.

You are confronted with a significant problem. Not only will there be tremendous costs involved in recruiting and hiring a new neurosurgeon for your hospital, but you will also be faced with a significant loss of opportunities for your hospital organization to provide comprehensive care. The hospital will no longer be able to provide neurosurgical services in general, and many other programs, such as surgical epilepsy management, trauma center care and spinal cord rehabilitation programs, will be handicapped. These are the opportunity costs of the situation simply because of a loss of intellectual capital (in the form of human capital).

Strategies to counter this will be discussed in subsequent chapters, but immediate costs are not the only effects that result from reductions in intellectual capital. Opportunity costs are often involved regardless of whether an organization is losing a neurosurgeon, an administrator or even a receptionist. Each individual has intellectual capital that is important to the organization, and each one provides unique opportunities for the organization to thrive within the market.

Knowledge Obsolescence

The goal of any organization is to recruit, hire and train individuals who possess the greatest intellectual capital. But we realize that each of us has different talents and abilities. Someone may be exceptional in creative design while another has expertise in organizational skills. Of course, pockets of ignorance sneak into the best organizations. This variation in knowledge among individuals of an organization accounts for some degree of knowledge obsolescence.

More importantly, however, knowledge obsolescence occurs even among the brightest stars of an organization in industries where change is rapidly occurring. Knowledge obsolescence is directly proportional to the velocity of change within a given industry. If technological advancement, innovative discoveries, market trends and competitive rivalry are intense and quick, then everyone in the organization must keep pace. If they don't, knowledge obsolescence becomes a very real threat on a large scale.

Consider the rapidly changing environment of newspaper media organizations. Almost overnight, technological developments forced this industry to adapt in order to survive. Failure to establish blogs, digital media outlets, online presences and a variety of interactive features meant certain doom for many traditional media organizations. In fact, many traditional newspaper journalists and companies have fallen by the wayside because they did not keep pace with the changes in the industry. Knowledge obsolescence became the disease that was eventually fatal to their companies.

The decline in an organization's intellectual capital as a result of knowledge obsolescence is easy to understand from the standpoint of individuals within the organization. But failure to keep pace with changes by altering structural processes and relational capital assessments can be just as devastating. Knowledge obsolescence can affect any of the three components of intellectual capital unless assertive knowledge management tools are implemented.

Duplication Costs

My first lesson in duplication costs came when I began working for a large bank in Toronto. I was young, energetic and determined to make a big impression. My first day on the job, my supervisor gave me a special project. I was to research and collect all the information and data available about the mutual fund industry in order for our bank to launch its own product. In essence, this was a competitive intelligence-gathering exercise.

After enthusiastically accepting my assignment, I went to check out my cubicle and prepare for the task given to me. In my tiny space stood a six-drawer filing cabinet, and of course my first inclination was to see what was inside. But all the drawers were locked (with no labels), and no one in the office had a key. Oh well. Even though it took up considerable space, I worked around it.

For the next several weeks, I went into each of our competitors' branches undercover, disguised as a customer. I elicited information from the branch managers all the way down to the call-center operators. I collected annual reports and mutual fund statements and prepared codified summaries of every interview and telephone call I made. In other words, I was collecting other organizations' intellectual capital. After I had gathered all of this data, I then analyzed and prepared my report for the bank's executive staff with my own recommendations. I was ready to make a big impression on my superiors.

Being that the presentation was the following day, I wanted to keep the final draft of my report in a safe place. The filing cabinet was an obvious consideration, but it remained locked.

After asking everyone in the bank about how I might open it, I finally gave up and called my friend Hank. Hank can break into anything. For twenty dollars and half my lunch, Hank had the filing cabinet open within a few minutes. It was then that I realized that I should have called Hank four months prior. I stood in horror as I peered into each folder! Inside the filing cabinet lay every mutual fund report and database for every bank throughout Canada. Needless to say, I was devastated.

I confronted my manager about the files; she knew nothing. I then confronted her manager about the files; he knew nothing. Finally, I climbed this ladder of ignorance all the way to the bank's president. He casually put his arm on my shoulder and said, "Nick, sorry, I forgot. We asked another intern to compile that report six months ago. I guess we won't need that report from you after all, and by the way, we should cancel that presentation you have scheduled tomorrow for the senior executive team. Have a nice day."

For four months I had invested countless hours in researching, analyzing and summarizing data for this report. Think of the costs in payroll hours and benefits this accrued for the organization. Then think of the lost-opportunity costs that resulted from my not working on another project. Then consider the lack of utility the report in the filing cabinet had provided. All of these represent duplication costs. It is often the case in very large organizations that the right hand does not know what the left hand is doing. Intellectual capital is being duplicated because the structural processes in place are causing a poor utilization of knowledge. The end result is poor efficiency, poor organizational learning and one very unhappy employee—me.

A couple of weeks later, I attended a regional orientation

meeting along with other new employees working for the bank. As it turned out, I met a guy in my same position from the Montreal branch...and guess what. He was working on a project researching and compiling data on the mutual fund industry for his supervisor as well! This confirmed for me a simple truth: the bank was dumb! There was very little appreciation for intellectual capital and surely very little evidence that any knowledge-management processes were in place. Instead of learning as a company and increasing its intellectual capital, it was slowly becoming more ignorant and more stupid every day. Duplication costs were running rampant.

The Next Step

In today's business world, knowledge is power. Intellectual capital imparts the greatest value to an organization. Minimizing the threats to intellectual capital loss and maximizing the acquisition of knowledge are the keys to success today. The entire purpose of effective knowledge management is to create a flow of information within the organization that encourages learning while protecting the intellectual capital stock of the company that is already present. Failure to invest in these efforts will result in a declining value in the best-case scenario and possibly organizational failure in the worst.

We have now seen how the effective management of information (or lack thereof) affects individuals, groups and organizations differently. Next we will look at institutions. With each successive level, the stakes get a little higher. Individual problems with knowledge management gaps affect personal lives. Group problems affect team efficiency and growth. Organizational errors in knowledge management cause significant costs and lost market opportunities. But with institutions, the risks are even greater.

FURTHER READING

Price to book for valuation: http://www.investopedia.com/articles/fundamental/03/112603.asp

P/E and P/B ratios: http://lloydsinvestment.blogspot.com/2007/09/are-stocks-with-high-price-to-book.html

Organizational collaboration: http://www.NickBontis.com/BontisHRProInterview.pdf

Assessing knowledge assets: http://www.Bontis.com/ic/publications/IJMRBontis.pdf

Misalignment of stocks and flows: http://www.Bontis.com/ic/publications/JMSBontis.pdf

Turnover and knowledge management: http://www.business.mcmaster.ca/mktg/nbontis//ic/publications/JICStovelBontis.pdf

Cost of turnover: http://tinyurl.com/32j48b6

Knowledge obsolescence in journalism: http://www.american.edu/soc/news/Journalism-Alumnae-Discuss-Reinvention-Amidst-Ever-Changing-Industry.cfm

Scan QR code for direct link to website,
hypertext links and other resources:

CHAPTER 16

Impact at the Institutional Level

President Bill Clinton once said, "Being president is like running a cemetery: you've got a lot of people under you and nobody's listening." Perhaps this was his feeling about the distribution of information throughout the government. President George W. Bush, on *Good Morning America* six days after Hurricane Katrina, stated, "I don't think anybody anticipated the breach of the levees." Of course, experts for days before had warned of the levee disruption as part of the massive potential for damage. Knowledge management was far less than optimal in this situation.

More recently, President Obama stated, "The US government had sufficient information to have uncovered this plot and potentially disrupt the Christmas Day attack, but our intelligence community failed to connect those dots." Again, the shortcomings in information sharing among intelligence sources were identified. Even large, multinational corporations could do no better. When the CEO of BP finally responded to the oil spill crisis in the Gulf of Mexico, he said, "I'm sure many of you have been watching the plume. All I can say is it is unlikely to give us any real indication of what is going on. Either increases or decreases are not an indicator of either success or failure at this time." Pardon me, what the &#@%

does that mean? How about the pending eruption of the Eyjafjallajökull volcano in Iceland? Why was their no integrated coordination of the implications for cross-Atlantic airline travel? Isn't it scary to consider that some airlines chose to continue flying as usual while volcanic ash was spewed into the stratosphere, though others cancelled flights?

Another example is the debt crisis in Greece and the corresponding market malaise of the EU. One of the main culprits that precipitated the financial crisis was the selective (i.e., reported and unreported) revenue and income reporting of many businesses in Greece. Essentially, this is another example of hoarding information and the resulting repercussions.

Problems with knowledge management become even more significant when we look at things from an institutional level. Individuals have the ability to choose for themselves how they will manage their own productivity. Groups and organizations likewise have some degree of internal control over their intellectual capital and knowledge processes. But a declining degree of control often occurs among organizations and within social institutions. Policies and procedures are less stringent and subject to a variety of external pressures. While all the same barriers to positive information sharing exist within organizations, the ability to implement effective strategies of knowledge management among institutions at the cross-organizational level is a greater challenge.

In 2005, one of the deadliest hurricanes ever to strike the US devastated the city of New Orleans and many areas of Louisiana and Mississippi. The number of lives lost was more than 1,800, most of whom were elderly and/or disabled. In the aftermath, it was evident that this loss of life could have been prevented. In fact, one year before Hurricane Katrina struck, an institutional exercise among multiple agencies was conducted to simulate the effects of a catastrophic hurricane. Under the name Hurricane Pam, this fictitious storm portrayed nearly the exact same characteristics as Katrina.

Local city officials, state officials, members of FEMA (the Federal Emergency Management Agency), DHS (the Department of Homeland Security) and representatives of the National Weather Service were involved in the development and results of this simulation exercise in emergency management. But a few months after they adjourned, and after they agreed to implement steps toward an effective solution, funds for developing the needed infrastructure were cut by the Bush administration. Communication, transportation and other emergency services were never completed as promised. The group never reconvened to consider alternative options.

When Katrina actually hit, local emergency services were overwhelmed. Communications broke down as the storm leveled the city. FEMA officials blamed the federal administration for a lack of support and blamed local and state services for lacking adequate mobilization of transportation. Local and state officials blamed FEMA for a lack of support and a failure to activate federal assistance. National Guard teams were rendered ineffective due to lack of communication. Nursing home staff aborted policies and procedures and chose to save themselves, leaving patients behind to die. What little information planning was in place was either inadequate for the situation or aborted, or both.

Despite the lessons learned during 9/11 regarding the vital need of portable communications for emergency service workers, no system had been devised in the four years leading up to Hurricane Katrina. In fact, a $7 million grant had been given to the city of New Orleans by the DHS in 2003 for the development of such a system. But the program had stalled due to lack of federal guidance and standards for the use of funds. One side blamed the federal government while the other blamed universal state resistance to federal intervention.

Furthermore, there was a high level of miscommunication between Louisiana Governor Blanco and FEMA with regard to assistance for southeastern parishes. Her letter to FEMA indicated a dire need for assistance, but this was not reflected in the president's state of emergency declaration. Perhaps the US government wasn't even aware of the levees breaching. Were there egos involved? Or are there specific examples of information hoarding?

As a result of poor knowledge management, the primary concern was not divorce, loss of a job, loss of a business contract, loss of profits or even failure of a corporation. In this case, the concern was the loss of innocent people's lives. Within and among institutions, ineffective information flow and access carry greater risks compared to the areas already covered in this book. Additionally, larger hurdles exist for institutions as well. As demonstrated during Hurricane Katrina, the oil spill in the Gulf of Mexico, the volcano eruption in Iceland and countless other instances, the inability to convey information efficiently and effectively can have tremendous repercussions. Issues affecting such institutions will be addressed here to provide some perspective on how we, as a society and a nation, must devise better systems if we truly care about the security and safety of human lives.

Institutional Knowledge Management

How do institutions differ in processing and sharing information compared to organizations? When referring to institutions, I am referring to any type of macro-level social structure in which multiple organizations share a role. For example, education is an institution affected by many organizations ranging from PTA groups to state and federal agencies. The national institution of criminal justice is composed of branches of Congress and the Constitution all the way to local law enforcement departments. Of course the financial institution includes international entities such as banks, investment corporations and multiple national, governmental and regulatory agencies. In each of these, multiple organizations, groups and individuals must collaborate and share knowledge for effective functioning.

To a great extent, institutions have some of the same difficulties that organizations have. They are composed of multiple parts. Therefore, codifying all the intellectual capital that falls under the umbrella of the institution is a challenge. Creating the appropriate knowledge management pathways and infrastructure that promote a flow of information is critically important. In other words, structural capital plays a significant role at the macro level of analysis.

However, institutions rely more heavily on relational capital than organizations do. Within an organization, a degree of hierarchy and policy control is naturally present. An executive team or board defines what procedures are most likely to be effective and which ones will be implemented. The boundaries between supervisor and subordinate are clearly defined. However, in many institutions this leadership role can be vague. When multiple groups or organizations are part of an institutional process, one entity may not be permitted to provide leadership. There are often subtle conflicts and territorial wars that have lasted for years (e.g., FBI versus CIA, RCMP versus CSIS). This absence of clear governance can result in a lack of accountability and direction. Ultimately, this can lead to poor knowledge management.

Accelerated information sharing is best promoted when an aligned team atmosphere is present, and leadership can play a vital role in creating this culture. In the events surrounding Hurricane Katrina, plenty of teams were part of the emergency services institution. However, no one took a lead role. FEMA, DHS, local officials and state officials all failed to establish a lead position to facilitate knowledge sharing and create an effective outcome. Ultimately, every entity was left standing, pointing their fingers at everyone else. As a result, catastrophes occurred.

In other situations, too much leadership can squash information sharing and effective knowledge management. Let's take the war on terrorism for example. After 9/11, the nation was in a state of fear, and national patriotism was running high. In a knee-jerk response, President Bush, with the support of Congress, launched an all-out war not only against terrorism but also against Iraq and Saddam Hussein. Alleged weapons of mass destruction were described, and allegations that radical Islamic terrorists were being supported by Hussein were spread. This paved the way for billions of dollars and thousands of human lives to be mobilized in an effort to combat terrorism.

Unfortunately, information did not support such action. Intelligence provided to the Bush administration demonstrated that in reality, al Qaeda had little to do with Iraq. In fact, American support of radical Islamists during the Soviet War in Afghanistan had a greater role in strengthening al Qaeda than anything Iraq had ever undertaken. We also now realize that weapons of mass destruction did not exist but were simply an imagined threat. The authoritative style of leadership prevented a transparency of knowledge to those who assisted in making the political decisions, and it pushed political and emotional agendas forward unguided by factual knowledge. Thus the institution of war on a massive scale ensued.

In one of my own research studies, I assessed which parameters best promoted positive knowledge management in the setting of multinational corporations. The corporation I chose to examine had multiple subsidiaries in six different countries, and as a result it functioned as an institution composed of several organizations. In the results, I found that the reverse transfer of knowledge was a significant part of overall learning and performance improvement. What is the reverse transfer of knowledge? This is when, instead of the traditional hierarchy in most organizations, where knowledge is passed from the top downwards, the allowance of knowledge to flow also from the subsidiaries to the parent corporation (reverse transfer) is equally important.

Institutional knowledge management and learning require a balance between leadership and an open flow of information in multiple directions. Each organization or group comprising the institution has unique intellectual capital. In order for the institution to benefit, this knowledge must be available and must be shared among the other components. In addition, direction and guidance in implementing action based on this information must be in place. Failure to have both results in situations like Hurricane Katrina on one hand and the war on terrorism on the other.

A Culture of Information Sharing

On Christmas Day 2009, Umar Farouk Abdulmutallab boarded Northwest flight 253 headed for Detroit carrying enough explosives in his underpants to kill the nearly 300 people on board. As the evidence surrounding this young Nigerian was released, it became clear that a complete lack of information sharing had occurred. The number of red flags surrounding the would-be terrorist was concerning to a nation that thought such a thing could never happen in today's world of airport security.

Earlier, in May of that year, London authorities had placed Abdulmutallab on a watch list after identifying that his application for a student visa listed a bogus school. He was also known to have spent a great deal of time in Yemen, where al Qaeda cells exist and young extremist soldiers are trained. In 2009, US intelligence intercepted messages describing a Nigerian as part of a terrorist plot. The boy's father then notified the US embassy in November of his concern that Abdulmutallab may have been on a suicide mission. Yet despite this, Abdulmutallab's US tourist visa was never revoked, and he was never placed on a no-fly list. No one made the connection between all of these pieces of information until after the fact.

The classic "failure to connect the dots" was described by President Obama in the debriefing to follow. This epitomizes the culture in which (a lack of) institutional information sharing exists today. More often than not, information hoarding takes place between agencies fearing political repercussions. Incentive structures favor privacy and security at the demise of open collaboration. Critical knowledge is poorly indexed and becomes difficult (if not impossible) to access. Worse yet, rarely is someone individually held accountable. This current culture of security and safety is counterproductive to information sharing.

The Markle Foundation Task Force on National Security presented a report early in 2009 listing the key criteria needed in order to promote an environment and a culture of information sharing. Among these criteria, increased metrics of data, greater accountability, increased transparency and a change in incentive structures were included. Institutional problems in these areas had been found to exist as they pertained to national security, and these problems hindered knowledge flow among agencies and organizations. Unfortunately, these strategies have yet to be fully implemented and realized. as shown by the Christmas Day terrorist plot.

Problems within institutional cultures are not uncommon and are not specific to national security organizations. For example, consider the status of electronic medical records (EMR) within the health-care industry. Comprehensive EMR products have been available since the late 1990s, but even today different physician offices and hospital systems have medical databases that cannot be easily shared. This inability to share information still exists because numerous vendors who produce different EMR systems have no incentive to communicate with each other. They do not want to risk market share or profitability by investing in enhanced communication with other EMR systems who might steal away clients or trade secrets. So as a result, the entire healthcare institution suffers.

Useful metrics are not available on an institutional level because EMR systems "don't speak to each other." Transparency is therefore absent from one system to the next, resulting in medical tests and procedures that are often repeated. No one is held accountable because leadership demanding that these databases be transparent is lacking. Plus, there is no financial or other type of incentives for EMR companies to pursue information sharing solutions. In fact, disincentives are actually in place.

The one thing that the health-care industry and national security systems have in common is the ultimate price that is paid when information is not shared. If security intelligence fails and actions are not taken, terrorist attacks or other catastrophic events can occur. If patient information is not available fast enough in emergency situations, tragedies can ensue. Information hoarding at an institutional level carries the highest stakes if not carefully addressed.

Security and Privacy Issues

In November 2009, a Virginia couple was having the time of their lives. Well-dressed and posing with President Obama for a picture, the two had waltzed into the White House as presumed guests. The only problem was that they hadn't been invited. After several minutes of what started as a spectacular evening, the two were escorted out of the White House and threatened with criminal charges. Plenty of finger pointing ensued, as usual. The social secretary of Obama could offer little explanation as to why the couple had not been stopped at the gate, and DHS promptly blamed the social secretary for the lack of security. In the end, it was a lack of information sharing that led to the crashers gaining entry to the party.

In a time when terrorism is a constant fear in America and in an age when we have accepted many inconveniences for the sake of greater security, having two people enter the White House and shake hands with the commander in chief is unimaginable. But is it really? Once again, breakdowns in communications and information allowed a breach in security. While this is an important aspect to consider in institutional knowledge management, this is not necessarily the biggest impact poor security and violations of privacy have on institutional function.

The development of intellectual capital is best facilitated when a culture of information sharing and trust exist. Trust between individuals, groups and organizations does not always come easily, especially when the world is on edge, waiting for the next catastrophe to happen. If I don't think the information I share with you will be used wisely and protected according to its level of importance, I will likely choose to hoard it instead. I have to feel a sense of security in order to share my knowledge. Organizations and groups are no different in their decisions on whether or not to share information.

Part of the problem in many institutional settings is that privacy and security are actually too intense and deter necessary information flow. This stems from a culture of needing to know rather than being privileged to know. In the former culture, which still permeates many government and business organizations, information is only given to members or organizations that need the information to function. But defining who actually needs to know is difficult and often occurs after a need is obvious. The question is whether a need for information should be defined according to an ability to function or whether it should be defined more broadly. This definition of need has a limiting effect on information accessibility and sharing depending on how narrowly it is defined.

A culture that promotes knowledge privileges, in contrast, allows access to information based on other measures of security. A person is privileged to access information if it falls within his or her scope of possible duties. This opens up the flow of information to anyone in the institution who has adequate security clearance. Even if a need to know does not exist for a specific task, organizations and/or individuals have information access because it falls within their broader domains of responsibilities. This can enhance creativity, innovation and intra-organizational communication because each institutional component now has a better view of the big picture. Greater flow of information among components of an institution promotes teamwork and knowledge sharing. Reduced flow has the opposite effect.

Of course, security and information privacy is still very important. If entities feel that privacy rights, civil liberties or security is in question, knowledge sharing will decline regardless of accessibility. The use of information audits, access logs and technology can help in this regard. Let's not forget that technology is a big part of the reason we are being bombarded with data and information to begin with. We may as well use some of its benefits to accelerate the flow of information.

Encryption algorithms, digital rights management and IP anonymization are useful tools that promote privacy and enhance appropriate security measures.

In April 2003, the Privacy Rule became part of the Health Insurance Portability and Accountability Act, better known as HIPAA (Canada's equivalent would be PIPEDA (the Personal Information Protection and Electronic Documents Act) and Europe has the European Union Directive on Data Privacy). In essence, privacy rules for handling sensitive information, including medical and financial records, were brought under strict regulations with which the health-care and many other industries had to comply. The initial concerns of health-care administrators, doctors and nurses were that these regulations would add even further bureaucracy to the system and limit efficiency and effectiveness to an even greater extent. But what has happened since?

Like any type of change, resistance was greatest at first. Subsequently, everyone became acclimated to the change, and streamlined policies and procedures ensued. But the most significant benefit of HIPAA has been the added reassurances of patient privacy, which have enabled patients to feel more comfortable when divulging personal information. More importantly, these privacy measures have increased the abilities of systems, doctors and other health agencies to share information, which was more cumbersome previously. In other words, increased security and privacy led to better information flow. As a result, the entire institution of health care advanced in its ability to manage knowledge. This is the positive effect of knowledge flow if appropriate privacy and security measures are implemented.

Institutions Are Ultimately Composed of Individuals

The features described so far that pertain to institutional intellectual capital and knowledge management are among the most important. Security, privacy of information, accountability, metrics, accessibility and incentives are key factors in creating an environment that is trustworthy and conducive to both information sharing and collaborative behaviors. However, it is important to realize that even large institutions are still composed of individuals, and individuals are still the main sources of intellectual capital.

This fact does not preclude the greater importance of relational and structural capital in an institutional setting, but people are still the drivers of knowledge transfer and flow. In my own research I have found that person-to-person communication is essential for effective knowledge management. This pertains to institutions as much as it does to groups or organizations. Direct access to individuals within and between organizations is thus a necessary feature for institutions to promote institutional learning.

Let's consider one of the biggest institutional blunders of recent times: the Great Recession of 2007. What began as the collapse of the housing bubble quickly led to the collapse of several large banks and financial institutions that had heavily invested in mortgage-related securities. With these developments, widespread stagnation and ultimately recession occurred. In America and throughout the world, economic markets began to enter a downward spiral as governments struggled with the right solutions to minimize the damage.

It is quite easy and appropriate to assign blame in this situation to many organizations. Banks and mortgage companies that chose to lend money well above the actual value of the housing market are easy targets. Financial corporations who made credit card access at high interest rates overly accessible to consumers likewise should be considered. Investment firms who became wealthy through mortgage-based securities and then received bailout funds are certainly strong suspects. Even the government and its lack of regulation can be blamed. But in all of these instances, agencies, organizations or companies are being blamed.

The fact of the matter is that individuals within these groups, companies, firms and agencies are the drivers of information as well as behavior. Loan officers and bank executives examined information to make their decisions about mortgage risk. Stockbrokers and hedge fund operators bought and sold investments based on their knowledge of the market. Consumers chose to overextend themselves in credit debt and mortgage payments without adequate self-control. Speculators may have actually facilitated the recession based on profit-based incentives for short selling. The institution and its components created situations that favored the financial collapse, but it was individuals who made decisions one by one that resulted in the economic downturn.

I am not making this point to detract from the responsibilities of institutions and organizations. Instead I point this out to show that millions of individuals were behaving with limited information. Each group of individuals did not have an overall concept of what was transpiring throughout the entire economy. In other words, individuals only saw (or chose to see) one piece of the bigger puzzle. If more open transparency and better informational flow had been evident, perhaps the events would have not been as catastrophic as they were. Several economists predicted a collapse of the housing and credit markets more than a year in advance. But widespread knowledge sharing and direct communication between lenders, regulators, investors and consumers did not occur (and still doesn't today).

In order for institutions to thrive, individuals have to be incentivized to share knowledge and not to hoard it. They also must be in an environment and culture that favor not only knowledge sharing but also assertiveness in distributing information to others. When individuals leave an institution, their intellectual capital must be considered and retained for the sake of the institution. These are all very real and significant challenges at the institutional level of analysis.

Costs of Poor Knowledge Management

Information mismanagement at an institutional level is without question more costly than other levels of analysis, as has been demonstrated. Whether you measure the costs in dollar figures, in quality of life or in the number of human lives, knowledge hoarding and miscommunication carry significant prices within larger social institutions. Consider some of the following statistics:

Hurricane Katrina

- 400,000 jobs lost
- 600,000 pets lost or made homeless

- $110 billion in direct damages
- 1,836 deaths (third-most deadly hurricane in US history)

Great Recession

- 8.6 million jobs lost
- 15.3 million Americans out of work
- $11 trillion in US stock market losses
- 20 percent drop in median home values

9/11

- $2 trillion lost in stock market wealth
- 430,000 jobs lost
- $100 billion lost in property, goods and services
- 2,976 human lives lost

War in Iraq

- $900 billion spent or approved for war spending
- $10 billion wasted or mismanaged
- 4,390 human lives lost
- 31,762 soldiers with significant physical wounds
- 30 percent of soldiers with mental health problems after returning home

In each of these events, the losses can be attributed to a significant degree to poor knowledge management. The inability of multiple agencies and organizations to plan effectively for Katrina has already been described. The miscommunication and hoarding of information between many branches of US intelligence provided a barrier that could have prevented 9/11. Lack of leadership and oversight was a major cause of our recent economic crisis. The War in Iraq (as well as the war on terrorism) reflects a degree of autocratic governance and a resistance to the full utilization of the intellectual capital available. In each case, billions of dollars were lost and thousands of human lives affected.

As we move from our personal problems related to information bombardment toward higher macro levels of analysis, the stakes become more significant. We might suffer from poor relationships, poor mental and physical health and an overall poor quality of life if we manage knowledge poorly; and at a group and organizational level, poor knowledge management can lead to poor efficiency and productivity, causing risks of organizational failure and losses of jobs. But at institutional levels, all of these areas are affected in addition to the general society. Often, institutional crises even affect global function, as was evident in the Great Recession and in 9/11.

Properly managing knowledge and information begins with us as individuals. If this can be done effectively in our personal lives, then we can manage information more effectively in the groups and organizations to which belong. Subsequently, the same tools used to improve intellectual capital and knowledge flow in these settings can be applied at institutional levels. We are the building blocks that lead to better knowledge management, and we are the ones who can reduce the costs to society.

A Positive Note

In October 2002, two men traveled by car around the Washington DC beltway, randomly targeting suspects in shopping malls, gas stations and parking lots with sniper fire over a seven-and-a-half-week period. They become known as the DC or Beltway snipers, and all totaled the two men killed ten innocent people and wounded five others. These statistics do not sound positive in any capacity. However, the methods that led to the eventual arrest of these two men reflect how institutional teamwork, leadership and individual participation can lead to effective dissemination of information.

Multiple agencies and organizations were involved in the investigation. The FBI, the Secret Service, the Bureau of Alcohol, Tobacco and Firearms, the Virginia Department of Transportation and multiple police departments in the Washington DC, Maryland and Virginia areas collaborated on solving this crime. Notable also was the leadership of Charles Moose, the police department chief of Montgomery County, Maryland, where the shootings began. Despite federal and state involvement, he was an effective leader, coordinating all these resources while maintaining adequate transparency of information for the public.

During the investigation, the two snipers boasted about another unsolved killing in Montgomery, Alabama, which provided a key clue in solving the case. Crime analysts in Alabama and Virginia were able to match some lifted fingerprints, identifying one of the men. Federal and state background checks then led to a historical association between this man and the other killer as well as a recently purchased vehicle registered to one of them. Multiple local police departments then confirmed that the vehicle had been in the vicinity of three of the shootings.

Chief Moose immediately released a public statement to the media regarding the identification of the vehicle and the two men. On October 24, 2002, a civilian notified police of the vehicle's being parked at a rest stop along interstate I-70 in Maryland, and the two suspects were finally arrested. This real-life story is a great example of how the full intellectual capital of all entities was harvested and leveraged efficiently and effectively for shutting down the perpetrators.

Despite the challenges of holding a multistate investigation with many agencies involved, the criminal justice institution worked effectively with the public and all of its resources in solving the crime. Strong leadership, a proper balance between transparency and security, information sharing and accessibility enabled a team success that even involved the public. Though many lives were lost, countless others were saved because of the efficiency and effectiveness of how information was managed. This is the real impact and benefit of good knowledge management.

REFERENCES

Christmas Day bomber: http://tinyurl.com/32nfdfe

Markle report on national security: http://www.markle.org/downloadable_assets/20090304_mtf_report.pdf

National intellectual capital index: http://www.Bontis.com/ic/publications/JICBontisUN.pdf

White House crashers: http://tinyurl.com/39jftrf

Subprime mortgage collapse: http://tinyurl.com/2cejpfe

Market manipulation: http://www.globalresearch.ca/index.php?context=va&aid=10529

Hurricane Katrina facts: http://www.hurricanekatrinarelief.com/faqs.html

Great recession continues: http://online.wsj.com/article/SB10001424052748703837004575013592466508822.html

Great Recession statistics: http://www.huffingtonpost.com/2009/10/10/the-statistics-of-the-gre_n_316548.html

Iraq War stats: http://usliberals.about.com/od/homelandsecurit1/a/IraqNumbers.htm

Washington DC sniper case: http://www.pbs.org/newshour/bb/law/sniper/

Digital state: http://www.digitalstate.org

Scan QR code for direct link to website, hypertext links and other resources:

CHAPTER

17

Individual Prescriptions

Diagnosing a problem is usually easier than solving it. The National Weather Service forecasters knew well in advance that Hurricane Katrina was headed for the Gulf Coast, but addressing how to handle the catastrophe was a different matter. BP and the rest of the world understood that a breach in machinery had caused an underwater oil geyser, but finding a time-efficient solution was another issue altogether. Likely, you also realize that you are overwhelmed by information in your personal life, but because of pressures to stay informed you don't have the answers to help you make an effective change.

Never fear! While a large part of my discussions have been spent identifying and explaining the problems of information bombardment and poor intellectual capital management, I will now offer several therapeutic solutions to help you. Some tools are effective at individual levels of analysis while others assist with intellectual capital management at group, organizational or even institutional levels. These techniques and strategies are means by which you can gain control over the ever-increasing volumes of information headed your way each and every day.

Depending on which areas are of the greatest interest to you,

I have categorized my prescriptions for action into different levels. If you find that you lack personal time for yourself and your family because the knowledge era has gradually chipped away at this resource, individual prescriptions will guide you toward effective resolutions. On the other hand, if group or organizational duplication costs, information hoarding and knowledge attrition are bigger concerns, other prescriptions can show you how intellectual capital can be fostered and properly managed. For many of you, more than one level will attract your interest. After all, information affects us in many different ways and in many different aspects of our lives.

Seeing a problem and complaining about it is much simpler than devising effective solutions for change. You only need to surf through the television news shows to see pundits and professionals pointing out various problems and pointing fingers of blame in one direction or another. But instead of defining information bombardment as a problem, let's take a different approach. Let's accept that we now live in the Information Age and that information is something we must learn to manage well if we wish to be successful.

Certainly identifying the problem and understanding it are key components of effective change, but taking action in a positive direction is equally important. With this in mind, I offer what I have found to be great remedies to the dilemmas information bombardment has created. I use these in my own life and in my own organizations, and without question they have enhanced my quality of life greatly. For anyone living in today's Information Age, these prescriptions for action are invaluable.

In pursuing change to help deal with information bombardment in your personal life, several steps can be easily taken. By making changes in how you communicate information, the negative impact of information bombardment can be greatly diminished. Consider the following steps from an individual's perspective.

Use Rule Wizards

No matter what e-mail program you use, e-mail is the dominant program running on everyone's personal computer. E-mail is even becoming a dominant function on cell phone and smartphone devices. Whether you use Gmail, Hotmail or Outlook, the use of e-mail rule wizards is a fantastic way to gain greater control over daily information. By implementing some of the inherent tools of these programs, information can be much better organized and managed.

First of all, *prioritization* is a useful tool for managing e-mail messages. Each message you receive or send has a prioritization attached to it. Most messages are sent as normal priority messages, but e-mail programs typically offer options of high-, normal- or low-importance choices. By defining an e-mail message as one of these three priorities, the receiver is able to view those messages of greater priority first. If time is limited (as it always seems to be), then low-priority messages can be deferred to a later date.

The important point here is to be courteous in your e-mail messaging. If you are simply sending a message about a book you read last week to a friend, mark the e-mail as low priority. This simple courtesy to the recipient allows them to better manage the information they receive. In the same fashion, request that your e-mail contacts return the same courtesy to you. Being responsible and achieving reciprocity in tagging e-mail message priorities is an effective tool in better organizing the information you receive.

The second means by which e-mail rule wizards can be used is *auto-foldering*. Every e-mail program enables various ways to implement rules that define where a message should be placed. For example, all e-mails received from your boss might automatically go into a corporate folder rather than your inbox. Perhaps you are working on a project within the company. You and all the project participants may agree to label the subject of all e-mail messages pertaining to the project as "company project A." Auto-foldering then automatically places all of these e-mails into the project folder rather than your inbox. You still receive the information, but the information is already organized upon receipt into the appropriate location.

In addition to sender and subject, e-mail messages can be organized by priority, sensitivity, date and a host of other variables. You have complete control over how e-mails are organized as they arrive at your desktop. This prevents you from using your inbox as a storage location for incoming e-mails, which is a notoriously inefficient way to manage daily information. Instead, visit specific folders when you are focused on that subject matter. This improves data processing and reduces the number of distractions to our already challenged attention spans.

The bottom line is that the cleanliness of your inbox reflects the cleanliness of your mind. If you have 5,264 e-mails in your inbox, then this likely says something about how overwhelmed your brain is with information and data. The average knowledge worker receives eighty-six e-mails every twenty-four hours, and the inability to organize and effectively manage these e-mails can be a tremendous problem. I have thousands of clients, students, colleagues and friends who send me dozens of e-mails every day, but rarely do I ever have more than twenty e-mails in my inbox. That should be your goal as well. Remember: a clean inbox equals a clean mind.

The last subject under rule wizards pertains to e-mail subjects. While auto-foldering can be used to organize e-mails according to their subject lines, using and encouraging the use of *descriptive subjects* by colleagues and others provides a way to augment the rule wizards of your e-mail program. Too often we send (and receive) e-mails without any subjects whatsoever.

The simple addition of a descriptive subject line to an e-mail can allow much greater organization and efficiency. For the same corporate project mentioned above, different aspects of the projects could contain different subject lines ("project budget," "project calendar," "project milestones," etc.) These e-mails could then be sub-foldered automatically if everyone participating used consistent, descriptive subject lines. Think how much easier it would be to locate, organize and manage a project in this way!

Push Alerts

For many, the pursuit of information occurs through search engine tools on the Internet and through other efforts designed to seek data through various resources. In short, this type of activity is referred to as *pulling* information since we must find and extract the data we want. No matter how efficient we become at pulling information, there are always some search costs involved.

In contrast, when we push information toward ourselves, the search costs are minimal because we have established criteria by which certain filtered information arrives at our desktops. Therefore, the goal is to push the information we desire to us in order to eliminate the time and energy required in pulling information. Having information pushed toward us is much more efficient than pulling it from a smorgasbord of resources.

Two Web sites are worth mentioning in relation to creating a means to push desired data toward our attention spans. These are http://www.google.com/alerts and http://www.socialmention.com/alerts. Both of these sites allow you to type in subjects of interest that are subsequently automatically searched for on the Web daily. If content is found that matches your subject request, the information is pushed to you via your e-mail in the form of information alerts. In this way, you can stay up to date and informed without having the burden and cost of searching for the data.

Google Alerts tends to be more comprehensive when searching blogs, news, videos and discussions on the Web while Social Mention Alerts tend to have a more social focus. Twitter, Facebook and other social media are better represented on Social Mention Alerts, including bookmarks and microblogs. Between these two, the vast majority of information available on the Web, particularly within Anglophonic resources, is well represented and can facilitate access to information most efficiently regardless of your particular interests.

As an aside, I would encourage you to add your own name, company, product or other specific identifiers to your list of alerts. This practice is an easy way to stay abreast of what is happening in relation to your own situation. Whether personal or professional, having this knowledge can be useful, and with these alert mechanisms it takes hardly any effort to remain well informed.

Receiver Customization

The addition of e-mail communication has revolutionized the efficiency with which we distribute information. Not only can I send a fifteen-slide PowerPoint presentation to a colleague within seconds, but I can even distribute it to an entire multinational corporation if I want. While the distribution is efficient, the processing of the received information is often not. In fact, for many of the people to whom we send information, the mode of how information is received can cause significant inefficiency.

Instead of simply sending a copy of an e-mail to a distribution list of people or replying to all, we need to be more attentive to the people to whom we send information. In other words, we need to be less lazy and more knowledgeable about the people to whom we send data. As individuals, we are all unique, and we each like to receive information in a different way. In order to promote efficiency, you and I should know the preferred means by which our acquaintances like to receive data and abide by those preferences. In the long run, this is what creates efficient information transfer and management.

For example, Joe does not like to receive e-mails. Instead he prefers voicemail because it allows him to hear the intonation and exclamations in my voice. This provides him with greater information than the use of caps in an e-mail message. On the other hand, Sarah doesn't like e-mail or voicemail. She prefers social interaction face to face. In order to facilitate information sharing and progress, visiting her office is much more efficient than e-mail or voicemail (she has a harder time deleting me when I am standing in front of her!). Lastly, Bill only likes face-to-face dialogue at certain times of the day. I have learned that visiting Bill at 10:00 a.m. (when he is beginning to have a mid-morning snack attack) with a chocolate donut is the most effective way I can communicate with him.

Receiver customization is the process by which we define how the people with whom we communicate best prefer receiving information. I log this data into their contact pages of my e-mail program and honor their preferred means of communication. Not only does this show respect to them, but it also provides greater efficiency in the process. In return, they have less unwanted information in their inboxes and reciprocate respect in their communications with me. Receiver customization allows greater qualitative information sharing with less noise and distraction.

Speed Reading

Improved organizational skills and better filtering mechanisms of informational processing are undoubtedly skills that will enable better information management at an individual level. However, improving personal skills in the ability to absorb information is also helpful. One of the ways information efficiency can be increased is through the ability to read (and comprehend) at a faster pace. This is where speed reading becomes an important tool in the knowledge era.

The average person today reads at a rate of 200 words per minute and comprehends at a rate of approximately seventy-five percent or more. Imagine that instead of reading 200 words per minute you read 400 words a minute. In essence your ability to absorb information would be twice as fast as the average person in the Information Age. Unfortunately, the converse also is true if you fall below this average figure.

After years of practice and using techniques that I have developed, my current reading speed is 1,200 words per minute. Through graduate school, during my academic career and even in my business endeavors, the amount of information I've had to read has been tremendous. If I wanted to have a life outside of academia, I had to learn how to absorb data faster and more efficiently. Speed reading was my answer. Now I am able to comprehend six times the amount of information in the same amount of time compared to my abilities in my early days as a student.

Believe it or not, learning to increase your reading speed is not that difficult. The first step is to test your own personal reading speed by visiting http://www.NickBontis.com. Once there, select the "Fun Stuff" tab and provide the password "123," which will enable you to then select the speed reading test. If you score more than 200 words a minute in your speed reading ability, celebrate! You are above average in your information-absorbing abilities. However, if your speed is less than 200 words a minute, you might want to keep it to yourself. You don't want everyone to know that you are one of the bottlenecks in today's information flow.

The Web site also provides an overview of exercises that can be performed to enhance your reading skills and speed, and with enough practice you are likely to increase your abilities to well above average. Think of all the free time you would have by doubling or tripling your reading speed. Bill Clinton is reported to have a reading speed of 1,200 words per minute, and we can only imagine what extracurricular activities he enjoys with his additional free time!

FURTHER READING

Google alerts: http://www.google.com/alerts

Web 2.0 alerts: http://www.socialmention.com/alerts

Speed reading test: http://www.nickbontis.com/win_main_fun_stuff_speed_reading.swf

Brain games: http://www.lumosity.com

E-mail rule wizards: http://www.slipstick.com/rules

Scan QR code for direct link to website,
hypertext links and other resources:

CHAPTER 18

Group Prescriptions

In moving from an individual level to a group level, information sharing versus hoarding becomes a more significant issue. Prescriptions that pursue effective information strategies at a group level encourage greater trust and social communications favoring knowledge dissemination. Consider the following group-level prescriptions as they pertain to intellectual capital and knowledge management.

Socialization

In centuries past, socialization was a significant part of the learning environment. During Ancient Greek times, citizens would gather in the square to listen to philosophers and teachers. Socrates, Plato and Aristotle would pontificate to hundreds in a very social atmosphere. Even cave people and primitive cultures sat around campfires, passing down stories of their ancestry as a means to educate their tribes. Unfortunately, today's corporate and non-corporate environments do not favor this type of interaction as readily.

The problem with this lack of institutional socialization is that it fails to foster the trust and relationships needed between colleagues to facilitate information sharing. People who are isolated due to different geographic locations may never get to know personally others with whom they collaborate. Perhaps they are in remote cubicle spaces within the same building, in different towns or even several time zones apart. Despite frequent interactions through e-mails, phone conferencing, video conferencing and other modes of telecommunications, the old-fashioned face-to-face interaction that builds relationships happens only rarely.

In order to reestablish this effective mechanism that promotes information sharing, social opportunities need to be created for colleagues, coworkers and group members. Summer meetings, holiday parties, weekly coffee socials, town hall forums, corporate getaways and a variety of other social events can be structured so that personal interaction between group members is increased. This in turn promotes trust as people come to know each other. In addition, social opportunities strengthen common goals that further enhance project efficiency.

The other benefit of institutionalized socialization is for new employees or group members. Social events and opportunities allow new members to become acquainted with existing members and vice versa. Knowledge is intuitively shared in this setting as group patterns and behaviors are more efficiently explained and demonstrated for those just coming into the group. If you recall, a social event alerted me about my colleagues within the banking firm who were working on the same mutual fund project. If these events had been more frequent (not four months later!), I would have known much sooner that my project was simply redundant and a waste of time. If you would like to promote greater information sharing within your group, investing in greater social opportunities should be a priority.

Knowledge Cafés

Socialization and knowledge sharing within larger groups can also be facilitated through knowledge cafés. Knowledge cafés are regularly scheduled events presented in a show-and-tell fashion. Periodically, a few individuals show the rest of the group their particular areas of interest and their specific functions within the group. Once everyone in the group has participated in this exercise, an improved understanding of the entire group's operations exists. In short, knowledge cafés are a great way to collect intelligence for the group systematically and make it accessible to everyone.

When I worked at the bank, knowledge cafés were held every Friday afternoon during the summer, one hour before everyone left for the weekend. Each Friday, a different department within the bank invited everyone to visit its section of the bank. People within that department would be introduced with explanations of their responsibilities. Workflows of everyone in that department would be described, and even file cabinet contents would be revealed (obviously, these knowledge cafés started months after my mutual fund project fiasco!). By the end of the hour, everyone knew about that particular department and how it fit into the overall schema of the bank.

These activities are excellent ways to help educate the entire group about tangible and intangible information while simultaneously enjoying a social environment that furthers working relationships and trust. For a brief time each week, people enjoyed donuts, coffee and their colleagues while receiving information about how the entire group and its components operated. Knowledge cafés are effective events that further promote an informational sharing environment.

Dynamic Corporate Yellow Pages

If you visit many Web sites, you will often find site maps outlining how the sites are organized and constructed. Similarly, many groups or organizations have directories identifying various offices, their phone numbers, key individuals and specific e-mail addresses. But what happens if you want to know more specific information about a group? For example, what if I were trying to find out if anyone else in the bank had an interest in competitive mutual fund accounts? The standard type of group directory would not be very useful.

Dynamic corporate yellow pages refers to an online directory within the intranet of a company or group that identifies not only contact information but many other knowledge variables as well. Various meta tags can be attached to individuals and departments describing their expertise, their interests and other aspects of their functions within the group. People can then quickly find other group members of interest because this information has been captured in a dynamic database.

For example, I would not only know that Dave was in the human resource department but also that he was active in professional training courses, had expertise in writing policy manuals and was adept at public speaking. This additional information could be very useful and reduce costs and inefficiencies of group activities and projects.

Corporate yellow pages should be fluid and dynamic, requiring constant updates and edits in order to be most effective. As people within the group acquire new skills and expertise, and as group members come and go, this glorified group directory needs to be kept current to facilitate efficiency and optimal information sharing. Creating and maintaining such a resource for a group will add significantly to making information more accessible.

Knowledge Exchange Auctions

With the advent of companies such as eBay and Craigslist, the effectiveness of online auctions and bidding communities for services and products has been quite obvious. Since knowledge is intellectual capital, information and knowledge can be treated in a similar fashion. This is the concept behind knowledge exchange auctions, including one that I have cultivated through a company called Knexa.com (http://www.knexa.com). In short, these auctions encourage and enable people to share knowledge with others in a marketplace wherein they are rewarded for information sharing.

For example, suppose a multicity corporation in the US has many networks working in parallel in different regions. The East Coast region functions independently compared to the West Coast and southern divisions. In this scenario, an East Coast manager could post a PowerPoint presentation on mutual funds on the corporate knowledge exchange auction for the other division managers to have. As a result of this posting, the East Coast manager would receive electronic tokens that could be held in an electronic savings bank for the company. In time, these tokens could be traded in for corporate rewards. These might include an increase in a department's budget, additional vacation hours or even lunch with the company president.

Knexa.com offers the same platform on a global scale, so that information can be traded among individuals or corporations throughout the world. Research, white papers, presentations, experiences and a variety of intellectual capital can be bought and sold for real money in this type of setting. The same type of trading auction could be established for any group, utilizing whatever type of currency was deemed appropriate. Knowledge is power, and intellectual capital has value. In order to encourage information sharing, people must be rewarded for providing their knowledge to others. Knowledge exchange auctions are innovative ways to help promote such activities.

FURTHER READING

Knowledge exchange auction: http://www.knexa.com

Selling expertise: http://www.NickBontis.com/BrettBontisKMReview.pdf

Parallels in knowledge cycles: http://www.Bontis.com/ic/publications/CuradoBontisCHB.pdf

Knowledge café: http://www.theworldcafe.com

Knowledge markets: http://www.skyrme.com/insights/28kmkt.htm

Scan QR code for direct link to website, hypertext links and other resources:

CHAPTER 19

Organizational Prescriptions

Addressing intellectual capital and information processing at larger organizational levels requires a more comprehensive commitment to knowledge management. Group-level knowledge management focuses on the ability to create an environment of information sharing, but organizational prescriptions are more concentrated on how information flows and how it is captured. The following prescriptions provide effective solutions of knowledge management that best protects an organization's intellectual capital and fosters its growth in the future.

Diagnosing E-Flow

With increased computer-mediated communications, electronic mail has become the preferred mechanism of communication for most organizations. This is the means by which large quantities of information and knowledge are passed from one area to another within the organization's structure. Therefore, evaluating the efficiency and functionality of information flow is important. Fortunately, this can be assessed fairly accurately by examining the e-mail flow within an organization. I use the term *e-flow* to define this electronic informational flow.

If an organization wishes to evaluate how well its informational flow is operating, diagnosing how well (or how poorly) e-flow occurs is an excellent exercise. This graphical representation of knowledge flow is constructed by taking the organizational chart and superimposing the velocity and direction of e-mail flow among different individuals, departments and hierarchies. This exercise will not only identify the direction of e-flow as horizontal or vertical between different areas but it will also identify trends and tendencies where information may bottleneck or be hoarded. Once the latter are identified, these areas can be the target for specific efforts to improve knowledge sharing and management.

In research exercises that have examined e-flow diagnoses, it has been interesting to find that organizational members tend to overestimate the flow of information. Reliance on subjective assessment is therefore not as accurate as the objective tool of e-flow analysis. Further information and an example of its usefulness can be found in my article "The E-flow Audit: An Evaluation of Knowledge Flow Within and Outside a High-Tech Firm."

Appointing Senior Leadership

For more than a decade, trends within organizations have been to increasingly invest resources into better knowledge management. One of these efforts has been the rising need to appoint senior management to oversee and direct knowledge management. This senior position, most commonly known as *chief knowledge officer* or *CKO*, is critical in today's Information Age. Organizations that utilize chief knowledge officers understand that proper knowledge management is essential to compete today and that a senior executive must be accountable for safeguarding a company's intellectual capital.

Duties of a CKO involve establishing the proper information technology that promotes information sharing as well as cultivating a climate that avoids information hoarding. By aligning processes, policies and programs geared toward encouraging knowledge collaboration and sharing, the organization can excel with its oars moving in the same direction. Without a senior leader at the mahogany table of the firm safeguarding proper knowledge management, the chances of success in today's competitive environment drops significantly.

Why is it important for a chief knowledge officer to exist among the senior executives of an organization? Why can't effective policies and procedures simply be installed to accomplish this task without another high-paid executive? In short, it is because the senior leadership is a microcosm of the entire organization. If a problem exists within the organization, more than likely the problem originated within those seated at the mahogany table. Whether the organization is experiencing disengagement, knowledge hoarding, stress responses or work bombardment, the senior management team likely holds the reason for why such problems are present.

If your role is to control-alt-delete and reboot the way knowledge is being managed within the firm, start at the top. The root cause of the underlying dilemma will become crystal clear as you examine how senior leaders conduct themselves within the organization.

Throughout the last decade, the position of chief knowledge officer has been increasing among Fortune 500 firms. Development, accountability and progress of effective knowledge management are essential activities in the information environment of today and have accounted for this trend among organizations. For further reading regarding CKOs, my articles "The Rising Star of the Chief Knowledge Officer" and "CKO Wanted—Evangelical Skills Necessary: A Review of the Chief Knowledge Officer Position" can provide additional details.

Developing Causal Models

Traditional models to assess how different parts of an organization are related have mostly consisted of correlation analyses. In other words, correlations are drawn between two or more sets of activities or variables. But unfortunately, these traditional models examine associations and offer little to explain actual functional issues between the parts present. Simply because two things are associated does not mean there is a cause-and-effect relationship.

Causal models, on the other hand, offer greater insight into the drivers of actions, behaviors and results. By looking at both qualitative and quantitative antecedents and consequents of various components of an organization, a much clearer picture can be seen. This in turn allows specific changes to be made that have greater impacts on operational results for the entire organization. Relationships between variables can be assigned values that indicate their strengths or weaknesses of causal effect. In addition, the degree of change in policy or procedure needed to promote the greatest benefit can be more readily determined.

In regard to intellectual capital, the human capital component can best be evaluated by developing causal maps for an organization. Items such as employee turnover, employee retention and business performance can be measured against different policy changes. Through surveys, interviews and other tools, causal maps can and should be developed on a regular basis because this allows opportunities for more-informed executive decisions based on empiric evidence. If it isn't measured, it cannot be improved.

Examples of how causal maps have been assessed in some organizations and industries can be reviewed in my articles "A Causal Model of Human Capital Antecedents and Consequents in the Financial Services Industry" and "Intellectual Capital ROI: A Causal Map of Human Capital Antecedents and Consequents."

Entry and Exit Interviews

Under the umbrella of succession planning, significant amounts of intellectual capital can be either gained or lost depending on how well an organization manages its human capital. The senior management team is not the only resource of intellect and knowledge in the firm. In fact, knowledge is universal, and every single member of the organization holds unique and specific information that no one else has.

Consider the call center operator who speaks to customers all day long. Do you think she might have some valuable information? What about the newly hired human resources assistant who incidentally has a degree in psychology and conducted research regarding the effect of colors on the human psyche? Do you think marketing might benefit from her talents?

Both entry and exit interviews are critical in accessing and quantifying this information, but there are some basic rules of thumb. First, entry and exit interviews should be conducted by a third party unassociated with the organization. This encourages open dialogue from the members being interviewed in addition to providing an objective perspective. Secondly, the data obtained from these interviews should be examined in aggregate and not on an individual basis. The anonymity awarded in this format also encourages candidness. Lastly, the information learned from these interviews should be incorporated into the organization's dynamic yellow pages and intranet through meta tags and other identifiers. These actions will allow optimal utilization of the information acquired.

In most organizations, this intellectual capital is rarely collected, and it walks right out the door. If we hear of someone leaving the firm, what is our typical response? We have a party! Coffee and muffins for everyone! And if the person leaving has been at the firm for more than five years, then we simply raise the bar by getting chocolate cake instead of muffins. Forget about trying to access what he or she might know or might have learned about the organization during his or her tenure. All too often, that important knowledge is simply ignored.

New employees should be interviewed in order to understand what intellectual assets they bring to the organization, and they should be encouraged to speak out so that any cultural barriers that might stem from being new can be erased.

Likewise, members leaving the organization should participate in training their replacements through job-shadowing programs. Indeed these investments have costs associated with them, but the opportunity costs of losing this valuable intellectual capital is much, much greater. Without succession planning, an organization will undoubtedly have a perpetual leak of information as members come and go.

FURTHER READING

E-flow audit: http://www.Bontis.com/ic/publications/JKMBontis.pdf

Chief Knowledge Officer: http://www.Bontis.com/ic/publications/BontisIBJ.pdf

CKO wanted: http://www.Bontis.com/ic/publications/KPMBontis.pdf

Human capital causal model: http://www.Bontis.com/ic/publications/JICBontisFitz-enz.pdf

Five ways to save intellectual capital: http://www.NickBontis.com/BontisHRProIC5waystosaveit.pdf

Onboarding and exit interviews: http://www.nobscot.com

Scan QR code for direct link to website,
hypertext links and other resources:

CHAPTER 20

Institutional Prescriptions

Knowledge management solutions discussed in the previous sections have been confined to aspects that lie within a structured environment. The prescriptions provided for the individual, for groups and for organizations thus far have been confined to internal changes and activities. However, at an institutional level, organizations look externally to find additional solutions for how to manage information best. From standards to collaborations, these prescriptions examine a much broader perspective.

As an academician and entrepreneur, I have spent a great deal of time in both research and consulting work addressing remedies at an institutional level for various organizations and business firms. From developing metrics and benchmarks to devising ways of innovative networking and collaboration, I have come up with solutions that hold the keys to much larger and complex problems facing not only big business environments but social environments as well.

Benchmarking and Metrics

Remember: if it is not measured, it cannot be properly evaluated. I have spent much of my consulting work specifically in the area of devising metrics and benchmarks for organizations so that they can indeed measure how well they are doing within the realm of knowledge management. A significant aspect of this addresses issues surrounding human capital, such as training and development costs as well as turnover costs. However, measuring performance can be applied to any area of intellectual capital.

Concerning metrics, performance can be measured against one's competition, against the industry in which a firm exists or even against societal measures. But once it's measured, how does an organization know if its performance is good or bad? Benchmarking holds the key. Developing a benchmark or standard provides a goal that can be attained or surpassed. This is routinely done for many financial and production metrics, and successful organizations are now developing the same benchmarking practices for intellectual capital.

Benchmarking can be assessed in three different ways. Longitudinal benchmarking measures changes from year to year. For example, did the organization spend more on training this year compared to last year? Cross-sectional benchmarking examines changes across an industry. For example, if Bank A had a turnover rate of twelve percent, what were Bank B's and Bank C's turnover rates during the same period? Lastly, benchmarking can be applied to an accepted standard published for an industry. Saratoga Institute—founded by metrics guru Dr. Jac Fitz-enz and now owned by PriceWaterhouseCoopers—provides industry standards for several areas concerning HR management.

While several resources are available to provide standard benchmarking for industries, some organizations fall outside the fray. For example, credit unions traditionally do not like to be compared to banking industry standards or traditional financial benchmarking parameters. An alternative to this is to develop your own consortium model composed of friendly firms so you can devise your own niche of standards. I have specifically performed this task for the credit union industry by serving as a third party and collecting data from a dozen or so different credit unions. Once the data from the consortium was compiled, all the credit unions involved had an excellent set of metrics and benchmarks by which they could assess their individual performance.

Metrics and benchmarking are essential in today's environment of scarce resources. Imagine sitting in front of the mahogany table, requesting an increase in your budget for training and development. The CFO will certainly ask for justification, and you don't want to find yourself replying with answers like, "Because more training is better" or, "Because I want it." You want objective facts and data, benchmarked internally and externally, to support your request. In dealing with knowledge management, these tools are essential.

Alumni Networks

Alumni networks offer tremendous opportunities to foster and protect the intellectual capital of a firm. As employees retire or leave the organization, their bases of knowledge about the industry, the organization and even the customers and vendors are extremely valuable. Some of this will be captured during the exit interview, but why should it end there? Utilizing these individuals as part of an alumni network continues to foster good relationships between the organization and the retirees, and the information obtained there will far exceed any information received from an industry consultant.

Alumni of an organization can be used to harvest intellectual capital and information in a variety of ways. For example, these individuals can be used as secret shoppers, as focus group participants for new products and services, and as research and development consultants. Often these alumni will provide insights and information for free simply because the organization respects their knowledge and continues to care about their opinions. After dedicating years of their lives to the organization, alumni have a degree of loyalty to a firm. If the organization continues to value them even after retirement, this trusting and caring relationship can continue and foster information sharing well into the future.

In short, alumni networks begin with the exit interview. Knowledge and intellectual capital is harvested then, but utilization of these individuals' knowledge can be enjoyed for a long time afterwards by establishing these opportunistic networks. These are always win-win situations if instituted effectively.

Macro Wikinomic Tools

In today's knowledge era, information is everywhere and failing to harness its power will likely be the pitfall of many organizations in the twenty-first century. Taking a perspective from my colleagues Don Tapscott and Anthony Williams, authors of *Wikinomics* and *MacroWikinomics*, I believe that innovative firms and organizations will take advantage of the huge collective abundance of knowledge that is simply there for the taking.

In 2001, Wikipedia was formally launched as an online

encyclopedia resource. The wiki aspect defines its core concept, which enables fast and easy creation and editing of information on numerous topics by millions of users. What began as a small online resource has now grown to more than fifteen million articles in over 200 languages. How long do you think it would take a business organization to develop the same volume of information and, more importantly, how much do you think that would cost? For Wikipedia it took less than a decade and cost practically nothing!

Macro wikinomic tools offer the same advantages to institutions across the globe. Imagine a collaboration of experts in any particular field contributing to an online wiki database generating the best solutions in the shortest amount of time. Think of the expansion of creativity and genius such an open forum would allow among top talents all over the world.

In addition, such tools are not time-sensitive. A contributor in China works his entire work day adding information to the database only to pass the baton to another person in France hours later. Collaboration is ongoing, twenty-four hours a day, seven days a week. Macro wikinomic tools are not only expansive in their breadth of information access but also time-efficient. With these tools, institutions can enjoy full horsepower globally when generating intellectual capital and information.

As described in *Wikinomics,* these collaborations have been ongoing and are increasing in prevalence in today's world. For example, the thirteen-year Human Genome Project, which defined the entire human DNA sequence, was the result of online collaborations between multiple nations including the US, the UK, Japan, Germany, France, China and others. Flickr and YouTube are similar online wikinomic collaborations of photo images and videos, respectively. With 1.8 billion people online, what a shame it would be to fail to tap into this tremendous pool of knowledge and intellectual capital.

I would encourage you not to underestimate the power and potential that macro wikinomic tools have for global change and reform. Imagine if British Petroleum had created a macro wikinomic platform to resolve the Gulf oil spill. How much time would have been saved in finding an effective solution? How much more of our environment and wildlife would have been rescued? These tools have great potential to help us make positive impacts on our world. In fact, failure to utilize them may soon be considered not only short-sighted but negligent. On the flip side, we must also appreciate the power such tools can have and the harm they may cause. WikiLeaks is one example of how communal publication of information can be simultaneously reviled and celebrated

Practicing Accountability

While this final category is less of an action item and more of a philosophical change, it remains important nonetheless. With the barriers between nations and societies becoming more permeable, and with the greater dissemination of information, an even-greater tendency to focus on the big picture has evolved. For example, when we receive less compensation than expected, the firm or government taxes are to blame. When a minority is ostracized, society or a specific culture is to blame. And when wars break out between nations, ideologies are held accountable as their causes.

While some of this may have merit, the real truth is that groups, organizations, institutions and policies do not cause problems related to information mismanagement. At the root of all of these situations, an individual is ultimately accountable for what transpires.

Groups do not make decisions or hoard information; individuals within the groups do. Organizations do not choose to share information within their industry; individuals within the organization do. Agencies do not recommend action or inaction; people within them do. In every situation, somebody has made a decision either to share or to hoard information and then act accordingly. This decision influences the larger collection of individuals, but regardless, a single, solitary person is accountable for the end result.

For example, why do half the population in Greece work for the government and receive pensions well beyond the amounts of other similar nations? A political party's platform, an administration's philosophy or a legislative action is not the reason. Who claimed that Saddam Hussein hid weapons of mass destruction (WMD) that led to the Iraqi War? It wasn't simply an agency report or a subcommittee's investigation findings. Who decided to withhold or ignore information that could have thwarted the 9/11 attacks? Again, it wasn't the FBI, the CIA or any other intelligence organization. Ultimately a single person made the decision either to share or to hoard information that led to decisions and actions. This is where true accountability needs to be placed.

The prescriptions listed at each level of perspective by necessity assume that information and knowledge are managed to an extent at different hierarchies. Therefore, different strategies can be employed at different levels to encourage more effective knowledge management and the use of intellectual capital. However, individuals lie at the core of every level. People choose how to use, manipulate and manage information. If a change is needed, regardless of the level of hierarchy, the strategy must be directed toward how people behave, and holding them accountable for their decisions regarding information behaviors is essential.

Almost overnight, information bombardment and the rapid acceleration of knowledge dissemination have occurred. The effects on us as people occur at a variety of levels. We feel the onslaught of data in our personal lives as we struggle to keep up with an endless amount of new and changing information. We become frustrated with the inefficiencies at work and in social groups as information is hoarded. We are sensitive to poor knowledge management within the companies and firms to which we belong as our intellectual capital is undervalued. And we all experience major catastrophes at institutional levels when information flow is poor. Indeed, the explosion of information in the knowledge era has created many dilemmas for us.

Fortunately, there are solutions. The prescriptions in this chapter are devised to help you, at every level, make a difference in how intellectual capital is managed. These tools can make your personal life more enjoyable, your professional life more satisfying, and everyone's world a better place in which to live. When it comes to information and knowledge management, we don't need to work harder. We simply need to be smarter. The time has come to control-alt-delete and reboot. Take a step forward with a new perspective and begin to manage information more effectively rather than letting it manage you.

FURTHER READING

T&D Benchmarking: http://www.NickBontis.com/BontisDrake.pdf

PwC Saratoga: http://www.pwc.com/ca/en/people-change/sara-toga.jhtml

What's measured counts: http://www.NickBontis.com/BontisWhat'sMeasuredCounts.pdf

Predictive learning impact model: http://www.NickBontis.com/BontisPredictiveLearningImpactModel.pdf

Corporate alumni networks: http://www.corporate-alumni.info/survey_corporate_alumni_networks_summary_english.pdf

Wikibrands: http://www.wiki-brands.com

Macrowikinomics: http://www.macrowikinomics.com

Scan QR code for direct link to website,
hypertext links and other resources:

Speaking Testimonials

Professor Nick Bontis is not only a pioneer in the field of intellectual capital, but one of the world's real experts as well.

Thomas Stewart, Former Editor, **Harvard Business Review** and ***FORTUNE* Magazine**, New York, New York, USA

Nick Bontis is a brilliant, provocative thinker who understands the deep changes underway in our society. His presentations are perceptive and persuasive, and always done with great gusto and humour.

Honourable Bob Rae, 21st Premier of Ontario, **Government of Ontario**, Toronto, Canada

There are a few rules you should know about having Dr. Bontis speak to your management team about the future of the workplace environment in the Information Age. First, do NOT follow him as another speaker. Second, do NOT skip him as a seminar participant. Third, do NOT design a program without him as a conference producer. He is, defacto, the reason why any one should attend an event he speaks at!

Anton van Elst, Management Training Officer, **ING Bank**, Amsterdam, The Netherlands

Nick Bontis seems always in motion. Whether he's speaking to conference audiences or his university students, Dr. Bontis delivers fast-paced presentations that find him prowling the room, popping animated slides on the screen or spilling water from a glass to illustrate ideas. His energetic discussions embody his specialty of study: the accumulation and flow of intellectual capital.

Steve Barth, Editor, ***Knowledge Management* Magazine**, San Francisco, USA

Dr. Bontis is a unique individual who mixes together three key ingredients. First, his academic credentials are terrific and his thought leadership is recognized and appreciated globally. Second, his entrepreneurial spirit drives him to present a practical business orientation in every issue he discusses. Third, his energetic and warm personality acts like a magnet for all those who meet him. Most importantly, whenever I put together a world-class conference I know that I can count on him to consistently deliver a high- performance keynote that leaves the audience buzzing.

Jane Dysart, Program Director:
KM World, **Internet World**, **InfoToday**, Toronto, Canada

Many of the evaluations we got back from our top performers at our annual UNIGLOBE Chairman's circle event in Sonoma identified you not only as the best speaker/resource they had experienced through UNIGLOBE, but many also said you were the best speaker they had ever seen anywhere period!

Martin Charlwood, President,
Uniglobe Travel International, Vancouver, Canada

Nick's reputation as a world expert in his field is indisputable. However, the real magic occurs when he steps in front of a crowd. His charisma acts like a magnet and captures everyone's attention. He will be sure to leave a lasting impact with your audience.

Maen Nsour, Regional Programme Advisor,
United Nations Dev. Program, New York, USA

Few people actually live up to their advance press, but Nick Bontis exceeds it. His presentation was superb, both in content and style. Our sophisticated audience was enormously entertained while being challenged with new ideas and approaches. We'll have Nick back as many times as we can, assured that the message and research will always be fresh and provocative.

Carla O'Dell, President,
American Productivity and Quality Centre, Houston, USA

Dr. Bontis was the perfect ending to our customer conference. He was able to bring together a number of very different telecommunication technologies under one banner and drive home a message that was engaging both professionally and personally.

C. Scott Robinson, Sr. Marketing Manager, **Allstream**, Toronto, Canada

Dr. Bontis is a stunning speaker. He has a rare combination of entertainment value which will keep you on the edge of your seat; high energy to keep you engaged; scientifically intriguing research results with real, relevant, and immediate business value; an uncanny ability to present complex concepts in easy to understand language; and the ability to ignore the irrelevant or misleading in favour of the key insights. The ideas come so fast you can't even afford to blink. Wow!

Joe Weinman, Director Strategy & Technology,
AT&T Business Services, Bedminster, USA

Dr. Bontis created a significant impact with our audience, many of whom were leading exponents in the field of KM. His engaging and highly interactive delivery kept everyone enthralled; more importantly, he delivered some challenging and valuable insights into this complex field, based upon his extensive research background and practical experiences. Thanks to Nick's presentation, we closed our conference with style and credibility among our customers.

Carrie Hamer, Marketing Manager,
Dataware Technologies, Cambridge, USA

Bontis continues to be one of our highest evaluated speakers at the Enterprise Intelligence World Summit. His presentation provides food for thought and plans for action as well. He is insightful, provocative and inspiring!

Bill Doherty, President,
International Conference Development, Marlborough, USA

Dr. Bontis has special skills that are obvious to those of us who have heard him. He spans the boundaries between academics and managers, summarizing and illustrating how theories may be transformed into decisions and deeds. Nick brings a dynamic, crowd pleasing sense of knowing and humour to his presentations.

Gary Anderson, Regional Manager,
HRSDC, Government of Canada, Ottawa, Canada

I have engaged him on several occasions as a speaker and consultant. I have found him to be consistently entertaining and extremely well-founded in the topics he offers. His style is engaging and his knowledge of the first order.

Dr. Jac Fitz-enz, Founder & Chairman, **Saratoga Institute**, Santa Clara, USA

Bontis combines interesting content, wit, and a smooth speaking style in a way that makes one want to invite him back often. Nick has spoken at several events I have hosted.

Dr. Patrick Sullivan, President, **ICM Group**, Palo Alto, USA

Dr. Bontis did an outstanding job at our recent Global Executive Seminar. Out of a total score of 5.0, participants rated him 4.86 for the overall topic and 4.94 for whether he was effective. Comments from participants included: he was the highlight of the conference; his stories and metaphors were useful and fun; his was one of the most compelling presentations I have seen; he was the best speaker I have seen in years, he taught me how to sell KM to clients and his high energy level and enthusiasm offered many new perspectives.

Christian Winslow, Marketing Manager, **Accenture**, St. Charles, USA

Nick Bontis brings alive the topic of KM in such a way that everyone understands this new and complex field. His energetic approach, his sound research base, his practical application of the knowledge is an absolute delight for his participants. My colleagues in Jamaica are still talking about his presentation at the conference and the radio interview afterwards. We are truly grateful for his input.

Nsombi Jaja, Principal, **Quality Management Consulting**,
Jamaica, West Indies

I jumped at the opportunity to have Dr. Bontis keynote one of my larger training conferences. His topic (Knowledge Management & Intellectual Capital) was very timely. His style was interactive and exciting. His passion was undeniable! There is no doubt that Nick and I will do a lot more work together in the future.

Curtis Skene, Training & Certification Manager,
Microsoft Canada, Mississauga, Canada

Dr. Bontis' presentation was inspirational, motivating, and fulfilling. Thank you for taking the time to speak with us and I hope you know, that you truly made a difference for this public servant.

Aileen Chiasson, Escalation and Review Unit,
Canada Student Loans Program, Hull, Canada

I just wanted to say thanks to Dr. Bontis for sharing his knowledge and expertise with members of the federal government. Nick has ignited the sparks and they will be hard to extinguish. I have to admit that this is the first initiative, in a very long time, that has lent itself to immediate credibility. There have been many flag wavers of various principals and theories that have come and gone over the years—none sustainable and none that have struck me in a way that I wanted to have any personal investment in them. This is not the case with knowledge management theory and practice. My attendance at Dr. Bontis' one day introduction was as a result of the very high recommendation from a colleague. Nick's session has created the same sense of enthusiasm and wanting to share inside of me. Both of us made a presentation to the rest of our Division this week and we believe we have enough of an impression to create a desire for our peers to attend your session(s). This includes our Director who is in a position to incorporate KM theories and principals into his initiatives. He champions and leads a variety of HR working groups and has contact with all levels across the government and in the "real world" too. My colleague and I have both said that your workshop was a topic of conversation at each and every meeting that we have attended this week. My background in marketing taught me that you can't buy this kind of advertising at any price. Just wanted Dr. Bontis to know that I personally very much enjoyed his dynamic and refreshing presentation and that his efforts and dedication are already showing rewards. This is a testament to him and his dedication

Craig Peabody, Manager,
Treasury Board of Canada Secretariat, Ottawa, Canada

Nick's presentations illuminate content while challenging and enervating audiences. A presenter with flair and panache, Nick provides a learning experience not to be missed.

Debra Wallace, Assistant to the Dean,
FIS University of Toronto, Toronto, Canada

Dr. Bontis is an engaging and compelling. He clearly has his finger on the pulse of key management trends in the new economy. His work on intellectual capital management is influential and important, and I expect his influence to grow considerably over time.

Britton Manasco, Senior Partner,
The Knowledge Capital Group, Austin, USA

Dr. Nick Bontis is a fine presenter with a rare and deep knowledge of knowledge management, intellectual capital and organizational learning, created through a refined combination of practical business experience and serious scholarship.

Bryan Davis, President,
Kaieteur Institute of Knowledge Management, Toronto, Canada

Dr. Bontis has an outstanding ability to communicate complex concepts in a simple concise manner. This coupled with his enthusiasm and in-depth knowledge enabled him to leave a lasting impression with us.

Neel Chauhan, Analyst, **Accenture**, London, United Kingdom

Bontis is an exceptional presenter. He provides credible, research-based content in a manner that is practical and useful. Nick is enthusiastic and engaging as he offers up several new and important ideas on the management of Human Capital.

Michael H. Mitchell, Founder & Principal,
Greenlight Management, New York, USA

Nick Bontis has the remarkable ability to define, demonstrate and then scope out the issues related to intellectual capital and knowledge management in a language that is accessible to a wide range of audiences. I have seen Dr. Bontis engage senior management and speak to large groups of employees from the federal public sector and in both cases he was successful in addressing their questions and concerns about this newly emerging field. He is dynamic, pedagogical, extremely knowledgeable and easy to comprehend.

Michelle Boulet, **Knowledge Management Advisor,**
Health Canada, Ottawa, Canada

Dr. Nick Bontis is not only an expert in the field knowledge management, but also an extremely interesting speaker. He surely knows how to catch and keep the attention of the audience.

Dr. Ante Pulic, Professor, **Austrian IC Research Center**, Vienna, Austria

Bontis is the kind of speaker people come to conferences hoping to hear: a speaker who combines the skill to communicate clearly and effectively, with the talent to inspire, provoke, and move his audience. Dr. Bontis is that rare coming together of energy and erudition.

Dr. Chun Wei Choo, Professor, **FIS University of Toronto**,
Toronto, Canada

Nick is an energetic and learned speaker, who bridges the world of the academy and business. Both professor and consultant, he is a knowledgeable and engaging thinker. Dr. Bontis ranges comfortably between the theory and practice of knowledge management and makes an engaging addition to any professional program.

Brook Manville, Chief Learning Officer, **Saba,** San Francisco, USA

Dr. Bontis is an enthusiastic and engaging speaker on Knowledge Management. He articulates leading edge thinking on both the theoretic and practical front—advancing both the "science" of KM and its understanding by the layman. He communicates using analogies and real-life examples that make the subject of intangible assets both concrete and compelling.

Dave Pollard, Global Director for Knowledge Innovation,
Ernst & Young, Toronto, Canada

Dr. Nick Bontis is worth every penny of his fee. At the Ontario Economic Summit he was given 20 minutes following a cocktail party to speak about intellectual capital in the same room where people were standing around with drinks in their hands chatting—within a minute, the room went quiet and he had us spell-bound—he's a university prof with star power!

Edward Barisa, Chief Executive Officer,
Ontario Real Estate Association, Toronto, Canada

I am pleased to support the credentials and the credibility of Dr. Nick Bontis as an expert in the KM field. He is an enthusiast who can inspire people to be more involved in Knowledge Management in the global economy through his very professional presentations. He takes pains to customise his material for a particular audience and theme. He mixes very well and is a good ambassador for his profession and his country.

Lyall Lukey, Co-ordinator, **SmartNet Workshops**,
Christchurch, New Zealand

Nick spoke to a group of business owners who have heard many "motivational" speakers. This time they were actually motivated! Nick's impressive research and his provocative and entertaining presentation left us entirely speechless, but seriously challenged. Not a single person left the room without a vision and a commitment.

Gordon D. Miller, Owner **UNIGLOBE Premiere Travel Planners,**
Ottawa, Canada

The field of KM is both vast and complex. Dr. Bontis has a unique combination of academic expertise and dynamic presentation style which makes this important new area very accessible to the corporate world.

Frances Horibe, President, **Vision Arts Inc.**, Ottawa, Canada

Energetic, enthusiastic and a great entertainer—a man who really knows what he is talking about.

Ken Standfield, Director KM Research,
Knowcorp Inc., Melbourne, Australia

Dr. Nick Bontis brought a rare combination of insight and entertainment to the subject of intellectual capital planning our Spring 2000 Government CIO Summit.. He achieved one of the highest session scores ever, 4.9 out of 5, from our knowledgeable and demanding audience of government Chief Information Officers.

Steve LeCompte, Vice President, **FCW Government Technology Group**,
Falls Church, Virginia, USA

Dr. Nick Bontis has a gift for making the complex subject of human capital valuation not only understandable but entertaining as well. His presentation at our annual conference received the highest rating among a field of impressive, knowledgeable speakers.

Gayle Selby, President, **Saratoga Institute**, Santa Clara, USA

Professor Bontis' presentation style was very inspirational and fuelled even more my desire to pursue a life long career in KM and related disciplines of organizational learning.

David Lett, Principal, **SYSDOC**, London, UK

Dr. Bontis' presentation at the V° International Human Resource Conference held in Buenos Aires, Argentina was a great success. It was full of interesting concepts and was greatly enjoyed by all the participants not only from the content point of view but also for the way it was delivered. He is an outstanding speaker who contributed enormously to our event.

Alejandra Saggese, Director of Learning,
AMA-Latin America, Buenos Aires, Argentina

With changing demographics, markets and technology such enormous issues for credit unions, I've booked many academic experts and business strategists as presenters at our conferences. None have connected with the audience with the ease that Dr. Bontis did. I was awed by his ability to zero in on the specific aspects of the knowledge revolution that are most relevant to our industry. The fact that delegates were charged up and receptive after his thought-provoking address enhanced the impact made by subsequent speakers. He garnered record- high marks on our delegates' evaluations. Reaction was unanimously positive, with a whopping 80 percent giving his presentation a "5" - the highest possible rating. He was complimented on his engaging speaking style and ability to inject some humour into the proceedings. Many delegates went out of their way to comment on the strength of his address.

Gayle Stevenson, Manager,
Credit Union Central of BC, Vancouver, Canada

Dr. Bontis was the highest rated speaker at the 3rd Annual Canadian Knowledge Management Conference hosted by Infonex. On a scale from 1 to 10, he scored an outstanding 9.56, whereas the average speaker evaluation score was 7.65. The audience indicated a very high level of interest in the issues that he addressed.

Christopher Graham, Vice President,
Conference Development, **Infonex**, Toronto, Canada

Dr. Bontis' presentation was right on target. It aligned very well with the workshop theme proposed to the delegates. Several conference delegates commented to us that they found his discussion on measuring knowledge very insightful. Some of the comments include: "Nick is a wow!"; "extremely knowledgeable and enthusiastic"; and "intelligent and good sense of humour." His presentation received one of the highest ratings.

Natalie Gagnon, Research Associate,
Conference Board of Canada, Ottawa, Ontario, Canada

Dr. Nick Bontis' keynote at Information Highways 2001 was unanimously declared "excellent" by all attendees. His presentation was dynamic and entertaining yet contained a good deal of substance. He used well-crafted visuals and presentation techniques to explain very complex concepts in a straightforward manner and impressively combined solid research results with practical advice. Everyone carried away plenty of inspirational, thought-provoking ideas that could be applied back at the workplace.

Vicki Casey, Director, **Information Highways**, Toronto, Canada

Dr. Bontis has energy, passion and a well-honed intellect. He is a pioneer in the field of knowledge management and just the kind of individual needed to make business sit up and listen.

Graham Westwood, President, **Domain Knowledge Inc.**, Toronto, Canada

If knowledge management hasn't made the top ten list in your organization's strategic priorities because your senior management still doesn't get it, at the very earliest opportunity, send them to the next workshop given by Dr. Nick Bontis—or better yet, get him to make a house call. A recognized leader in the discipline of intellectual capital management, Dr. Bontis delivers an engaging and insightful presentation. No one walks away without understanding the urgency of embedding KM into the organization's vision and business strategy.

Mary Hum, Senior Manager,
PricewaterhouseCoopers LLP, Toronto, Canada

Dr. Nick Bontis is a true global knowledge leader. He is the first PhD graduate in the world on the subject and has—as a most admired teacher—pioneered courses and conferences on the subject that have become world renowned. He is both an appreciated and an awarded speaker around the world advocating this new knowledge economy. He is also continuously and successfully pioneering new research.

Leif Edvinsson, CEO, **Universal Networking Intellectual Capital**,
Stockholm, Sweden

Bontis has justifiably developed a solid reputation both as a rigorous thinker and researcher in the area as well as an insightful and engaging presenter of new perspectives on the organization. He continues to make a very important contribution to this emerging domain.

Hubert Saint-Onge, Partner, **Saint-Onge Alliance**, Waterloo, Canada

The transition from the industrial paradigm to one focused on knowledge is more than a "mind-shift" it creates a need for a new kind of person, one who takes others with him by engaging their worldview. Nick does this when he talks Knowledge Strategy, opening this new world to his audience by making it human and accessible. In a field in danger sometimes of being overrun by recycled informationalists re-bottling the same offering in new ways, true apostles of the new age are rare.

James van der Westhuizen, Principal, **KnowHouse,**
Johannesburg, South Africa

Changing everyone's paradigm is tough job. Nick Bontis considers this to be his "day-to-day pursuit." He stands out as a pioneer in stimulating companies to embrace the vital role of intellectual capital through his strong presence and interactive presentations to create 21st Century Companies.

Frank Lekanne Deprez, Partner, **KPMG**, Amsterdam, The Netherlands

Nick Bontis was one of the first academic researchers to see the value in documenting the evolution of the knowledge movement. His techniques are thorough, his insights compelling and his broad initiative to innovate within the community laudable.

Debra M. Amidon, Founder and Chief Strategist,
Entovation, Wilmington, USA

Attendees gave you the highest rating of any speaker, a "world-class." Excellent! Your participation was greatly valued and appreciated by everyone who attended.

Ronald M. Cowin, Conference Program Director,
The Conference Board, New York, USA

All of our speakers are experienced and professional in their own right but Dr. Bontis always stands out above the rest. The average speaker scores were 3.9 for Style and 3.8 for Content. Dr. Bontis scored 5.0 for Style and 4.9 for Content. Absolutely amazing!

Sally Swinamer, Conference Director,
Int'l Quality & Productivity Centre, Toronto, Canada

As a keynote speaker Dr. Bontis delivered a powerful, motivating and exciting presentation that challenged us as individuals and as an organization. Dr. Bontis was able to relate his knowledge and experiences to our (foodservice) industry. He also offered thought provoking insights as to how we could apply his knowledge management principles to enhance our business and achieve our full potential. Overall "Nicky B." made a very positive impact and impression and I am confident that both he and his presentation will be remembered for years to come.

Nils Kravis, President & C.O.O. , **Kelsey's International Inc.**, YPO Member

I am a YPOer from the BC Chapter. My first experience with Nick was at the Canadian Conference in 2002 when he spoke there. I have to say he was probably the funniest, yet most insightful business speaker I have ever heard. This was not just

my view, but I think the view of almost everyone in the room. As a result of that session, I encourage the event chair for an upcoming event I was helping with to drop the "Harvard" resource we were considering and bring in Nick. He did not let us down and produced one of the highest rated "business" events we have had in years. Nick has an amazing ability to deliver critical business content in a way that makes it fun (and at time hysterical), but gets the message across so you won't likely forget. I can recommend him as a resource with absolute confidence.

Terry M. Holland, **Krystal Financial Corp**. Vancouver, USA

Dr. Bontis spoke at the 2003 Best Practices in Knowledge Management and spoke at several IQPC Canada events. Mr. Bontis always rates above conference average and has several times been given a 5 out of 5. He is a very energetic speaker and delegates appreciate his contribution and expertise.

Michelle Tampoya, Conference Director,
Int'l Quality & Productivity Centre, Toronto, Canada

I was fortunate enough to have the opportunity to see Dr. Nick Bontis, not once, but twice within a 6 month timeframe. The first session was fantastic and left me wanting to know more. Dr. Nick's mix of professional experience and dynamite speaking personality make him a must see! You leave his sessions not only feeling energized but having also learned so much about information flows or lack thereof, within a work context. The second session I attended was about causal models. I didn't know exactly what I was in for and found myself to be overwhelmed when I took a look at his handout. Within a one hour period not only did I understand his handout, but I could fully relate it to the first session and begin to realize instances of it (good and bad) within my own organization. I would highly recommend Dr. Nick Bontis to any organization wishing to improve their own knowledge transfers and management.

Janice Brooks , **Bank of Montreal**, Toronto, Canada

Dr. Bontis' presentation was outstanding! As a conference producer we ask our delegates to rate all our speakers. The overall average out of 10 was 7.23 which is quite high. Nick's score was 9.58 which is truly remarkable.

Laszlo von Altmann, President, **Infonex,** Toronto, Canada

Nick Bontis delivers a workshop on reality in the workplace. No matter what his credentials are, Nick captivates an audience and enlightens the participant by cleverly disguising the content with an entertaining delivery. If you go to one self help seminar this year, make it this one. His energy is matched only by his wit and the relevance of his message, and he will no doubt leave a lasting positive impression with you and your staff.

John Baxter, Internal Auditor, **Royal Bank**, Toronto, Canada

Nick provided a stimulating and dynamic presentation on a very difficult area of interest for the RCMP. He created excellent understanding and initiated some important discussions on the topic and process. Thank you and well done.

Geoff Gruson, Deputy Commissioner,
Royal Canadian Mounted Police, Ottawa, Canada

I didn't get a chance to talk to you yesterday but I just wanted to thank and congratulate you on your amazing seminar at the CCGD conference. It was very enlightening for me. I am a firm believer in the Sam Walton phrase, "Learn all you can, share all you know."

Peter Brisbois, Marketing Manager Tropicana,
Quaker Tropicana Gatorade, Toronto, Canada

I found the presentation that Dr. N Bontis gave on Knowledge Management and his predictions for the future to be highly energized, informative and inspirational. He is a very dynamic speaker with a great message of a challenging yet positive future. The audience seemed very involved, entertained and appreciative of Dr. Bontis'style, wit, and message. By far the loudest and most joyful applause of the ARMA conference went to Dr. Bontis.

John T. Wilson, Record Systems Analyst,
Calgary Board of Education, Calgary, Canada

Good Morning Nick, I attended your presentation yesterday. It was an absolute pleasure to listen to you talk. It is amazing what you talk about makes such common sense with so few companies looking at knowledge in that way. The succession plan is also a very important step for companies as well. I have seen this in working with Honda a few years ago where a person was getting a promotion and he had to train his replacement for 2 years. Keep up the great work and I look forward to listening to you talk in the future.

Daniel Collins, Key Account Manager,
Retail Food Brands, Toronto, Canada

Thank you for your contribution to the IC Congress! Your presentation was the highlight of the conference according to the "grapevine"! Your slides were filled to the brim with content, yet you were able to set a tone of closeness and warmth which then continued to characterise the whole congress. I and the organisers owe you a lot for this!

Karl-Erik Sveiby, Principal, **IC Partners Helsinki**, Helsinki, Finland

Dr. Bontis' depth of knowledge and engaging presentation style on the aspects of Knowledge Management is unparalleled. Dr. Bontis is a "must" for any event on Knowledge Management - at our recent event he captivated the audience during

his presentation and provided all participants with valuable food for thought on Knowledge. Dr. Bontis provided us with the kick start needed to engage all employees and management in realizing the importance of knowledge management and organizational learning to our organization.

Dave Goods, Director Government On-Line Project,
Environment Canada, Ottawa, Canada

Dr. Nick Bontis wowed our Management Team with his presentation on Knowledge Management. He is an informative and entertaining speaker with a very powerful message. He left everyone in the audience asking questions and wanting more. I highly recommend him as a speaker—just don't be the one to present after him, he is a tough act to follow.

Anna Grolle , Director of Corporate Operations & HR,
Cactus Restaurants, Vancouver, Canada

I looked back over the participant feedback comments (which was optional) and have pulled out a sampling for you: excellent leave behind knowledge; best I've enjoyed through YPO; tremendous presentation; dynamic and well organized; thought provoking; fantastic; excellent topic and phenomenal delivery; very appropriate and key to awakening new management priorities; fabulous speaker and great presence. From my perspective as the meeting planner of the event, Nick was a pleasure to work with. He was well prepared, very low maintenance and delivers a high voltage, content-rich presentation. It is always a challenge to find new, interesting and thought provoking speakers for a YPO audience, given that they have had so much exposure to so many events. Nick proved to be an excellent fit for this group.

Andy Weinkove, Meeting Planner,
Young Presidents Organization, Niagara Falls, Canada

I organized a YPO program with Nick as the keynote speaker. The event was very well received and Nick was considered to be among the better speakers ever invited to present to our group. He was dynamic, entertaining, and thought provoking. He did a great job.

Paolo Kalaw, CEO, **DTI Dental Technologies**, Vancouver, Canada

When I began putting a speaker series together the name at the top of my list was Dr. Nick Bontis. Dr. Bontis did not disappoint. His presentation is packed with information and insights, and gives you a real sense of not only the topic but of the man. One of the most memorable presentations I have heard.

Gordon Neufeld, Principal, **The Best-Half**, Hamilton, Canada

Dr. Bontis' enthusiasm and eloquence filled me with electricity—I could feel the learning happening at a cellular level in my body.

Dan Randow, Director, **GroupSense,** Christchurch, New Zealand

I thought Dr. Bontis' presentation was energising and his content thought provoking and leading edge.

Terry Neill, Managing Partner,
Knowledge Management, **Accenture**, London, UK

Nick's speaking style is engaging, his material is rock solid, and his enthusiasm is positively contagious!

Verna Allee, President, **Integral Performance Group**,
Walnut Creek, California, USA

Dr. Bontis has the rare combination of an outstanding and engaging presentation style together with the academic brains to back it up. He is inspiring, motivating, and quite frankly, a brilliant role model in the knowledge world.

Rob Crawford, Partner, **KPMG Consulting**, Vancouver, Canada

His delivery, ability to relate and communicate to the audience was crafty and clever.

Margo Stutesman, Business Alliance Manager,
SAS, Cary, North Carolina, USA

Knowledge Management is not a new topic and is generally viewed as adding value to information. But Dr. Bontis' approach with his dynamic presentation demonstrates that KM is in fact part of our daily work. He shows us how we can contribute individually to make it part of our organizational culture thus deriving all its benefits in simple actions.

Thierry Chen, Senior Business Analyst,
Environment Canada, Ottawa, Canada

I went into the Nick Bontis presentation expecting a stimulating discussion that covered the genesis of knowledge management as well as its applicability in the enterprise given its growing prominence. I was not disappointed. Dr Bontis delivered a thorough and thought provoking presentation that was well crafted and insightful. I particularly liked the stats he had researched which are ample reason to enlist knowledge management solutions and his clever analogies for the flow of knowledge across the organization.

Ken Gikunda, Business Analyst, **TAP Ventures**, Vancouver, Canada

I was fascinated by Dr. Bontis' presentation on KM. It was not only entertaining but also had wonderful content and examples that the students could relate to easily. I have attended expensive conferences in the US, Europe and Canada over the past 20 years (e.g., Conference Board, HRPAO, IBM and SHRM) and I felt he was better than other big names who present there. With teachers of his ability, entrepreneurship, and energy, it makes me proud to sell the McMaster Business School to all of our alumni and stakeholders as one of the world's best.

Maurice Dutrisac, President,
DeGroote McMaster Alumni Association, Hamilton, Canada

There are very few people I have met so far in my life that have left a such a strong impression in my mind .... Nick's presentation this morning was dynamite and it certainly sparked a real interest for me to want to learn more about his area of expertise. I arrived back to work with a feeling of enthusiasm and a recharged passion for what I do. After listening to Dr. Bontis, I found myself so excited to think about all of the interesting areas of work and research that are out there and I trust that one day I will challenge myself to explore all my options. Thanks again for opening my eyes to new ideas and possibilities.

Bev Jones, Human Resource Administrator,
Omista Credit Union, Moncton, Canada

Prof. Nick Bontis is a leading expert in the field of IC specifically as relates to the leveraging of human capital through structural capital and into value. Nick produced the first Ph.D. thesis on IC in the logical positivistic School. Dr. Bontis is continuing to make important contributions to the IC field using communication channels appropriate for the speed at which the field develops.

Industrial Professor Göran Roos, Chairman,
Intellectual Capital Services Limited, London, UK

My wife just burst in the door, gushing about the speaker that she had heard at the CCGD conference in Mississauga earlier today. She said that I MUST contact you. It is rare that either of us even remembers what was said (or who said it) after one of these all-day affairs; usually my eyes are rolling around in the back of their sockets and drool is running down my right cheek by about 1:30 or so. You, however, captivated her. She felt confident that your message would be as relevant to a small group like ours (under 20 employees) as it was to the 1,300 who heard you speak today.

David Frank, Partner, **Bell Financial**, Toronto, Canada

When it comes to knowledge-sharing, I have heard no one with as much expertise and enthusiasm. Dr. Bontis is a public speaker with extraordinary talent.

Mady Gorrell, Director, Corporate Communications, **BrassRing**, San Francisco, USA

Bontis' presentation was insightful, challenging to my basic assumptions, extremely dynamic, tremendously well-focused to the audience, very practical and evangelistic to the KM movement. He delivers true wisdom. I felt motivated to carry the message to almost anyone who would listen. Further, Nick made me want to learn more. It was a real treat. I would be more than honoured if Dr. Bontis would speak for us again.

Pat Selden, Executive Producer, **The Strategy Institute**, Toronto, Canada

Your captivating and passionate lecture this afternoon has truly inspired me. For many years I've held an awareness that I have had something more to offer to this world. Exactly what it was eluded me, until now. I see the imminent change you speak of, and I am excited about the possibilities. Thank you for your insight, energy, and time. It has made an important transformation to my life.

Danielle Durand, Manager, **Coast Hotels**, Calgary, Canada

Professor Bontis' style of humour and talent for forcing the audience to think differently was of great benefit to both us and our vendor partners. The feedback we received has been especially positive—a completely new view on the power of information, and on how organizations can be left behind should they decide not to change. Professor Bontis challenged the audience with the concept that companies can use collective information and knowledge for a competitive advantage. We would recommend Dr. Bontis to any organization that wants to challenge their people, and learn how to harness the power of knowledge within their organization.

Clint Mahlman, Vice President, **London Drugs**, Vancouver, Canada

I was in attendance today at the conference and was astounded by your presentation. I've been to a lot of these events, and invariably the keynote speaker is either entertaining or educational. Until now I've never seen both. So, thanks very much for your time, I think a lot of people took a lot away from it.

Dan Plawiuk, Manager, **Van Houtte Coffee**, Toronto, Canada

I want to thank you for your great presentation to us. I came away with some great new perspectives on some very interesting and important issues. I have already started on your list!!! In fact, I have dusted off the speed-reading books and tapes that I bought some time ago and have been procrastinating on ever since. As someone who experiences a lot of such meetings (I have had my UNIGLOBE business for

23 years now), I can candidly say that I do not recall as energetic or interesting a presentation. You did a great job of presenting and making interesting what could be "dry" material, and you did it in world-record time! I am now going to do more research and also I will share my insights with colleagues and my management team.

Mike Foster, Owner, **UNIGLOBE Instant Travel Inc**, London, Canada

I just wanted to say thank you for a very interesting and engaging VoIP seminar that you presented in Vancouver. Being that I'm in sales and not really that technically savvy, but do need to keep up on new trends etc, I usually find myself glazing over after about 10 minutes of a technical presentation. Your seminar kept me engaged and you related it in such a way that even us non-techies could completely follow it ...again thank you!

Jocelyn Rheault, Sales Manager, **InfoChip**, Vancouver, Canada

With impressive credentials, Dr. Bontis is invigorating and captivating. He delivers with a sense of humour and energizes your brain to a higher level.

Vrishti Singh, Senior Project Manager,
Bank of Montreal, Toronto, Canada

Nick did an incredible job presenting to our group. He is extremely professional and designed his presentation to meet our needs and ensure it fit with the objectives of the conference and the atmosphere in the room. He entertained, provoked much thought, and left us with some concrete tools and ideas to make our organization better. We look forward to seeing him again.

Ed Jager, Senior Business Analyst, **Parks Canada**, Ottawa, Canada

You have to hand it to Nick Bontis for exceeding already high expectations. It was with no small anticipation that I, generalist policy wonk and admitted techno-peasant, toughing-out Day Two of a conference amidst a sea of IT and IM professionals, looked forward to his presentation. Now, here at last, was an accessible (and dear) subject for this wretched non-techy, that would be delivered by a guy whom I had heard called one of KM's foremost authorities and practitioners. So I was expecting to experience a rich, stimulating and thought-provoking presentation. But what Mr. Bontis managed to accomplish—by whipping together a captivating intellectual gumbo that mixed pinches of pantomime, humour, irony and compelling stories, all delivered with the fervour of a seemingly incorrigible optimist, (with the worldliness to temper views of a shining future with some 'wicked' little insights into the more self-serving side of human behaviour)—was a surprise and a rare gift. There aren't a lot of people that can pull off this kind of performance and remain credible. Perhaps that's the best compliment I can pay Nick Bontis—he is a very bright, very funny, apparently genuine guy who has a lot to say about a subject that increasingly bedevils this crazy world we are challenged to figure out.

Steve Sullivan, Senior Policy Analyst,
Agriculture and Agri-Food Canada, Ottawa, Canada

Dr. Bontis is a charismatic speaker with captivating style. He has an ability to weave detailed concepts with practical examples, leaving his audiences with meaningful, applicable and memorable knowledge that can only benefit their work and their organizations. Knowledge management is a resourceful key to success and Dr. Bontis has opened the door to a new approach with unique insight into the leading role of technology in the future of our business and personal lives.

Randy Borron, Vice President and Director,
Royal LePage Commercial, Toronto, Canada

Nick was a consultant on a project I lead for a major property and casual insurer, and I found him to be an extremely knowledgeable resource. He is a great presenter—full of energy and enthusiasm for his topic—and he offers credible research to back up what he has to say. We would hire him again.

Kaye Vivian, Director Strategic Intelligence, **The Hartford**, Hartford, USA

Let's face it, Dr. Bontis has supreme confidence in his ability to engage an audience. I mean who else gets up in front of a crowd of 1,400 (just AFTER they've eaten lunch) and begins to talk while half the room is already healthily engaged in idle conversation. Most speakers I've ever seen have either waited in silence like an elementary school teacher, or they "ahem" their way to audience attentiveness. Dr. Bontis just started talking once on stage and within 30 seconds the entire room went from 'chatter-chatter' to complete silence. After 5 minutes people were afraid to cough in fear of missing something he said. The information given during the entire day-long staff meeting was interesting and relevant—and so was his keynote session—but the difference is HOW he engages people. Dr. Bontis is what people mean when they say that someone is dynamic.

J.P. Surette, Labour Unit,
Human Resources and Skills Development Canada, Ottawa, Canada

I had the pleasure of attending the keynote address by Nick Bontis at the Government of Canada's IM Day 2005. It was a great way to kick off the day. Back by popular demand, this was a repeat performance for Dr. Bontis as keynote speaker at IM Day. The audience appreciated his wit, energy and insight. Dr. Bontis brought us back down to basics with an astute analysis of user expectations and behaviour.

Louise Houston, Manager, Information & Library Systems,
Supreme Court, Ottawa, Canada

Nick, I would like to personally thank you for your presentation to HRSDC's "Investing in People" conference. You brought your boundless energy and vast knowledge to help make this event a resounding success. Your contagious enthusiasm captured the attention of the audience, helping us to place our daily challenges in the context of global change, and engaging us in a fun and exciting way. I have seen you speak on many occasions, and am always amazed at how each time you arrive with a dynamic presentation and leave behind laughter, applause and new ideas.

Alan Nymark, Deputy Minister,
HR & Skills Development Canada, Ottawa, Canada

Immediate feedback indicates it was one of the most well received presentations we have offered in many years. The subject matter was fresh, the pace was perfect and your own energy level was infectious. For the duration of the convention, delegates were quoting your presentation and engaging in considerable discussion about it. One of a meeting planner's most challenging tasks is to find speakers from event to event that bring something new to the audience, either a new subject area or a new way of looking at things that can captivate an audience. Your presentation met these objectives and more. Knowledge management is a relatively new idea to our industry. After your presentation however, it is clear that many will pursue further some of the subjects you raised in the context of how they can improve their businesses. My only regret about the presentation is that we only gave you about 90 minutes to introduce a huge new subject area. Recognizing that we have only scraped the tip of the proverbial iceberg, I do hope to have you back to the ORBA convention next year to speak to members directly about how they can begin managing their corporate knowledge pool to enhance their productivity and efficiency. Thanks again for an extremely interesting and very professional presentation to ORBA members. We look forward to working with you again in the future.

Rob Bradford, Executive Director,
Ontario Road Builders Association, Toronto, Canada

Nick Bontis is a truly remarkable man. He has worked with our small health care organization and shared KM and intellectual capital with all levels of our staff. His passion, absolute credibility and commitment to our journey have inspired us. We have been working with him since 2001 and look forward to many more joint endeavours.

Mary Raithby, Executive Director,
Country Terrace Long Term Care Home, Komoka, Canada

When I say "thank you for last night" I absolutely mean the enlightening, eye opening, and super fantastic presentation that I had the opportunity to enjoy last night at MPI's first meeting of 2006. WOW, what a way to start the new year. Just wanted to let you know that you have given me a "mental hernia" and I haven't stopped thinking about all that you had to say. I brought the handout back to my office, and I am now trying to implement some of your strategies in my everyday life. Again, thank you so much...you are great at what you do. Not to mention extremely funny!!!

Rosanna Foti, Business Development Manager Canada,
Puerto Rico Tourism, Toronto, Canada

During our Government of Alberta Supervisor's Conference, Dr. Bontis' keynote presentation engaged the audience as demonstrated by participant feedback such as: "Dr. Bontis was amazing", "His knowledge mixed with his energy was a great way to start the morning", and "Excellent speaker—engaged audience in light hearted humorous ways while sharing important information" Other quotes from participants included: "A hugely dynamic speaker! We need him at 6-month intervals!! Very invigorating talk. No wonder he is highly regarded as a professor", "Normally I find inspirational speakers to be plastic and not true. Dr. Bontis was different. He was engaging and managed to keep my attention from start to finish. I laughed hard, and also learned much. Not to many people can leave you laughing, inspired, and educated", and "What a smart man! I wish I was one of his students. He has a lot to teach the rest of us."

Andrea Hayes, Employee Engagement Consultant,
Government of Alberta, Edmonton, Canada

Dr. Nick Bontis sure hits the MARK! Never before has the pace of change become more rampant and rapid. Nick's presentation and style energized and inspired the team while giving us specific actionable steps to apply in our daily life. It was much more than just a keynote presentation. I have no doubt that Nick's contribution will have a lasting and noticeable effect on myself and my team for years to come as we continue to "Embrace Change Through Leadership!"

Mark Outram, Director of Pharmacy Operations,
A&P Drug Mart Limited, Toronto, Canada

Nick is absolutely one of the best public speakers with whom I've ever worked. He appeared at one of our conferences and scored off the charts. A true intellectual and "Renaissance" man, Nick is an expert communicator.

Mike Dover, VP, Syndicated Research, **New Paradigm**, Toronto, Canada

Dr. Bontis' work is a significant breakthrough in quantifiably defining the benefits of knowledge and information management. His methods, which are grounded in well-defined and accepted mathematical approaches, are uniquely applied to real business applications. He provides much-needed expertise for organizations to determine the most beneficial budget allocations for various HR and KM initiatives. Using these techniques may help us from "flying blind" and trying to guess at the most appropriate approach to addressing fundamental business and human performance problems.

Greg Reid, CEO, **InFuture LLC**, Andover, USA

Thank you for your presentation at our Customer Focus meeting. You did an outstanding job! The best speaker I've seen in 15 years! From humorous to inspirational speaking you have offered a motivational message like no other. You have brought excitement, expertise, and inspiration to the members of our group. Your topics were key in opening the mind with refreshing thoughts and visual gestures. On behalf of Cascades Boxboard Group, I wish you continued success and would happily recommend you to anyone looking for quality motivational speaking. You contributed greatly to the success of our meeting. Looking forward to the next opportunity to work with you!

Mark P. Roy, VP Sales & Marketing, **Cascades**, Montreal, Canada

Imagine a group of senior executives, who having arrived from all parts of the globe; spend a long day actively involved in intense workshops determining what the best Knowledge Management solutions were for their firm. Perceive the group dinner that night where these same executives are feeling wrung out, jet lagged and exhausted. Then: Nick Bontis stands and delivers a speech on "Thinking Ahead: Taking the Knowledge Journey'. Within seconds these same executives are brighter, engaged, enthused and full of new thoughts for the future of the firm and are very ready for day 2 of the workshop. There are very few people in this world that are as engaging and as knowledgeable as Nick, never ever miss an opportunity to see him in action.

Peter Dyson CEO, **SKA Learning**, Victoria, Australia

Expectations were high for Nick's session at the HRPAO Talent Management Conference, but they were indeed surpassed! Dr. Bontis was as clever and provocative as ever. He challenges HR professionals to be the best business partners they can be, bringing seemingly complex points home by employing relatable analogies and injecting a healthy dose of humour. You cannot help but want to implement what you have learned and share it with others. Nick Bontis is a must at every conference, but other presenters beware: You do not want to follow him.

Lisa Padula, Director, Org. Effectiveness, **Yum! Restaurants International**, Toronto, Canada

Thank you for following up on Dr. Bontis' speaking engagement at our leadership meetings. He did a great job! Very energetic at exactly the right time. I continue to get positive feedback from the attendees. He is entertaining and very knowledgeable at the same time. His presentation style is indeed quite unique. Thank' s again for all your efforts in helping me find the right fit for our needs.

Marissa Poratto-Cleghorn, Manager Bus. Inf.,
MDA MacDonald Dettwiler, Richmond, Canada

I thoroughly enjoyed your presentation today in Kingston, Ontario at St. Lawrence College. Of all the numerous seminars I have attended including some by Zig Ziglar and Tony Robbins, I found yours to be the most dynamic and entertaining from an intellectual and presentation basis. I was most impressed with your double algorithm module.

Perry Windsor, HR Manager,
Ludlow Technical Products, Gananoque, Canada

I thoroughly enjoyed and was intrigued by your comments made at the Valley Business Conference in Fresno California last month. I believe that your assessment of future skills' needs is right on and have already used your rationale to support my statement that people should invest in themselves—it will provide the best return on investment that they'll ever get.

Bill Syvertsen, Professor of Business Administration,
Fresno City College, Fresno, California

It was my pleasure to meet with Dr. Bontis at the PMAC event in Niagara Falls. Personally, I thought Dr. Bontis represents new age thinking in a way never before approached in Canada. His insight into practical every day matters and how KM process is key to human life makes him an asset to Canada. His vivaciousness and positive energy set him apart from others and his approach reminds me of Malcolm Gladwell. He connects with the audience in a Clintonesque manner.

Sankar Krishnan, SVP/Director & Trade Finance Head,
Citigroup, Toronto, Canada

Nick Bontis is quickly becoming one of our great Canadian Leaders. His charisma on stage must be seen in person to appreciate a universal message that encompasses all segments of business. Nick is truly one of the best speaker's available, to deliver an extraordinary philosophical message suitable for any event.

Stephen Bauld, VP, **Ontario General Contractors Association**,
Mississauga, Canada

If you need a speaker, Nick is your man. His 90 minute presentation went by in a flash, absolutely fantastic. Listening to him for another 90 minutes would have been easy. Without any hesitation I would attend his presentations again & again. You will not be disappointed.

Barry Wyner, Director, **Altus Group Limited**, Toronto, Canada

On behalf of the Edmonton Police Association, I want to express my sincere thanks to you for coming to Edmonton to present to our members. Your reputation as an effective and dynamic speaker who captivates and engages an audience preceded you; however, your performance, energy, and passion for knowledge management exceeded our already high expectations. Your presentation was extremely informative, thought provoking, and quite the revelation in terms of what to expect in the coming years with all the technological advancements in the world and in terms of the capital knowledge currently held in our own organization and in our police service. You delivered a significant message which was exceptionally timely, especially given the global trend surrounding employee retirement and retention issues. Your academic reasoning that underpins and supports the philosophy of knowledge management and intellectual capital resonated with our members, particularly in achieving a balance of sustainable capital knowledge within an organization. Your passion and zeal for this very unique discipline shone throughout the presentation and your unique, no frills, gimmick free delivery was very refreshing. The time flew by in what seemed like a few minutes and the audience was left wanting more. I would have no hesitation in recommending you to any organization that is seeking to understand intellectual capital in order to increase performance and productivity.

Michelle Stolarchuk, Director,
Edmonton Police Association, Edmonton, Canada

It has been our pleasure to work with you during the preparation period in advance of the conference and on-site during the event. Keynote speakers are a critical component for a professional conference and a major draw factor for registrations. Our registration numbers exceeded our expectations and we believe our program was the draw factor. The more than 700 delegates who attended the "World of Opportunity" conference rated it as one of PMAC's best yet. The evaluation results for all four of our keynote speakers were 'excellent' and your session was specifically noted as exceptional. We thank you for your contribution toward such a memorable event. Once again, please accept our gratitude for your participation in the PMAC annual conference.

Emily Eyre, Conference Co-Chair,
Purchasing Management Association of Canada, Toronto, Canada

Dr Bontis' presentation on improving leadership skills within your organization is a must see for anyone in management positions or aspiring to be. His knowledge and understanding of the concepts of intellectual capital management are only surpassed by his delivery and zest as a communicator. We strive to bring the best possible information the busy Fire Chiefs of the Canadian Fire Service in order to better prepare them to meet the new challenges they face. Nick delivered the importance of being organizationally sound and prepared in a way that flawlessly related to the Fire Service. I was impressed by how quickly he created a bond with the group. The final result, a standing ovation! Great work.

Pierre Voisine, Manager,
Canadian Forces Deputy Fire Marshal, Ottawa, Canada

I first met Nick Bontis in 2005 at a Coast Hotels & Resorts Sales retreat. All of us left the room chuckling and floating with new knowledge which is exactly the way one should feel after a 3 day conference but rarely does. Recently I had the pleasure of recommending Nick to a key account who was overwhelmed by the speaker options available. I was thrilled to learn they had booked him strictly on my word and invited me to attend. This time I was introduced to even more fascinating stats with which he amazes his audience. My client was thrilled. Thanks Nick!

Monica Zeniuk, Sales Manager,
Coast Edmonton Plaza Hotel, Edmonton, Canada

I had the privilege to attend Dr. Bontis' presentation at an Executive Forum of the HRPAO. Dr. Bontis is an unsurpassed speaker who challenges status quo while bringing potential complex issues to actionable objectives. An entrepreneur at heart, his enthusiasm and passion is contagious. You can't stay indifferent when you come in contact with this individual.

Josee Dykun, Vice President, Human Resources,
Yellow Pages Group, Montreal, Canada

Nick Bontis is not your normal PhD, Nick is one of North America's best and brightest and definitely cutting edge. We found Nick to be extremely insightful and above all entertaining!

Brent Gingerich, President, **Entrepreneurs Organization**, Toronto, Canada

Dr. Nick Bontis provided a riveting presentation during a very important high level meeting for our company. He described important strategic concepts in a simple way so that everyone understood. He also provided actionable methods to implement them easily. The results of his presentation caused a variety of significant changes including a more positive attitude among our employees as well as helping us with our integration process. For a global firm like ours, small changes make a big difference. A total of 97% of all attendees during the presentation rated his performance as either good (21%) or excellent (76%). Given the sophistication level of our audience, this is an outstanding achievement.

Adrián Vázquez Ramírez,
Planeación y Desarrollo, **Nemak**, Monterrey, Mexico

Entertaining, engaging, and without a doubt, the most energetic keynote speaker I have ever seen. Dr. Nick Bontis captures your attention with a deep and perceptive understanding of intellectual capital. His dynamic approach in his presentations, along with his insight to rapid change in our society, will leave you amazed and full of ideas as to how to manage a fast paced business environment.

Lou Cafazzo, Associate Director Alumni Advancement,
McMaster University, Hamilton, Canada

My feedback is simple. Wow. Well-done Nick. Very, very informative, funny, dynamic, interesting. Made perfect sense. Refreshing to listen to. You tapped into the frustration I feel that we (HR professionals) are often just 'spinning our wheels'! GREAT ENERGY!

Cathy La Fontaine, Officer Program Planning & Development,
Ottawa Hospital, Ottawa, Canada

WOW, I thought Dr. Bontis did a fabulous job. His persona, energy and enthusiasm set the stage with a firm belief on past / present / future economics, business theory and daily occurrences that cross each and everyone's paths. I thoroughly enjoyed listening to Dr. Bontis speak and asked opinions of many attendees. They, too, thought he was very entertaining and provided excellent points to follow (and keep), and of course, always a few with constructive criticism.

Tracy Okonski, Marketing Communications Manager,
Angiotech, Reading, USA

Nick Bontis is brilliant! He is one of the most energetic speakers I have ever met. Nick has the ability to bring his sessions to life. He is provocative and pushes the envelope in our thinking and how we do things. He does an amazing job in helping people focus on issues which would otherwise be brushed off as "unimportant" or "irrelevant." I have seen Nick at a few events and after every event I am left in awe of how he manages his audience and how he is able to engage the entire room. For our session, he was able to engage all levels of the organization in a fun and interactive way. He manages to create a sense of urgency and priority to the issue he is presenting. It is difficult to capture Nick's essence into words, but when trying to describe him and his presentations, the words talented and thought-provoking definitely come to mind.

Julie A. Giraldi, Chief HR & IT Officer, **Ontario Hospital Association**,
Toronto, Canada

Having hired Dr. Bontis for both our Century 21 Canada Conference, and for our UNIGLOBE Travel International top franchisee event in the past, I can say that he received some of the best Event Reviews we've ever had from the attendees of these two recurring events. Additionally, through my membership in YPO (Young Presidents' Organization) BC Chapter, I have also had the pleasure of seeing Dr. Bontis deliver two different Presentations, both of which were extremely well received by a good cross section of some of the best business minds in the province. As such, if are still considering working with Dr. Bontis, I highly encourage you to do so—your audience will not be disappointed.

Martin H. Charlwood, President, **Uniglobe Travel & Century 21 Canada**, Vancouver, Canada

Nick Bontis is a high energy, provocative speaker who helps teams understand and embrace the rapid pace of change. It's not surprising that his students and corporate audiences love his presentations—they are full of insight and passion.

Stephen D. Graham, Executive VP Corporate Marketing, **Rogers Communications**, Toronto, Canada

I thought your presentation at the Government 2.0 meeting the other day was the best of the bunch! Really great stuff and your presentation was so engaging.

Steven Green, Manager Cabinet Office Com., **Government of Ontario**, Toronto, Canada

Thank you Nick for your highly positive presentation at the National Conference of the PMAC I attended in June, 2007. I really appreciated the way you managed to get the serious points across while maintaining the light-hearted atmosphere. Everyone felt comfortable and I am now actively taking a reading and comprehension course. Looking forward to seeing you again at a future conference.

Glynn Hancott, Purchasing Manager, **Ministry of Health and Long-Term Care**, Toronto, Canada

I have contracted Nick Bontis to present on a number of occasions on a variety of business and government topics related to IT and HR and their ultimate impact on competitive advantage. His performances are always eye-opening and typically rated at a par with our top speakers. His innovative content is solid, his energetic style is engaging and he uses humour to great advantage. He has never let us down.

Don Tapscott, Chairman, **nGenera**, Toronto, Canada

As the keynote speaker at the 2008 Northeastern Ontario Fire Education Conference in North Bay, Ontario, Dr. Nick Bontis' energetic delivery of his informative

and thought-provoking 90-minute presentation was easily the highlight of the conference. The 450 delegates, spell-bound in attentiveness to the key messages pertaining to knowledge and intellectual capital within organizations, gave him a spontaneous standing ovation. In the written evaluation of this presentation, delegates used superlatives such as "awesome", "excellent X 4 and X 7", "amazing", "informative", "humorous", "perfect", "entertaining", "captivating", "a great mix of comedy and seriousness", and "worth every cent you spent." I highly recommend Dr. Nick Bontis as an extremely knowledgeable, engaging, and dynamic speaker.

Dr. Fred McLennan, Principal, **Ontario Fire College**, Gravenhurst, Canada

I have conducted these Professional Development days for my staff for 5 years now. To date I have never received such an overwhelming positive response from the participants. Comments like, "best Speaker yet", "Dr. Bontis was engaging, informative and Dynamic", "we want to hear Dr Bontis again", are but a few of the positive unsolicited comments I received. Personally I found your presentation and delivery to be refreshing, extremely relevant and entertaining. Hard to believe how much information was exchanged in such a short period of time. Thanks again and we will be seeing you again soon.

Tony Tollis, Director Budgets and Finance,
City of Hamilton, Hamilton, Canada

Dr. Bontis was by far the most popular speaker at our tradeshow. His insights were engaging, thought provoking and at the same time highly entertaining for our diverse group of delegates. At his conclusion, he left attendees wanting more.

Tamera Olsen, Executive Director,
Mortgage Brokers Association of BC, Vancouver, Canada

Nick spoke at the 2008 HRIA conference as a keynote speaker. Nick's approach was superb in taking some highly statistical information and making it very understandable (and humourous!) to everyone. I highly recommend him to anyone looking at booking Nick for a keynote address.

Chantelle Pinder, VP HR,
Calgary Winter Club, Calgary, Canada

Dr. Bontis is a quantum-thinker, pushing your grey-matter harder to think about the pace and promise of the future both in both business and society. He'll take you on a fact-based journey that spans millennia, exploring the power of the human-mind and its connection to global and accelerating trends in information, communication, industry and technology. He will educate and entertain, leaving you awe-struck and eager to think about tomorrow, today.

Kent Hatton, Brand Group Director, **Energizer Canada**, Toronto, Canada

Dr. Bontis is a globally recognized expert in his field of study. He is even better as a speaker and moderator. He has the rarely-perfected, highly-valuable ability to give his extensive understanding of intellectual capital a very practical perspective. He lights up a room with his enthusiasm and keeps things alive, relevant and provocative. He challenges the mind and causes everyone in his audience to think hard about ways to raise their game.

Darryl White, Executive Managing Director,
BMO Capital Markets, Toronto, Canada

Nick has a rare combination of energy, humour and intelligence that make him a great speaker, and his area of expertise—knowledge management—is timely and one that any group would benefit from hearing more about.

Carolyn Rogers, President and CEO, **Hydroxyl Systems**, Victoria, Canada

Dr. Nick Bontis combined energy, dynamic delivery and world class content to kick off our annual national conference. He engaged and energized our members, but more important he challenged them to think and act in response to the rapid changes affecting our communities and our organizations. We could not have asked for a better speaker to launch our annual conference.

Dan Clement, VP Learning, **United Way of Canada**, Toronto, Canada

Dr. Nick is a high energy and provocative speaker who engages his audience to break previous thought patterns and consider new paths to improved performance.

Court Carruthers, President, **Acklands-Grainger**, Port Coquitlam, Canada

Nick Bontis is an incredibly engaging speaker. In a very unique and dynamic manner, he bridges academics, business and "real life" knowledge. He made me think differently. His knowledge and energy is contagious. His presentation compelled me to talk to my wife about some of his thinking!

Greg Hicks, Chief Operating Officer, **TSC Stores**, London, Canada

On behalf of the Conference Board of Canada, I would like to thank you for your participation in our annual Top Talent conference. This event was rated exceptionally well by our delegates and we truly value your contribution to its success. Your presentation was masterful. The audience greatly appreciated your perspective on the challenges they face as change accelerates in their environment and the steps they can take to build continued success. Thank you for providing our delegates with considerable value at this event. I am certain they will find plenty of opportunity to apply what they learned upon returning to their respective organizations.

John Brewer, Executive Program Developer,
Conference Board of Canada, Toronto, Canada

Exciting, engaging, intelligent, energetic, straightforward, insightful, dynamic, fun—these are some of the comments we have received from our participants following Dr. Bontis' presentation of "Leadershift" at our annual HR Conference. His seamless presentation enthralled the crowd, and kept everyone tuned in and engaged. Even when challenged by one of the participants, he rose to the occasion and went above and beyond our expectations.

Roman Turchyn, VP HR & Business Ethics Officer, **L-3 Wescam**, Burlington, Canada

Thanks Nick. When I was in the office on Friday, I received continuous positive feedback about the day. You did an amazing job in keeping everyone's interest with your humour and high energy. Well done!

Marc Beaudry, VP and Chief HR Officer, **Providence Healthcare**, Toronto, Canada

Nick is a rare breed. He can pack hours of compelling content into an action-packed 90 minutes; all while keeping his audience energized, laughing and entertained. His presentation and thought-provoking ideas were water-cooler fodder long after our event.

Carole Stevenson-Roy, Dir. Corporate Com., **Alberta Motor Association**, Edmonton, Canada

The decision to bring Nick Bontis to our organization was a very good one. We had begun to explore the concept of "Knowledge Management" ... tough to define and understand and yet clearly a strategic direction we wished to go. Nick...through his enormous energy, wisdom, stories and experience was able to spark the leaders in the room onto bigger thinking about human capital metrics and organizational performance. He challenged us to establish action items ... and to begin them immediately. Yes ... we had a great day ... but more importantly we have seen the positive impact of what we learned. In the time since Nick's visit, our organization has gone on to plan for, and ultimately establish a balanced scorecard approach based on solid data and derived from reliable tools. We are able to make better decisions based on information available in "real-time." We now use the language of Knowledge Management in day-to-day conversation. Thank-you Nick for teaching us and challenging us.

Barbara O'Neil, Director Org. Development, **Chatham Kent Health Alliance**, Chatham, Canada

Dr. Bontis is engaging, entertaining, informative and thoroughly enjoyable! With delegates from around the world, his topic was timely and opened the eyes of everyone in the room. His interactive approach had the audience completely mesmerized. He should be at the top of everyone's "must have" list of speakers.

Richard McKeagan, President & COO,
Mechanical Contractors Association, Ottawa, Canada

I found Nick's presentation energizing and enlightening. He shared his ideas on intellectual capital, but also showed us techniques on how to manage it within our workplaces.

Bev Hendry, Chief Administrative Officer,
Township of Scugog, Port Perry, Canada

Our son has had the privilege of having Dr. Bontis as a professor at McMaster University and since that time his name has been a perpetual one in our household. To hear our son speak of this man, one would wonder if such a person really exists!! This week I was finally able to meet with Dr. Bontis, at the OHA Convention, where he was a guest speaker. And what did I come away with? Our son, while holding Dr. Bontis in the highest esteem did not nearly say enough about him!!! This man, as a guest speaker, was riveting, captivating, humorous , thought provoking and just downright enjoyable. His views on "changes" and "unlearning is harder than learning" are so relevant in today's workplace. My students came away from Dr. Bontis' presentation with a whole new perspective on how an experienced person who has worked at the same job for years would find the "unlearning" difficult. As these students gain employment in the Health Care field, they go in as innovative, fresh, dynamic young people, ready to "change the world"! They now, thanks to Dr. Bontis, will have a clearer understanding of not just how the veteran employees struggle with change, but, how to make that change easier for them. During this presentation we also learned that Dr. Bontis is a proud and loving family man. This too, was a great lesson for the students, to know that in this world of "change" your family may be the only constant in your life. So you must protect, value, nourish and give it the time it so richly deserves because without it, when the work day is over, you will have a great void in your life. So, if there is anyone out there who has not seen Dr. Bontis give a presentation, or had the privilege to be one of his students ...look for him and see him in action! For you truly have not seen "the all round best"!!! I sincerely hope that one day I will see you "perform" again!

Jane Piribauer, Health Record Manager,
Kingston General Hospital, Kingston, Canada

An engaging and entertaining speaker, Nick Bontis helps us to think strategically about the workplace of the future. Every day that future world arrives at light-speed, a tsunami of new information challenging us to embrace change as the new steady state - the perfect message for today's business environment.

Ken Tremblay, President and CEO,
Chatham-Kent Health Alliance, Chatham, Canada

Nick Bontis brought his unique brand of energy and intellect to our annual Management Forum Retreat. His humour entertained us and his insight inspired us. Our evaluations indicated that this was one of the best retreats ever!!! The Knowledge Café exercise that he introduced resulted in numerous realistic actionable items specifically linked to our strategic plan, providing direction for the upcoming year. Don't pass up an opportunity to see this man in action!

Susan Holden, Corporate Services,
Providence Healthcare, Toronto, Canada

I had the pleasure of hearing Nick Bontis for the first time at a recent hospital conference. The last of several speakers—including a retired Prime Minister, Chief of the Defence Staff, and a Governor General—Nick was an outstanding surprise and, in my opinion, the best speaker. His hour long presentation was funny, inspirational, and re-energizing. His subject, intellectual capital, is highly relevant to everyone.

Dr. David Broderick, Chief of Staff,
Northumberland Hills Hospital, Cobourg, Canada

Nick's presentation was a very insightful and forward looking view about the future impacts of information technology on the way we will work; delivered in an audience engaging manner, full of energy and highly entertaining. This presentation garnered excellent feedback from all the participants at our 25th Annual Symposium and energized the group for the entire day.

Rick Tolkunow, Director,
Utilization of IT in Public Works, Mississauga, Canada

It has been my pleasure and great fortune to work with Nick Bontis over the last few years on many occasions. He has presented and facilitated at our Inaugural Executive Forum, Keynoted at our Annual Conference and other professional development programs for HRPA (Human Resource Professionals Association). Nick takes a strategic yet practical approach—meeting the needs of Strategic HR Partners, and adding a cornerstone of development for Human Resource professionals—so important in today's uncertain workplace environment. Nick's consultative process is thorough and thoughtful. We look forward to future opportunities to work with Nick and recommend him highly to others.

Marta Pawych, Director Professional Development and Sponsorship,
HRPA, Toronto, Canada

Dr. Nick Bontis is such a dynamic and energetic speaker. He brings enthusiasm to his audience with great intellect and knowledge. His presentation was so well received we had Nick come back the following year.

Casey Thompson, Director,
Credit Union Professionals' Association, Toronto, Canada

Nick is a dynamic and enthusiastic speaker- his presentation definitely kept our energy levels up on a Friday afternoon! His presentation was a perfect blend of KM information and real life told in a humorous way to help us work better as individuals and work more effectively as a team. Based on the feedback received, everyone thoroughly enjoyed Nick's presentation and would love to hear him speak again. Thanks for an outstanding presentation!

Sammi Ha, Senior Manager Tax,
PricewaterhouseCoopers, Calgary, Canada

Dr. Bontis is a dynamic and motivating speaker; he engages the audience from the start of his presentation and keeps them entertained while sharing his valuable insights and knowledge. He was the highlight of our conference and left our participants wanting more.

Francine St-Martin, Manager,
Can. College of Health Service Executives, Ottawa, Canada

Dynamic, articulate, and thought-provoking speakers are hard to find. It becomes even more complex when we are seeking speakers who are passionate about a particular subject matter. Add to the mix that the speaker must be able to connect with the audience and you will have some idea as to why we are delighted with the glowing comments we received from our delegates about Dr. Nick Bontis' presentation at our conference. Comments included: amazing speaker that actually knows something, one of the best speakers I ever heard in all respects, very entertaining and funny, terrific energy and excellent communicator, great stuff, highest rated of the conference, too good - want more.

Deborah Klein, Director,
Investment Funds Institute of Canada, Toronto, Canada

On behalf of TD Bank Financial Group I want to share how pleased we were with the presentation delivered by Dr. Nick Bontis. Dr. Bontis' dynamic, thought provoking, presentation educated and engaged the minds of our recruiters. I personally was very impressed with the information, concepts and ideas that were shared. Feedback, by way of written comments from the conference participants included, "interesting and inspiring", "challenged me to think about things differently", to "I am now intrigued by the knowledge management topic." Dr. Bontis' presentation was talked about over the two days of the conference and beyond.

A.J. Filip, VP Staffing,
TD Bank Financial Group, Toronto, Canada

These are direct quotes from audience members of the Human Resources Professionals Association of Northern Ontario conference: awesome, great, wow, excellent speaker, very entertaining, engaging, high energy, great Friday afternoon speaker, great finish, bring him back, informative and interesting, interactive, funny, incredibly enlightening, different from any presenter, motivating and inspiring, looking forward to website, ridiculously good, and unbelievable speaker.

Lata Viseu, Specialist, Prof. Dev.,
HR Professionals Association, Toronto, Canada

With a combination of massive energy, intellect, humour and charm, Dr. Nick Bontis is the ultimate keynote presenter. While delivering substantive, relevant, and thought-provoking content, Dr. Bontis can keep any audience on the edge of their seats.

Alicia Rollo, Manager, Prof. Dev.,
HR Professionals Association, Toronto, Canada

Energy??? Excitement??? Thought Provoking??? If that's what you're looking for, Nick Bontis will deliver. As the opening keynote to the 2009 ECNO Conference, Nick was everything we were looking for, and then some. He had the audience eating out of the palm of his hand for the full hour! If you're looking to kick off your conference with someone who will challenge your audience to rethink how they are doing things, and ensure they take something from the day, hook up with Nick,

Wayne Toms, Board Member,
ECNO Conference Organizing Committee, Ottawa, Canada

I saw Dr. Bontis at the 2009 BC Human Resources Management Association conference speaking about causal models. What a shocking revelation—when an organization collects simple data points over a period of time, they can extract a wealth of information of what HR activities actually have an impact on the bottom line!

We're living in a new world where economic growth is taking on a new meaning—we may no longer see the accumulation of money and goods as a definition of success but instead the focus will be on sustainability and quality. Dr. Bontis leads us in the right direction to gain maximum impact with less input using our human capital and those that get that message will be generating the real growth in their organizations. Nick is the innovator of this new movement.

Helen Luketic, Research Associate,
BC Human Resources Man. Assoc., Vancouver, BC

Be ready to think and absorb if you have the pleasure of a presentation by Nick. He is a dynamic speaker that hits real world issues and challenges. I enjoyed every minute and would recommend everyone to spend some time perusing his website.

Gary Koetters, Senior Manager, **Intermatic**, Brampton, Canada

I was impressed by Nick's website, which intrigued me to pursue the possibility of Nick speaking to our customers at our annual customer conference, I'm glad I made the choice to partner with Nick for our event. The website is impressive, Nick in person is mind-blowing! I say that because admittedly, I feel as though we provided Nick with a very challenging topic to present on (Sustainability Imperative: Greening the Path to Accelerated Performance), he not only educated our audience, he engaged them, he entertained them and he left them feeling comfortable enough to approach him and start up a conversation as though they'd known him for years! Nick is unique in his delivery whether he's on stage or conversing one-on-one, he's refreshing to listen to and speak with and will definitely leave a lasting impression on anyone you choose to have him speak to! It was a pleasure meeting Nick and I look forward to the next opportunity we have to work with him!

Carly Patryluk, Senior Sales Leader, **SaskTel**, Saskatoon, Saskatchewan

This is the second occasion that I have had the privilege of inviting Dr. Bontis to speak to our organization; the first being with a large group of our worldwide HR professionals and this time, with our own local leaders, supervisors and managers. His engaging delivery in encouraging us to think outside of our own walls, both within our organization and externally was truly enlightening. As well, his quick wit and high energy kept our group riveted to their seats throughout the entire presentation. Our leaders were all thoroughly impressed with the presentation and have all agreed that they are anxious to put his words into action.

Roman Turchyn, VP Human Resources & Business Ethics Officer,
L-3 Wescam, Burlington, Canada

One of the most energetic presentations that I have ever seen. Bontis provided great insights into the enormously difficult issues that we will all face as we struggle to deal with exponential growth of data and information.

Paulin Laberge, Program Chair, **AceTech**, Banff, Canada

When Nick took the stage to speak to over 200 health department staff on intellectual capital and knowledge management, they were immediately captivated and riveted by Nick's high energy, fast paced presentation. Nick provided both superb entertainment and more importantly, a wealth of information with many practical examples and tools to illustrate his concepts. He received rave reviews from everyone I spoke to and is one of the best speakers I have ever heard. We certainly want him back for Part II!

Dr. Bob Nosal, Medical Officer of Health,
Halton Region, Oakville, Canada

Dr. Nick Bontis is an inspiring and engaging speaker and let's not forget humourous! The knowledge that I gained from his presentation has changed my approach to business and life. I have reclaimed time back. Thanks.

Barbara Kosterski, General Manager, **Banff Aspen Lodge**, Banff, Canada

Sincere thanks for making the Hancock Lecture at Hart House a resounding success, and a stimulating exercise in learning, unlearning and speed-reading. Preliminary reports from the post-lecture surveys indicate excellent audience engagement, due to the content and the interactive presentation. Congratulations on your 3M teaching award . . . we are honoured to have had you grace Hart House and the University of Toronto on the eve of such a prestigious and well-deserved honour. Have a wonderful weekend with your family!

Laney Marshall, Director of Programme,
Hart House—University of Toronto, Toronto, Canada

Dr. Nick, not only took his speaking engagement at our Annual Conference to a new level, he left the crowd wanting more. His inspirational talk and truthfulness about the future was a great addition to our program and is going to be talked about for many years.

Meredith Karosas, Director,
Ont. Sewer & Water Construction Assoc., Mississauga, Canada

Thank you for a fantastic delivery to the Canadian CEOs at the Executive Roundtable. Your passion and energy are contagious and your depth of knowledge a privilege to work with. I have thoroughly enjoyed our growing professional relationship ... very cool website, hat's off!

Heather McLachlin, VP Corporate Marketing,
CUMIS, Burlington, Canada

We were very pleased with Nick's presentation. Even with a very diverse audience, he was still able to capture the whole group's attention immediately, and keep it for the whole session. I'm still getting positive comments six weeks later. You've grown our outlook on the world today - thanks.

Steven Gemmell, Manager,
Grand River Conservation Authority, Cambridge, Canada

I wanted to provide you with some feedback on a luncheon I attended last week with 400+ other Scotiabankers. The guest speaker was Dr Nick Bontis - he was passionate, energetic, entertaining and informative. If he is any indication of the calibre of profs you have at DeGroote - then my kudos to you!!!

Marianne Hasold-Schilter,
Senior VP Leadership & Top Talent, **Scotiabank**, Toronto, Canada

Dr. Bontis, top marks for both content and presentation!! I particularly appreciate the fact that you spoke to each and every delegate at the conference. Title, position, seniority: none of this mattered as we all laughed, learned and were fully engaged in your presentation.

Anne Markey, Executive Dir.,
Can. Assoc. of Career Educators & Employers, Toronto, Canada

Fantastic! His energy, enthusiasm, humour, personality and the message he delivers is thought provoking and extremely relevant. Nick's presentation is engaging and interactive. This is the second time that Nick has been a key note speaker at our Annual Training Symposium, always to rave reviews.

Suzanne Fich, Manager,
Municipal Finance Officers' Association, Toronto, Canada

When I was asked to put together an executive retreat, I wanted to impress. I had neither hesitation nor stress when I asked Dr. Nick Bontis to speak. I have seen Dr. Bontis' presentation three times now, and every time I learn and unlearn something. In an ever changing world, the default position for many executives is to hold on to what they know and what they do. As a speaker, Dr. Nick Bontis takes us on a journey that allows us to understand just how things evolve and the need for individual evolution. Every time, the reaction from the participants is unanimous: "he is so good—I was on the edge of my seat". Thank you. Really.

Francois Desjardins, Pres. & CEO,
B2B Trust, A Laurentian Bank subsidiary, Toronto, Canada

Combining the best of a top academic and a successful business person, Nick provides objective knowledge of proven strategies with practical pointers. He delivers both style and substance as an engaging presenter plus insightful analyst who truly wants his audience members to become more productive.

Allison Chan, Manager,
Can. Assoc. for Pharmacy Distribution Man., Toronto, Canada

As an academic and researcher, Nick's work is first rate - meticulous, meaningful and packed with deep insight. That in itself would be reason to recommend him, but he's also a wonderfully engaging speaker who can take complicated data and analytics and make them come alive. Dynamic, engaging, entertaining, informative and thought-provoking - he's got it all.

Mike Prokopeak, VP & Editorial Director,
Chief Learning Officer Magazine, Chicago, USA

Dr. Nick Bontis is a passionate speaker with a well-paced presentation. He displayed the same high energy during his entire presentation. He kept the audience engaged and motivated with his usual inspirational focus on raising their performance. He balanced his delivery with his own style of humour. He had interaction with delegates and had some visionary statement about future trends. We were very impressed with his presentation. This was the third time Nick presented to our audience, we invited him back because of his high ratings and popular demand.

Winnie Chan, Senior Conference Co-ordinator,
The MEARIE Group, Toronto, Canada

Dr. Nick Bontis is dynamic and informative. His vibrant personality combined with obvious knowledge and energetic delivery made this one of the most educational and enjoyable seminars I have attended in a long time! Dr. Bontis interacts with his audience and brings day to day realities of business and time management to the forefront using practical tools and reminders to maintain balance and keep a clear perspective on our business and personal lives for both the present and in the future.

Domenic Calce, VP, Food Basics Merchandising,
Metro Ontario Inc., Toronto, Canada

For those people who have not yet had the opportunity to see Dr. Nick Bontis in person all I can say is that you are truly missing out on one of life's most engaging intellectual experiences. If I did not know better I would have thought we were paying out annual incentives instead of listening to a business session aimed at having our people improve their level of workplace performance. Our team was so wired into discussions involving making your brain a more effective tool at both home and the office I was concerned it would be difficult to get people back to the office after such an exhilarating afternoon. We are now scouring our calendars looking for the next opportunity to invite Nick to participate with the group. Great Job!!

Tim Coleman, Sr. Director Merchandising / Procurement,
Loblaw Companies, Toronto, Canada

Dr. Nick Bontis was a smashing hit at our National Sales Conference. Choosing a speaker is a daunting task and a risky one I might add. Dr. Nick Bontis is an expert in his field; he was able to share his wisdom on the fast paced world of technologies, the generational differences in the workplace and how to work with them. His great sense of humor, charisma and high energy truly set the stage for our conference. He engaged our people from the moment he started speaking that they didn't stop talking about him for many months after the conference. I highly recommend Dr. Nick Bontis!

Frank Di Rocco, Director, National Sales,
Delta Hotels and Resorts, Toronto, Canada

When it comes to listening to keynote speakers at conferences Nick Bontis is certainly one of the best I have seen in action, and I mean action. You as the audience are absolutely engaged in his delivery as he his informed about the issues as well as the groups dynamics. Tremendous value of information that leaves you thinking about your future direction.

Robert J. Clark, President, **Atlas Van Lines Canada**, Oakville, Canada

I have heard Nick Bontis on two occasions at the national convention for our industry organization. The energy and entertainment factors are first class but the message is clearly the value proposition. The internet generation, the knowledge age and the message to respect and encourage the recognition of Human Capital come through in the increasingly electronic environment of our daily lives. Add in some fun experiments in speed reading and mental multitasking and the experience is exceptional. I'd recommend his programs to all.

Ernie Reynolds, V.P. & G.M., **ShawCor Ltd.**, Toronto, Canada

Dr. Nick Bontis weaved our theme of Charting Responsible Choices Today for a Sustainable Future magnificently into his provocative presentation. His high energy presentation style and real life examples resonated very well with our members. If this is a glimpse of the next generation of Canadian professors then there is strong hope for the next generation of students.

Ralph Suppa, President & GM,
Canadian Institute of Plumbing & Heating, Toronto, Canada

The crowd loved you Nick! What a goldmine you were to our charity event. Your energy, passion and inspiration to 'train my brain' and seek out opportunities to learn and grow was impactful. And your follow up material will help remind and enable us to make it so! Fabulous job! THANK YOU!"

Jill Donahue, Founder and Chair,
Bricks and Books Charity Event, Toronto, Canada

Please accept my genuine thanks for your phenomenal contribution to our Leadership Meeting. You deliver a powerful message and thank you for your efforts to tailor that message to our group as it made the content that much better. The entire group was motivated and energized by your insight, wit and inspiration to bring out our best in everything we do. Judging by the feedback I've received thus far, you can be confident that it was a very successful program. It was a phenomenal afternoon and you were the perfect fit for our meeting!

Joshua Karam, Director of HR,
Westin Harbour Castle Hotel, Toronto, Canada

As an executive member of the MDRT (Million Dollar Round Table), I was charged with finding a speaker that would impress one of the most discerning and sophisticated audiences around: an association of the top producing financial professionals in the world! My committee and I culled over 500 speaker videos and proposals from all walks of life. After dozens of hours of research, fact checking and comprehensive reviews, we selected Dr. Nick Bontis to speak at our Top of the Table event, an exclusive international MDRT conference for the world's top performing professionals. He did not disappoint. In fact, Dr. Bontis not only blew away the conference committee but provided one of the best keynote presentations I have ever seen. He was even more of a smash hit than we anticipated. The international audience absolutely loved him as he had spent considerable time and effort researching our needs and learning about our association membership. The result was a rousing standing ovation! The following year, as we planned for another global event, Dr. Nick Bontis' name was again on the top of everyone's list. It was extremely rare for our association to have a speaker invited back. But he is no ordinary speaker. His presentations are a perfect mix of serious business-based messaging, backed with academic credentials, along with a very funny and engaging delivery. Our committee selected Dr. Bontis again to present on our main platform stage as a keynote speaker in front of over 6,500 financial professionals. His presentation was beyond outstanding! Once again he delivered a highlight performance that resulted in a standing ovation. It was unforgettable for our audience. The professionalism and efficiency he brings to the planning, execution and post-analysis phases of event planning is fantastic. He made our committee look great and made my life a lot easier. It is so nice to know that when you work with Nick, he is an engaged partner and he provides you with a fantastic return on your investment. I have no doubt, I will be working with Dr. Bontis again in the future. He is a crown jewel in the world of professional speakers.

Frank Andreoli, MDRT member,
Andreoli Financial Services, Toronto, Canada

Dr. Nick Bontis' combination of energy, humour, insights and practical tools to better manage information and convert it into knowledge delighted and enthralled our audience, leaving them wanting more. He is an engaging, brilliant, dynamic and entertaining speaker. Bravo!

Alf Goodall, Senior VP Individual Marketing,
Canada Life, Great-West Life and London Life, London, Canada

What can I say about Nicky B ... except he is entertaining, engaging, energetic, funny, smart, thought provoking and relevant!!! It's so easy to bring in a speaker who can tell you about time management, priorities and delegation; but it's more difficult to find someone who can help you deal with continuous change in a fast paced environment, and to deal with managing information bombardment by using technology to leverage your capabilities. Our staff enjoyed Nick's presentation and we received great feedback from them. Some examples of direct feedback include one employee who commented that our meeting was actually "useful" and that they are able to incorporate Nick's examples and suggestions effectively into their daily routine to increase their efficiency. Another employee said that he was the best speaker they have seen in years, and that he was informative and provided real information. Employees never got bored throughout Nick's presentation and they actually had something to take away with them at the end of the day. Thank you Nick for making our meeting a success.

Andrea Chan, Senior Manager, Human Resources,
AXA Insurance, Toronto, Canada

Scan QR code for direct link to website,
hypertext links and other resources:

Addendum

Two final math questions:

1) What delivers 100 percent collaboration?

If A = 1, B = 2, C = 3 and so on until Z = 26, then the following is true if the corresponding numerical values for each letter are added:

Having the right...

K	N	O	W	L	E	D	G	E		
11	14	15	23	12	5	4	7	5	=	96% collaboration

H	A	R	D	W	O	R	K		
8	1	18	4	23	15	18	11	=	98% collaboration

A	T	T	I	T	U	D	E		
1	20	20	9	20	21	4	5	=	100% collaboration

2) What is the universal theory of knowledge and wealth?

Theory 1: Knowledge is power $K = P$
Theory 2: Time is money $T = M$
Theory 3: Power is work over time $P = W/T$

Merge Theory 1 and Theory 3: $K = W/T$
Insert Theory 2: $K = W/M$

Solve for M: $M = W/K$

Which means...
As your knowledge (K) approaches zero, money (M) approaches infinity regardless of the amount of work (W) done.

Or, in other words...
The less you know, the more it costs you!

Index

A

B

C

D

E

K

L

M

N

O

P

R

S

T

U

V

W

X

Y

Z

Scan QR code for direct link to website, hypertext links and other resources: